"If you have a vision, but don't know how to turn it into reality, this is the book for you. One of the biggest lessons I learned when I started my business was never to take 'no' for an answer. When one door closes, Ronna shows you how to find a back door or side door—to ultimately get what you want."

—Bobbi Brown
CEO and Founder, Bobbi Brown Cosmetics

"Ronna Lichtenberg makes sense of all the complex reasons why women have so much trouble with asking, and then lays out how to do it so clearly that any woman reading this will be able to put it to use and see immediate results."

—Jean M. Otte
Founder and CEO, WOMEN Unlimited, Inc.

"Any woman who wants to build her business needs to know how to pitch. This book will help both the woman ready to make her first dollar and the woman ready to make her next million."

—Marsha Firestone, Ph.D.
Women Presidents Organization

"Ronna's new book is chock full of useful information for women who already enjoy success in the business world as well as those who aspire to do great things. Her candid, no-holds-barred advice and real-life storytelling is a powerful combination that is bound to strike a chord with working women everywhere."

—Lisa Weber
President, Individual Insurance, MetLife

"In a style that is both entertaining and informative, Lichtenberg has translated scientific findings into a wealth of practical advice that will help women shatter the glass ceiling without losing their femininity."

—Laurie A. Rudman, Ph.D.
Associate Professor in the Department of Psychology, Rutgers University

"'Pitch like a girl' will become the ultimate compliment! Ronna Lichtenberg outlines all the steps women need to take to truly master negotiating. It's a must read for anyone who thinks pink!"

—Alexandra Lebenthal
President and CEO, Lebenthal & Co., Inc.

"This book is a valuable resource for women who want to take charge of their careers. Ronna shares a framework for understanding style and individual differences in a way that challenges us to own our strengths and maximize our impact. Very empowering!"

—Mae Douglas
Senior Vice President and Chief People Officer, Cox Communication

"New technology shows that men and women tend to think and act differently. Ronna Lichtenberg tells us how to turn that knowledge into helping women succeed."

—Judy B. Rosener, Ph.D.
Professor in the Graduate School of Mangement at UC-Irvine and
author of *America's Competitive Secret, Women Managers*

"*Pitch Like a Girl* is important for all women who may not consider themselves businesswomen. . . . Ronna's landmark work offers a valuable framework and practical strategies for [women] to create environments and build relationships that will amplify their voices and promote their valuable contributions. . . . "

—Theresa Rejrat
Deputy Executive Director, Patient Care Services/Nursing
Bellevue Hospital Center, New York City

All best —

PITCH
like a girl

how a woman can be herself
AND STILL SUCCEED

Ronna

ronna

LICHTENBERG

RODALE

The author wishes to note that the names and personal details of some of the women interviewed for this book have been changed to protect their privacy.

Mention of specific companies, organizations, or authorities in this book does not imply endorsement by the publisher, nor does mention of specific companies, organizations, or authorities imply that they endorse this book. Internet addresses and telephone numbers given in this book were accurate at the time it went to press.

© 2005 by Ronna Lichtenberg

Cover photograph © Karen Beard/Getty Images.com

Printed in the United States of America

Rodale Inc. makes every effort to use acid-free ∞, recycled paper ♻.

The Empathy Quotient test in Appendix 2 and the Systemizing Quotient test in Appendix 3 are from *The Essential Difference: The Truth about the Male and Female Brain* by Simon Baron-Cohen. Copyright 2003, Basic Books (Perseus Books Group), New York, NY. Used with permission.

Book design by Tara Long

Library of Congress Cataloging-in-Publication Data

Lichtenberg, Ronna.
  Pitch like a girl : how a woman can be herself and still succeed / Ronna Lichtenberg.
     p.   cm.
  Includes bibliographical references.
  ISBN-13 978–1–59486–009–6 hardcover
  ISBN-10 1–59486–009–2 hardcover
   1. Businesswomen.   2. Women executives.   3. Women employees.   4. Women—Employment.   5. Businesswomen—Conduct of life.   6. Women executives—Conduct of life.   7. Feminist economics.   I. Title.
  HD6053.L49   2005
  650.1'082—dc22   2004019988

Distributed to the trade by Holtzbrinck Publishers

  4   6   8   10   9   7   5   3   hardcover

WE **INSPIRE** AND **ENABLE** PEOPLE TO IMPROVE
THEIR LIVES AND THE WORLD AROUND THEM

FOR MORE OF OUR PRODUCTS
WWW.**RODALESTORE**.COM
(800) 848-4735

CONTENTS

Introduction

The shelves of bookstores and libraries are filled with volumes of self-help books that promise you can achieve your loftiest goals in life—if only you'll change some fundamental aspect of your behavior or character. If only you are willing to give up carbohydrates forever and commit to a lifetime of cheese and nuts, you'll be able to lose 50 pounds in a nanosecond. If only you start thinking like a rich man and acting like a rich man, you can be rich too, and you can teach your kids to make a bundle while you're at it. If only you adopt these seven habits, nine rules, twelve steps, five strategies touted by successful, powerful, famous, or infamous business leaders, athletes, coaches, motivational speakers, multimillionaires, and all-around swell guys and gals, you too can be successful and powerful, not to mention model thin and enviably wealthy to boot.

I'm exhausted just thinking about it.

Like most women I know, I'm already too busy with the various responsibilities of my life to feel up for the challenge of putting yet another item on my To Do list—and certainly not as gargantuan a task as a character makeover. Even if I had the time, I wouldn't exactly be leaping at the chance. I resent the underlying implication that there is something fundamentally wrong with the person I am now, that I have to change who I am to get what I want. Even if I could change, I'm not convinced the strategy would work, that changing the person I am will help me achieve the desired results. Actually, I know it wouldn't work because I spent a lot of years trying to do it and eventually figured out that it wasn't the way to go.

Which leads me to the heretical thought that is at the very heart of this book: What if you don't have to change who you are to get what you want? What if you can achieve your most desired professional and personal goals by simply tapping more fully and consciously into the power of the woman you *already* are?

That's what this book is all about: helping women get more of what they want by being more of who they are. It's about showing women how to bring more of themselves to work—and get more back from it as a result. It's about figuring out what you really want, feeling comfortable asking for it, and then drawing on a neglected source of power to achieve it.

I call this powerful new tool pitching like a girl. The idea is to use your natural powers of influence and persuasion to gain support for what you want and to use the skills that most women have developed at building and nurturing relationships to get people to share your views and do what you want them to do.

Pitching like a girl, I'm convinced, is the key for every woman who has ever felt stuck in her work, and in her life. It is a powerful solution for any woman who is feeling underappreciated, underutilized, underchallenged, unfairly compensated, overwhelmed, or all of the above. Pitching gives you power: the power that comes from being heard, from being clear about what you want, and from having the tools you need to persuade other people to support you.

Whether you work for money or for meaning, for yourself or someone else, are happy in your career or are looking to launch a new one, pitching like a girl will change your life for the better. I promise. And in the pages that follow, I am going to teach you how.

Ronna Lichtenberg

We all pitch, at various times and in various situations, to get what we need and want in life. We just don't usually recognize what we're doing as pitching.

A pitch is nothing more—or less—than using your influence, skills, and powers of persuasion to gain support and to get people to do what you want them to do. Pitching is about enlisting someone's support for your goals. It's about asserting your vision of what should happen, asking for support, and making it clear to the other party why it's in their best interests to come along with you for the ride. When you pitch, you are basically saying to someone, "I need your resources to make my idea happen."

In the classic business situation, you pitch a prospective client to land a new account or a current customer to get additional sales. You pitch your boss to get a promotion or a coveted new assignment. You pitch to get subordinates to follow you. You pitch to get the powers-that-be to pay attention to your project instead of a colleague's or a competitor's, and you pitch to get someone to work on your team, instead of another's. You pitch to get money: the starting salary you want and deserve, a raise, the funds you need for a pet project, a bigger budget for your department. You pitch for visibility and for opportunities for development. The heart of it: *You pitch to land a new job, launch a new career, or start your own business.*

Most of us spend a lot of time pitching in our personal lives as well. If you're a mom, for example, you've probably invested some energy into pitching to get the best teachers for your kids. You find out who the teachers are, get the whole scoop on each and every one, and maneuver cleverly to get your child into that class—you're relentless. (If women pitched for themselves the way they pitch for their kids . . . wow, talk about unleashing power.) You strategize endlessly to develop the right pitch to finally have Thanksgiving dinner at your house this year—or not at your house, as the case may be. You pitch your boyfriend to go where you want to go on vacation, or your spouse to agree to renovate the kitchen or end the tradition of going to his family's house for dinner every Sunday. You think that maybe if you just pitch cleverly enough, you can finally get the man in your life to put the toilet seat down.

That, by the way, is one of my big personal pitching failures: I have failed to convince my husband, Jimmy, that it's in his best interest to put down the lid to the toilet seat, even after more than twenty years of trying. Pitching to get someone to change his behavior, as you'll learn, takes endless repetition and isn't the best technique. But that doesn't stop me from trying.

The truth is, I pitch just about every day for something, and I suspect you do too.

So the important question is not whether you pitch but how consciously and how well you do it. Are your pitches effective? Do you pitch with power? Do your pitches get the results you want at work, at home, in your life?

If you're like most women I know, the answer is probably not—certainly not as often as you'd like, particularly at work.

Here is the solid, take it to the bank, I'm-only-telling-you-this-because-I-love-you truth. If you are a woman, you probably have some issues around selling yourself. And if you can't sell yourself and your ideas, you can't pitch effectively.

But why is pitching such a challenge for us?

At its core, pitching often feels like a form of self-promotion. It is, after all, about putting your own needs first—or, at the very least, making your needs equal to the needs of whomever you're pitching to. And therein lies the rub for most women I know: Self-promotion feels like a guy thing. It smacks of arrogance. It feels antithetical to our nature, which we've been taught from birth should be all about modesty and nurturing and putting the needs of others first. Men seem to find it easy to sell themselves to get what they want, or at least accept selling themselves as necessary to getting ahead in life. Women typically find it distasteful.

This, I'm convinced, is the main reason so many women feel stuck at work. We can't pitch well because it feels like we are being someone we're not and, frankly, someone we don't want to be. We don't want to get ahead by blatant self-promotion or by putting our needs and wants ahead of others'.

4
Ronna Lichtenberg

We believe in our heart of hearts that we shouldn't have to sell ourselves to get what we want. We believe that if we work hard and are good at what we do, we should be recognized and rewarded without having to beat our own drum, toot our own horn, or play any other instrument in a self-promotional band.

Moreover, when we do try to sell our ideas, and ourselves, we feel as if we're not very good at it. We feel like we lack the brag gene or whatever quality it is that allows guys to shamelessly toss off their accomplishments and push their own agendas, without self-consciousness or guilt. In fact, there is considerable scientific evidence showing that part of the reason we hate to sell ourselves is indeed the result of the way our brains are wired (more on that, I promise). This, by the way, is neither good nor bad—it just is.

Trying to be someone we're not is draining. We may be able to pull it off, at least some of the time. But the effort uses up valuable energy and often leaves us feeling emotionally and physically spent.

When we are that spent, it's easier to feel like a victim. Some days it feels like there's nothing better than sitting around with a bunch of women moaning about how hard it is to be us. Sometimes that's even healthy. The problem is that moaning doesn't create momentum; it reinforces feelings of powerlessness. And when we tell ourselves it's okay not to pitch, we give ourselves permission to be smaller, duller, and less complete than we otherwise could be.

The solution is not to give up on pitching but rather to make pitching our own, to promote ourselves and our ideas in a manner that feels natural and authentic to us *as women*. We need to build on our desire for connection and skill at fostering relationships. In other words, we need to stop trying to pitch like a guy and start pitching like a girl if we want to win in a way that feels right for us.

"You throw like a girl." In childhood, those five little words were the ultimate put-down, leveled by boys at girls entering traditionally male turf: the playing field of sports. If you threw like a girl, you threw a ball weakly and with poor aim, failing to hit your target. When you threw like a girl, nobody wanted you on the team.

Well, we're all grown up now, and it's time to take that old negative rap and turn it into a positive. We can apply the concept to another traditionally male turf—the business world—tweak it, and reclaim it as a good thing.

Start with the action: throwing versus pitching. As women, we need to be more conscious and deliberative about the actions we take to understand and then advance our goals. Pitching means taking your ideas and tossing them, with intention, to someone else who can help move them forward rather than simply throwing them into the air and hoping they hit the target, or at least land in a way that doesn't embarrass us.

Pitching like a girl means doing it your way, by incorporating the desire for connection into transaction. It means doing it in a way that isn't about creating advantage but about creating connection. In men's language, selling is about making a killing, creating a position of dominance.

Well, excuse me, but I don't want to kill or dominate anybody. And therein lies another essential difference: When you pitch like a girl, no one has to lose in order for you to win. Not only are we more apt to achieve a victory, but we will feel much better about the victory we achieve.

We all have a limited number of choices at our disposal to get support for what we want to happen: We can ask, we can pay, we can demand, or we can persuade.

You pitch in situations where you don't have the power to issue an edict, or don't want to overuse or abuse the power you do have. You pitch to your kids when you are trying to convince them to do something they don't want to do—finish their homework, clean their rooms, go to bed, stop fighting, or simply be quiet for a few minutes—so you don't have to say, "Do it because I say so, because I'm the Mommy, that's why."

If you're pitching, you are not powerless. Too often we feel powerless because we don't know that pitching is an option. Pitching gives us power and control.

But there is an underlying comfort in feeling that we don't have control, in being a victim, in believing that whatever happens is not our fault. If you believe that you're a victim—of a sexist workplace, a tyrannical boss, an unfeeling spouse, or whomever or whatever else has somehow done you wrong and is holding you back—you let yourself off the hook. That's a comfy place to be. Yet it's choosing to rip yourself out of your comfort zone that will make all the difference in your life. If you don't go where the fear is, you somehow live a lesser life.

Unlike many authors who write successful self-help books, I haven't coached a professional sports team to their league championships or to Olympic glory, nor have I been the iconoclastic, much loved (or hated) CEO of a multibillion dollar corporation. I don't have a gazillion dollars in the bank (although I'm doing just fine, thank you), and I haven't dieted my way to rail-thinness (although I've almost made peace with that). I don't even claim to know more about pitching than anyone else on the planet.

But I do have some serious business credentials, which I need to tell you about so you can feel confident about my advice. Like some of you, it feels awkward for me to just flat out tell you I'm Miss-Listen-to-Me. But I want to set a good example for you, so here's my story.

I've spent more than twenty-five years in the business world, rising steadily through the corporate ranks to a series of high-level positions. Seventeen of those years were spent at Prudential, including five years on Wall Street as head of marketing for Prudential Securities. During that period I rolled out a series of groundbreaking programs, including one of the financial services industry's first major initiatives on marketing to women. Seven years ago, I left corporate life to become an entrepreneur, founding a management consulting company called Clear Peak Communications, which I still run today. My clients come to me for my signature programs on business development, strategy, communications, training, and women's initiatives.

I'm also a contributing editor specializing in career and business issues at *O* magazine, Hearst's joint venture publication with Oprah Winfrey. Along the way, I've written two other business books, both of which have done quite well. I've been on national TV and radio often enough that both my dentist and my hometown high school sociology teacher saw me. And I'm also a regular five-figure speaker on the motivational talk circuit. On my good days, I take pride in the fact that I've been successful in three very different careers.

That's the professional me—that is, Mrs. Lichtenberg, and what I think of as the Me, Inc. offering (more on that in chapter 4).

But that's not why I feel comfortable asking you to listen to what I have to say. The real expertise I have about pitching is that I'm on the same journey you are, trying to figure out how to be true to myself and to find a success that feels . . . *right*. Because my work allows me to connect with other women who are on the same journey, I've had the chance to understand the pitching challenges we have in common.

I can't say that life is perfect because I've learned so much about pitching; some days are better than others. But in the end, I can say my life goals power what I do every day, and there are a lot of days I feel that I am moving toward realizing my goals. I'm proud of the corporate career I had and even more proud that my business is alive and thriving.

Because I pitch, I get to write about issues I care about, for an audience I care about. Between my consulting work and my writing, I get a chance to help people change their lives for the better, which I care about most of all, and I've made some money along the way. And I've done it all while managing to sustain my marriage, help raise two stepchildren, and enjoy the company of truly wonderful friends.

None of the above would have been possible without good pitching. The best things in my work life, and often in my personal life, have been the result of pitching like a girl. Tapping into the sources of power, passion, and persuasion that others believe come naturally to me has made all the difference in my life, and I'm convinced it can do the same for you.

Ronna Lichtenberg

I pitch all day, most days, and have done so since I started out in the business world. I owe the completion of my college education to a pitch, my first big jobs to pitches, and, in a way, even my marriage to a pitch. And what I consider the biggest mistake of my life was the result of not pitching for advanced medical care when I should have. I picked the stories I'm about to share just to give you a sense of the breadth and depth of what effective pitching can accomplish, not because I think you should be pitching for the same things.

The first big pitch came back in the '70s, three years after I'd dropped out of the University of Texas four credits shy of graduation. Initially, I left college to deal with a diagnosis of a breast tumor, which fortunately turned out to be benign. Then I decided that I better get married because I was so old I was at risk of turning into an old maid—astonishing to me now that I thought this at the age of twenty-three, but I did—and so my boyfriend, Ron, and I got married and we moved to Washington, D.C.

The only way to put Ron through law school was for me to go to work. The only way for me to get a decent job was to have a college degree because good jobs require college degrees, which left me with two choices: lie, which didn't seem like such a great idea, or finish it up.

The problem was that I lived in D.C. and the University of Texas was in Austin, and they had a policy of counting credits for classes taken in Austin, not on the East Coast. Before virtual learning, people used to care a lot more about these things.

I wrote a letter to the admissions office and got a form response that basically said . . . we don't do it this way. That's where the pitch came in. I followed up with a phone call, asking the young assistant dean I got on the phone if there wasn't any way to fix this mess I had made of my life. There was; we worked out a deal where I took more hours at George Washington University than I needed but that satisfied the number and kinds of credit hours UT needed to let me graduate. She was smart enough to know that a UT alumna was more likely to be a donor to the school than a UT almost-alumna.

So I pitched to get my college degree, and then I pitched some more to land my first real jobs—not the making-money-during-the-summer-vacation kind of jobs I'd had since high school, but serious, you-and-new-hubby-will-starve-without-it jobs.

So it was off to the want ads, sending out cold résumés and making cold calls to see who might be desperate enough to employ an English lit major who knew something about Virginia Woolf and who could type reasonably fast, although not well. I landed a few of them, too.

It so happened that I'd saved a rejection letter I'd gotten from the Center for Policy Process, an all-purpose Washington think tank that advised big companies on trends in the environment. Looking back, I think I saved the rejection letter just because I was so grateful that I'd at least heard something, instead of that vast job-hunting silence, and because the letter itself sounded like someone nice had written it.

So I called them again and told an assistant whose name has escaped into the mists of time, "I saved your rejection letter [which is already an attention grabber], and I know I wasn't right for the position you had open before, but I am right for your company and here's why you should hire me." Then I ticked off the reasons: I would work on a project basis; I knew all about the federal government; I knew how to write, and by that time my typing had improved. I think it must have also been clear to them that I would work really cheap. The head of the company, John Naisbitt, who went on to write *Megatrends* and become a big business guru, hired me as a freelancer. I ended up staying full time and learned a lot about futures research, research techniques, and how to write for a business audience.

In the decades since I left Washington, I've probably pitched hundreds of times in a variety of professional situations—to land a bigger job, earn more money, or open up new opportunities for advancement. I've pitched in my personal life as well—starting with Jimmy, who is now my husband, to be my date to such an important function that he knew my intentions were serious.

Sometimes I've won and sometimes I've lost. But I've never, in my personal life, had as big a loss as I did in a situation where I *should* have pitched but I didn't.

In my late teens, I had found out from my mother's obstetrician, an extremely honorable man, that he'd given my mom very high doses of DES, an artificial estrogen that was used in the belief that it would prevent miscarriage. It turned out that the drug didn't prevent miscarriages in moms but it did sometimes cause uterine cancer in their daughters. With that risk in mind, when I started having abnormal pap tests in my mid-twenties, alarm bells starting going off in my gynecologist's head.

I can't tell you whether the DES caused my cervical cancer; given the kind of cancer it was, it probably didn't. I can tell you that it seemed, at the time, that the early-stage cancer I had might kill me. I ended up in the emergency room, and in the middle of the night I had an emergency hysterectomy. I was twenty-six.

Now here is where pitching could've come in. Before I had that first surgical procedure, somehow I had heard that there was a doctor in Massachusetts who was treating cases like mine with lasers. I can remember thinking about calling him, and I can remember feeling like my cancer wasn't advanced enough and that I wasn't important enough and that somehow my needs weren't sufficient to justify making a call to find out if there was some way he could help me. Maybe if I'd made the call, maybe if I'd made the pitch, he couldn't have helped me. Then again, maybe if I'd made the call, he could have and I'd have been able to bear children. I will never know.

Two months ago, decades after this incident, I got suspicious results on a medical test, indicating that there was some chance that the cancer had come back. My doctor took another test, saying that if the results weren't what we hoped for, I would need to see an oncologist. First I freaked. Then I thought, "It's really early, no big deal. I have time. I can see any oncologist, it doesn't matter." It took me about half a day to realize that I had fallen into a negative self-belief trap (that is, "I'm not really important enough to get the best care") like the ones I'm going to talk about in chapter 3.

Determined not to make the same mistake twice, I moved into high pitching gear. Within 24 hours I had done my homework online and knew which oncologists specialized in cases like mine. I'd talked to my friends and felt comfortable about asking for help—just for sheer emotional support and also to find out who they might know who could help me get into the right docs if I needed help to do it. My brother, task oriented like many men (as you'll see), went to work online and was able to tell me which hospitals had the most experience with new techniques that might be right for me.

It turned out that the next set of tests looked okay. But no matter what, I feel better knowing that even if future rounds of tests aren't so good, I am ready to pitch—that I can do my homework, rely on relationships, and ask for what I need—and that being ready will make a positive difference in the outcome, and in how I feel about my life.

Now, a bid to complete college at a different institution, a bid to land a coveted job, and my failure to get the best possible medical treatment may not appear to have all that much in common. But in fact, these seemingly disparate situations turned out to have a lot in common, although I certainly didn't realize it at the time. The cases that worked involved pitching, straight-up. I began the process by figuring out what I really wanted the outcome to be and identifying a key person who could help me reach that goal. I thought about what value was in it for that other person—that is, why it would be in that person's best interests to help me achieve my goal—and then worked hard to communicate that added value.

So while each of these situations involved a kind of self-promotion—I was, after all, putting myself out there to get what I wanted—it was not the swaggering, testosterone-fueled kind of self-promotion that relies on bragging and domination to achieve its goals. It's the kind of self-promotion that says, "What's good for me can be good for you too, and here's why." It's the kind that relies on relationship-building skills and seeks to have everyone walk away feeling good about the outcome.

It's pitching like a girl instead of like a guy, and it works.

Ronna Lichtenberg

CHAPTER 1

pink and blue

In a way, the world would be easier if all women were the same and all men were the same. There would be those handy visual cues we could rely on to tell us everything; we could simply note a heavy beard and assume that everything coming up in chapter 3 is true and that would be that. Except that all men are not alike, and neither are all women. Most of us have found that out the hard way, by making assumptions that turn out to be completely wrong.

That's why even though I am going to go through the vast generalizations about brain sex and stereotypes, I'm also going to spend time on ways to get a better fix on individual differences. The first kind of difference I'm going to look at is the difference between the styles people prefer to use to do business: whether they put a higher emphasis on connection, or relationship, or whether they put a greater emphasis on task, the activity of business.

I call this preference pink and blue style because, more often than not, a woman will have a pink style and a man a blue style—but not always. Sure, these colors are less politically correct than, say, orange and green, but that makes them easier to remember, too. Over the past few years, I've found that pink and blue is a simple concept for people to "get"; it's easy to use, and it's really powerful. You can get a lot of "A-ha!" moments out of the concept of pink and blue styles, and I'm going to rely on it through the entire pitching process.

THE BASICS OF PINK AND BLUE

A person with a pink style is someone who wants to connect with you before doing business with you. A "pink" will first mention the weather, your bull dog, your handbag, your shoes, your vacation—something, anything, before getting down to the business at hand.

It's easy to find pink-styled women on TV and in the movies: The enormously successful *Legally Blonde* films are a great example. Elle Woods, the lead character played by Reese Witherspoon, is an over-the-top pink who not only wears it as her signature color, but dresses her Chihuahua, Bruiser, in it. Elle does well at Harvard Law and as a lobbyist, not despite her style but because of it. Her desire to connect to other people, and to be personal even in situations where personal is traditionally not valued, help her win.

If you're really in the mood to rent a DVD, there's a classic scene involving pink styles in the movie *White Man Can't Jump*, the only basketball movie that ever made sense to me. In the scene, the character played by Rosie Perez is in bed with her honey, played (adorably, in my opinion) by Woody Harrelson. She tells him her mouth is dry. Woody jumps up and gets her a glass of water, clearly expecting some kind of acknowledgment. Instead, she gets pissed off. She tells him that she didn't want the glass of water. She didn't want him to *fix* the problem; she wanted him to empathize with her experience of dry-mouthedness. Empathy over task, that's the height of pink.

But there are men with pink styles, too, even though most of them don't like it the first time they have to say so in one of my workshops (by the end, they realize it's cool to be pink). Former president Bill Clinton's style tended toward pink, and whatever else you might say about him, he is abundantly a guy. But equally abundantly, he wants connection, not to mention affirmation. Newspaper coverage of Clinton's first day out of office, for example, reported that he greeted a woman in the crowd by saying, "Love your shoes!" My rule is if they start a conversation by talking about your shoes, honey, they are pink.

In a training program I did with Steven Safier, Ph.D., from HayGroup (the

Ronna Lichtenberg

big consulting firm), we used a lot of movie references to start teaching people how to spot pink and blue. One of our favorite pink men is Dr. Wilbur Larch in the movie *The Cider House Rules*. Dr. Larch, played by Michael Caine, is a physician in charge of a 1940s New England orphanage. One of Dr. Larch's former charges is Homer Wells, played by Tobey Maguire. In one moving scene, we see Homer reading a letter from Dr. Larch, including a very straight-forward "I love you." The "I love you" is a dead giveaway of pink style be-cause normally in movies a man is only allowed to say "I love you" to another man under the following conditions: it's his partner, who is dying of something awful; the team just won, or the team just lost; he and his buddy are either about to be or just have been fired upon by serious weapons and one of them isn't going to make it.

But what about women, real business women, with a pink style? There are more of them than you might think, but my nominee for the most compelling triumph of pink style is Oprah Winfrey. Oprah puts connection first, so much so that despite the fact that she is one of the most successful businesswoman in the world, she's been quoted as saying that she doesn't think of herself as a business person. Oprah's ability—and her desire—to connect is the hallmark of everything she does, and it's key to the degree and nature of her success. As a *Fortune* magazine writer put it in a cover story about her, "Everything is per-sonal at Harpo," Oprah's production company. Including business.

Now blues, on the other hand, are the opposite of pinks. They place a high priority on what I call task—just getting the job done. Someone with a blue style either just isn't naturally a "people person" or wants to keep his or her emotional connections outside the office.

Blues like to know where people stand, literally. Rank and order matter to blues. A blue wants to know right away how you fit into the grand scheme of things. Blues introduce themselves with titles and accomplishments.

Blues value business relationships and form close ones, but they're able to see their success as independent of relationships. A blue who is well paid will feel she has achieved success, regardless of how she feels about her workplace relationships. The CEO of Boeing, a classic blue, distinguished himself from his predecessor by saying that he was more likely to shoot first and ask questions later. If you hear a blue say someone has "killer instinct," it is probably meant as praise.

It's getting easier to find positive examples of blue women on television and in the movies, too, but traditionally, blue women got a bad rap; hard-boiled, cold-blooded, overtly ambitious women are a standard movie cliché and a way that our culture expresses ambivalence about women and power. (In chapter 3 I'll talk about the female stereotypes that present particular challenges for blue women.)

One positive image of a blue woman, though, is in the James Bond film *Die Another Day*. Those of you who are longtime Bond fans (and who isn't?) may remember that Bond's boss, known as M, was always played by a man—until a few years ago when M began to be played by the incomparable Judi Dench. In a scene near the beginning, James, played by (in my opinion, a slightly too skinny) Pierce Brosnan, has just been released from a nasty Korean prison, which specialized in low-tech but effective tortures that involved a lot of scorpions and ice water.

Anyway, in the scene in question, Bond and M are having a little debriefing about the circumstances leading up to his negotiated release and M makes it clear that if it had been up to her, she would have let the enemy shoot him. She also makes it clear that he will get back to work only when she decides. Her part of the conversation involves a lot of steely-eyed glances and ends with her spinning on a heel and striding out of the room, dismissing the possibility that she has the slightest interest in what he has to say about his future. We know that she cares about him but that her duty, and her actions, will be based more on how she feels about the *job* than how she feels about him. Very blue.

Positive images of blue men, on the other hand, are everywhere in popular culture. One of my favorite blue men in movies is U.S. Marshal Samuel Gerard, played by Tommy Lee Jones, in *The Fugitive*. The U.S. marshal is on the hunt for a doctor, played by Harrison Ford, who is accused of murdering his wife. From the start, the marshal's team refers to him as "Big Dog," which

Ronna Lichtenberg

is a definite clue that he is probably not going to have a pink style. But any doubts you might have had about his style are erased when he takes over the case from some lame local authority and starts barking out directions about the kind of search he wants done.

Blue-styled women in real life are pretty easy to find, too, because women with a blue style were the first wave of big achievers in business. Margaret Thatcher, to reach back a bit, had a very blue style. Buttoned up. No nonsense. Martha Stewart has a blue style as well. She is interested in the thing, in the task, not the person. Fortune 500 company women CEOs also tend to be blue—or at least act as if they are, which is what I call having a "striped" style.

In every workshop I do, there are strong pinks and strong blues. But most people have had to adapt their styles to some degree. The truth is that since the world of business tilts toward blue rules, if you are a pink woman in business you probably have a few blue stripes.

What does a striped woman look like? The big-time women broadcasters all seem striped, although the width and depth of those stripes vary. Katie Couric, for example, often leads with a pink style: friendly, approachable, clearly wants to connect. But she gets to task quickly, and it is clear she is about the business of getting the story. And Barbara Walters seems to me to have given herself permission to be pretty pink in recent years, especially when she's just one of the girls on her TV show, *The View*. Anyone who specializes in making people cry has got to put a big emphasis on connection.

Most people with stripes have one that is dominant—a style that they lead with and that they default to when stressed. Others are pretty evenly balanced. For example, my friend Diane Perlmutter, who heads up Gilda's Club, an international nonprofit organization that helps families live with cancer, says she is striped. She does care about connection. But when running a meeting, she wants to "get to the point." And when writing e-mails, she often has to remind herself to "say something nice"; some kind of opening note about the weekend, or a holiday, or whatever. For a total pink, that note would come naturally. A total blue wouldn't bother.

think pink

Here's what's great about being pink.

You live your business life in a way that gives you the opportunity to connect and to leverage those relationships to create value. Sorry to say leverage—I know it sounds pretty blue and maybe even a little calculating, but the truth is that relationships hold value and help you get things done.

Chances are, if you're pink, you have more people to turn to who will help you get what you want. You probably know the names of your dry cleaner, your kid's substitute teacher, the gynecologist's billing clerk, and everyone in security and in the mailroom.

You probably also have times when whatever work you are doing feels really good because it helps someone else. What you do can feel meaningful. Sometimes it just feels *good* to have coworkers, or colleagues, or employees, or whatever work relationships you have—and if you don't have these connections, you can at least imagine a situation where work would feel good because of the chance to have good working relationships.

Here's what's not so great about being pink.

When you're pink, you care so much about relationships that they are always with you. Ask a pink why she has trouble asking for a raise (more on this in chapter 9) and she'll talk to you of her concerns about how her boss feels about her. Listen to two pinks trying to negotiate a business deal and you will hear immense awkwardness, apologies, and a lot of talk about how they both feel—and that's a good discussion. The bad ones are when both pinks feel that they sacrificed too much in exchange for making the other person feel better and then brood about it, silently and independently.

It's also hard to be a pink in business. The way most people think about business is blue; only the really smart ones get the value of stripes. So if you're pink and you work, you are already pretending to be blue some of the time. The more blue the company culture, the more you are pretending.

That's an enormous strain, and, I think, one reason women end up bailing

Ronna Lichtenberg

out of jobs in big companies. When you are a pink woman, you are living in what is essentially an alien culture, which has a high cost. The "price" of trying to be someone you aren't is part of why the price of success, at least corporate success as men define it, seems to be too high for a lot of women. If you are a pink woman trying to be blue all the time, you don't need me to tell you how hard it is. Chances are the effort to be someone you're not is making you unhappy and probably also a little angry.

Another challenge for pink women is that pinks spend a fair amount of energy monitoring and reacting to other people's emotions. The saying "it's not personal, it's business" was invented for pinks: A pink can get so caught up in relationship drama that she loses focus.

Finally, what's most hard is that a lot of blues have bad attitudes about pinks, especially pink women. They think pinks are a little flaky. They think that pinks are scattered. And they think a pink's focus on relationships is excessive and a liability when it comes to tough business decisions.

blues rule

What's great about being a blue woman?

A blue woman's style is more naturally consistent with how most big organizations are run. A blue woman's desire to get down to business, or be strictly business, is easier for blue men (and most of the guys at the top of the food chain are blue!) to understand. Because a blue woman, as opposed to a pink woman, tends to put a higher premium on being respected than on being cared about, it is in many ways easier for her to succeed in the classic definition of success: climbing the next rung of the ladder.

What's not so great about being blue? Blue women are more likely to make a classic woman's mistake: thinking that working hard and efficiently is all it takes to get ahead.

Some months ago, I met with a blue woman named Marci, who worked for a giant telecom company and who, after sixteen years of devoted service, had the feeling that one of the heads cut off during the next round of head-cutting would be hers. (She was right: She got the news not long after.) Marci, to put it mildly, was terrified. She was also amazed that this could happen to her.

She told me she'd worked really, really hard. Marci was in the office late most nights. She was in the office at least one day every weekend. She did what she was told, and she did it well.

But when I asked her who she could turn to for support internally, when it looked like it might be possible to get a lateral move in the organization that would keep her from getting cut, she couldn't come up with any names. And when I asked her about her outside networks, she drew a complete blank. Marci had been working; she hadn't been "wasting" her time socializing—classic blue, classic blue risk.

Another risk, particular to blue women, is the opposite of the blue woman's advantage. Because blue women more naturally fit into the "normal" rules of business, it is easier for them to get taken seriously, to be given visibility, and to be asked to join the right projects and teams. But the double bind is that "normal" rules of being feminine are the direct opposite of a blue style: Women are expected to be empathic, care more about connection, take a moment to smile, remember the personal.

Women who don't follow all of those rules in business are more likely to be admired, and also more likely to be feared and criticized, both by pink men and pink women. A blue woman, paying attention to task in a blue way—by concentrating on the job to be done rather than on those who are doing it—is more likely to be called a bitch.

In the high-tech years, there was even a camp for blue women, which was supposed to cure them of being "bully broads." The idea was that the same behaviors that are okay in guys are not okay for women. Here's just one example, as reported in a *New York Times* article: "Her clients loved her. Her coworkers didn't. She didn't say please and thank you or greet everyone as she walked down the hall. Many men at her company didn't, but she was sent [to a coach] for her 'intimidating style.'"

Ronna Lichtenberg

How Do I Spot a Pink or a Blue?

Here are some tips on how to tell who's who.

How to Spot a Pink

- First sentence after hello is, "I love your shoes!"
- Introduces herself by telling you something about herself, her family, or her pets.
- Has pictures of people in her life at work.
- Expresses discomfort with hierarchy, even when she's the boss.
- Makes a point of offering food/beverages whenever people meet.
- Seems to feel funny talking about money (other than talking about spending it!).
- Believes in win/win.
- Talks about creativity and passion.
- Starts meetings by asking for everyone's attention.
- Dresses to express herself.

How to Spot a Blue

- No greetings or sign-offs on e-mails.
- Introduces herself with credentials.
- Has awards on display.
- Proud of military service.
- Talks about wanting to make sure she is positioned properly.
- Talks about cost control and managing the balance sheet.
- Believes there are winners and losers.
- Very comfortable with hierarchy.
- Wants other people to "get to the point."
- Starts meetings by starting the meeting.
- Dresses conservatively, but with something that makes a statement (like big jewelry).

Blue women I know who've worked on adding a few pink stripes point out a hazard shared by both styles: feeling like a fake. Nancy, a blue friend, told me that she'd just written an e-mail and gone back over it to add a paragraph at the beginning that was more personal. She said that it made her feel bad to do it because it isn't who she really is. I hadn't realized until she pointed it out that her e-mails to me are all purely transactional—what needs to be done, how we are going to do it, etc. She feels comfortable enough with me to be blue and not to add something that isn't natural for her.

I've also run across a lot of women who pretend, even to themselves, that they are blue when they are really not because the superficial advantages of it are so strong and because it is so strongly reinforced. Employers have over the last few years spent a lot of money to teach pink women how to act like blues, starting with dressing for success in the '70s and continuing with power talk in the '90s. Management has hoped for a while that the way to create an inclusive workplace is to get women in general, and pink women in particular, to just suck it up and turn into guys, or at least blue women.

That is not going to happen, for all kinds of biological, cultural, and psychological reasons I'll get to in a bit.

TAKING PINK AND BLUE TO WORK

The reason you need to know your style is so you can adapt it to your prospects—I'll get to specifics in chapter 7.

Now that you know how to spot a pink or a blue, and before you take a test so you can be sure of your own style, let me share a couple of stories about the potential power that lies in knowing these styles.

The stories involve the same pitching partner, whom I'll call Tom. The first time we pitched Vicky, I decided to experiment by sharing my pink/blue system with Tom in advance. My natural style is pink, if you haven't already guessed, and so is Vicky's. She's a big deal at a big investment bank: We were pitching her on a substantial training project. As a blue,

Ronna Lichtenberg

Tom's first idea was to go to the meeting prepared with a big binder full of facts and figures.

Knowing Vicky is pink, here is how we decided to approach it instead. It was summer, and I knew she wasn't on a diet. How did I know? Another pink woman will always tell you which diet she is on within the first ten minutes of a discussion. I also knew that she loved chocolate. I know that because I am really off the deep end about chocolate and talk about it too much, so other pinks, wanting to relate to me, bond with me by talking about it, too.

When we arrived at the meeting, Tom brought with him fancy iced mocha drinks, and I brought my personal favorite brand of dark chocolate. She was happy to see the chocolate and tucked it away for later—I will confess, much to my intense disappointment. I had figured since she's pink, she would share.

Then Vicky and I talked about shoes for a while. Then we talked about her daughter. Then we talked sort of generally about issues related to the program we were there to discuss. And then, finally—and only because I thought Tom might explode if we didn't get on with it—we told her about what we wanted to do. But we didn't go through a binder. We didn't ever hear specifics about Vicky's current position or how that fit into the broader scheme of things. We agreed on one next step, which was that she would talk to someone she trusted to move things forward. She did. And we did eventually end up getting to Tom's binder; the formal presentation and all the detail would have been wrong to cover in a first meeting with a pink.

Shortly thereafter, Tom and I met with Jeff, a senior guy at an accounting firm. What we had heard about him in advance made us think he was blue, so we prepared for a blue meeting. We had a binder. We had a chart. We were clear about next steps.

Jeff was exactly on time for the meeting. He also announced at the start that the meeting would end on time. We met in a conference room. He had a pad and a sharp pencil in front of him. He made it clear that he wanted to get right down to business and that his preference was to start by providing his thoughts on how he saw the situation. Within a few moments, he had credentialed him-

The Difference between Mary and Joe

Edie Weiner, *the* well known and respected futurist, gave me the following scenario about Mary and Joe as an example of how responsive women are to relationship considerations. Mary is the average woman; Joe the average man.

John, the boss, calls Mary in. He says, "Mary, we had a great year. You got a fabulous bonus." He hands her an envelope and turns away to work at his desk. Mary walks out of the office and how does she feel? Eighty percent of the Marys (and, I must add, all of the pinks) feel upset after this encounter. "Why didn't he tell me he liked me? Why didn't he tell me how good I am? How come I'm getting this check, anyway?"

Now John calls Joe into his office and says the same thing. Then he turns around and goes back to work. Joe walks out of the office, looks at the check, and says, "*Yes!*" Eighty percent of the Joes feel great.

Now let's tweak the scenario. John the boss now calls Mary in and says, "Mary, you are the best thing that ever happened to this division. I can sleep nights because you work here. I can't tell you how many people come into my office wanting you on their team because they trust you and they like you. *But* . . . you know, we had a bad year, and I fought really hard for whatever I could get for you. It's really not a great check, but please know that I fought as hard as I could because I think the world of you." Most of the Marys take the check, leave the office, and are flying.

Now John calls Joe into the office and he says the same thing he told Mary. Joe walks out of the office, looks at the check, sees how small it is and how does he feel? Most of the Joes will say, "I'm out of here! I'm worth more than this!"

One final tweak. John calls Mary into his office and says, "Mary, we had a great year, and you have a phenomenal bonus check in here. But I have to tell you that we have some real issues here. People tell me they don't want to work with you on their team." How do most Marys feel? Devastated. And the Joes, after the same conversation? Ready to frame the check (after, of course, it's been cashed).

Ronna Lichtenberg

self and laid out where he thought the business was working and where it wasn't. Then he wanted to see the binder. We went through the document page by page. When he had questions, Tom drew answers in a model on a flip chart. Jeff, blue to the end, closed the meeting with the specific next steps he was going to take. Same program, different approach. Good results in both.

We're going to talk a lot about style adjustments in this book, and how I know it makes you more powerful, not less, but I'll limit myself to just one more story for now.

My husband, Jimmy, who has a blue style, often consults for people in publishing, which has a lot of pink folks in it. In his early days of consulting, he would come home complaining about how his what-I now-think-of-as-pink-dominated meetings went. Me: "How did your day go, honey?" Him: "I went to another one of those endless meetings. I can't figure it out. The meeting goes on for an hour. For the first fifty-five minutes, it is blah-blah-blah-blah-blah-blah. Then, in the last five minutes, they agree on everything and we're done. Why can't they do the last five minutes first?"

Eventually, after I figured out pink and blue styles, I said, "You know what? They can't do the last five minutes first. It is not their wiring. And it is just as efficient because once they bond, they can really agree on what they're doing and get it done instead of agreeing on specific tasks and walking out of the room and going their own way."

Being blue, instead of finding this interesting and wanting to share his feelings about my brilliant discovery, Jimmy said, "So, what do I do about it?" So, for a few years I taught him something to say at the beginning of meetings that would indicate a pink-style interest in relationships, and I also told him that after he said it he could space out and think about something else. Like baseball. The real high point came a couple of years ago when he came home one night and I asked, "How was your day, honey?" and he said, "The meeting was *great*. We all sat down and they were doing that pink thing. And I said . . . ," here he paused for dramatic effect . . . , " 'Do you think boots are the new pumps?' "

there's opportunity in them-there styles

Stacey Englander, senior vice president of investments at the Lebenthal Division of Advest, an AXA Financial business, sent an e-mail after hearing me talk about pink and blue and deciding to give it a try. The subject line was "It Really Works."

Stacey explained she'd met a prospect and gone, in a forty-five minute conversation, from talking about the woman's great necklace to going over the details of her portfolio. The prospect then spontaneously offered eight referrals, after Stacey asked her about what she did for relaxation.

"Now, I'm not certain that the necklace and asking about relaxing really won the deal, but it sure as heck didn't hurt it."

you know that woman you hate?

I will confess that I'm not from the "she's another woman so I should love her" school. I try not to diss or hurt another woman in business, but there are women I like more or less, just as there are guys I like more or less.

Having witnessed, though, some fights between women at work that look like 1940s Japanese monster movies, complete with fangs and claws and swishing scaled tails, I've come to this conclusion: Many of the worst fights are between pink women and blue women. A pink woman sees a blue woman and expects connection—after all, she's another woman, right? For whatever reason, it's not the blue woman's thing to connect, so she either doesn't even notice the pink's friendly nature or doesn't respond. Consider the sword-fighting scenes in the *Kill Bill* movies. As Uma Thurman's character fights her former gal pals, they pause to chitchat over a cup of coffee or discuss their pasts. In one scene, Uma even says, "Between us girls . . ." with sword at the ready.

The pink feels hurt, rejected, and then angry. The blue gets angry because there's no rational reason for the pink to get angry. Then it simmers until full boil. All for lack of a little slack about style.

Ronna Lichtenberg

FORGET MISSIONARY WORK

I will admit that I love this pink and blue concept. Being who *we* are, whether pink, blue, or striped, helps us relax about other people being who *they* are, which is essential if we want to really communicate. In a workshop I did for *Better Homes and Gardens* magazine, one pink woman said, "I just realized that I don't have to get the blues to be pink. If they don't want to schmooze at the beginning of a meeting, that's okay."

Steve Safier, a "mostly" blue, echoes this: "Pink and blue has become a great shorthand for me to think and talk about how to consult. In fact, my 'bluest' client just selected a particular type of business partner because he needed—and said—that his company needed a little 'pink' at this tumultuous time in their history."

It's a concept that is so simple that people get it quickly, and it provides a shorthand for talking about stuff that might otherwise be difficult. It is much easier to say, "Oh, I'm blue, and that doesn't work for me," than, "You idiot woman, don't you know that I don't want to talk about your book club?"

We'll also see that knowing styles makes it much easier for you to pitch, because you can't pitch if you don't throw to where they stand. That sounds simple, but we've all spent a lot of time throwing to where we want them to be instead.

For some of you, the very thought of adapting your style is hateful. I'd just done a workshop for a New York women's group when a woman came up to me and said, "I hate what you're telling me. Why should I have to adapt to blues? I'm sick of them. If I have to limit or change how I approach them, they've won. I want to live in a pink world. Why do I have to do this?"

I answered her question this way: "You don't have to pay attention to anyone else's style or need—*if* you're happy with the way your work life is going now. If it is going great, then ignore me. If you're well paid and fulfilled, doing what you want to do, forget you ever heard me. But if you're not, then you might want to consider a change."

Early in my Prudential career, I worked directly with the six members of what was then called the Executive Office, which was supposed to support the chairman and CEO of the company (it was an idea whose time came, and went). Anyway, one of the EO members was a man I'll call Todd, a brilliant man who had made his reputation in various types of financial analysis. Todd was also very blue. I think it is fair to say that we respected each other but found each other pretty baffling, and I felt that he was difficult to please. Okay . . . actually, I felt he was just plain difficult.

About that time, Deborah Tannen's first book, *You Just Don't Understand*, came out, and I was thrilled by it. Flush with enthusiasm, I bought a copy for Todd, took it to him, and basically demanded that he read it. I still remember the look on Todd's face while he was listening to me carry on about the brilliant insights in this book. To his credit, he was really trying to understand what I was saying, but it was as if I had come not from another country, but from another galaxy. He asked me what the point was to all of this. My point, although I don't think I put it even this clearly, was that if he read the book, he would understand me. Once he really understood me, he would value me more. If I felt more valued, our relationship would be better. And that would be wonderful. (If you're thinking of doing something similar, direct the guy to Appendix 1 first.)

I left the book with him and a few weeks later asked if he had read it. He said he had, but he was even more irritated with me; he basically said that he had no idea why I thought that book was relevant to him or my doing my job in any way. We went on to our next task.

Looking back, I realize that what I wanted was conversion. I wanted Todd to want to connect. I wanted Todd to be pink. In fact, at some level, what I really wanted was for Todd to see the light, renounce being blue, and see that pink was really better. Which, of course, didn't happen.

I'm not alone in trying to convert other people to my style. Recently I had a chance to meet with Keri, another high-potential corporate pink in a big company who had just been rotated in from a line job to a higher-level staff

Ronna Lichtenberg

position. She was invited to do a formal presentation to the muckety-mucks, which she was excited about because she took a lot of pride in how she presented.

Keri worked hard on her presentation. It was creative. Visually interesting. She was passionate about it. She was proud that she had come to it from a very different angle. As Keri told me about it, I could imagine her giving it—blonde hair flying, her vibrantly colored outfit catching the eye, her hands waving.

Then she told me how much they hated it. After the presentation, she was told that something was wrong. When she pressed for feedback, the only thing they could single out was that they liked PowerPoint slides that were blue.

Now on the face of it, that seems pretty silly. But what they were trying to tell her was that her style wasn't working for them. (Actually, there is more to it, which I will cover in the brain sex material in chapter 3, on how men perceive different kinds of information.) Keri had two reactions.

One was that they were asking her to be something she wasn't when she wanted to be who she is. That left her fluctuating wildly between two desires, the desire to accommodate them by giving them blue slides and the desire to have them value her for who she is. But the other part of her reaction was to want to prove to them how stupid they were for not seeing that she was right—that all of her pink style was superior to how they had been doing business. And it is that alternating between feeling like a victim, that we are totally misunderstood, and feeling like a missionary, that we are going to prove it to them, that can so often keep us from getting what we want.

And what's the point? The point is one that we all keep learning in relationships in work and outside it. We are not going to change other people. A blue is not going to be pink. A pink is not going to be blue. Adding stripes is good—I'm all for it, and you are going to learn how. But what you are *not* going to do is learn how to change other people. They are not going to change. You can only change how you approach them, which will increase the chance that you will get the reaction you want.

Are You Pink or Blue?

Read the questions below and check off whether each statement describes you or not. Then count the number of pink and blue responses and refer to the scoring key at the end.

YES NO

☐ ☐   1. When first meeting somebody, I like to know their credentials (where they work, their title, where they went to school, etc.).

☐ ☐   2. If I could, I would buy everything online.

☐ ☐   3. I try to answer the phone by saying hi and then my name.

☐ ☐   4. At office meetings, I like to connect with people before we get to the agenda.

☐ ☐   5. The most satisfying discussions I have at work are about how to get the job done.

☐ ☐   6. I've been called aloof or unemotional.

☐ ☐   7. It's important to know the person you are doing business with as a person.

☐ ☐   8. It annoys me when people talk about their feelings at work.

☐ ☐   9. Announcing accomplishments is self-promotion and mildly distasteful.

☐ ☐   10. I believe it's my job to put people at ease.

☐ ☐   11. It doesn't matter if you don't like your boss; you have to respect him or her.

☐ ☐   12. It bothers me when someone comments on my shoes or outfit.

☐ ☐   13. I like to know where I stand in the ranks.

☐ ☐   14. I've been told I'm too emotional.

☐ ☐   15. I try to stand up straight and take up space.

Ronna Lichtenberg

Now analyze your answers.

1. Yes = Blue	No = Pink	9. Yes = Pink	No = Blue
2. Yes = Blue	No = Pink	10. Yes = Pink	No = Blue
3. Yes = Pink	No = Blue	11. Yes = Blue	No = Pink
4. Yes = Pink	No = Blue	12. Yes = Blue	No = Pink
5. Yes = Blue	No = Pink	13. Yes = Blue	No = Pink
6. Yes = Blue	No = Pink	14. Yes = Pink	No = Blue
7. Yes = Pink	No = Blue	15. Yes = Blue	No = Pink
8. Yes = Blue	No = Pink		

How'd you do? Ten or more of one color: This is your dominant color. Anything under ten: You have stripes! Note your score. Later, you'll learn how to make your color work for you.

am I blue?

So, what are you? Before we go any further, stop reading and take the test, opposite. If you're pink, you will love the very idea of a quiz. If you're blue, you will want the test to be longer and more fact based. Blues, be patient. In chapter 3 I'll get to scientific support for the style differences I am drawing here and we'll take a couple of tests with a lot more questions.

Later in the book you will learn additional ways to think about and adjust for style, but pink and blue is really all you need to get started and to see your own world of opportunities in a fresh way.

So with your style in mind—pink, blue, or striped—we are going to get started by helping you get clear about what you want. Because without knowing what you really want, how can you possibly be effective in going after it?

CHAPTER 2

the quick-dry chapter

I know. When you are really in a hurry, even waiting three minutes for your nails to dry takes too long.

You may feel the same way about getting to the how-to part of this book, particularly if you are blue and ready to get right to the task.

Since I am pitching to you, you're the boss, and there is no way I could, or should, make you read something you're not in the mood to tackle (just a little pitching preview).

So, if you're in a big rush, here's the deal. I'm going to give you the highlights of the next chapter, "What's in Your Head That's Not in His," here so you can go directly to the how-to part starting with chapter 4. In exchange, I'm asking you to read chapter 3 later because I think it will really help you understand more about yourself and how to find the success you want. It's stuff you really need to know, even if you don't want to know it right this minute.

If you are pink, you are probably going to be really interested in chapter three and will want and value getting a relationship perspective before getting to the how-to of the book. You can skim these pages and just keep on reading the book in order.

THE THREE THINGS THAT CAN HOLD YOU BACK, IN QUICK TIME

No. 1: Biology

Biological differences between men and women are in our brains, as well as in our pants. Research into what scientists call "brain sex" has found that the average woman has more of an orientation toward thinking about, and valuing, relationships than the average man does. We women take in more information about other people and their emotions and are more aware of, and more likely to talk about, our reactions to those emotions.

Because business organizations were designed by men, for male brains, these female brain sex gifts have been considered a liability at the office. Organizations that are highly masculine in style tend to devalue styles that are associated with the feminine. Women feel devalued, in countless small ways, and it adds an extra burden to our working day.

Understanding biological differences, including the potential advantages of having a woman's brain, is the first step to becoming truly successful. It helps you understand how best to manage "them," but more important, how to manage yourself—your own reactions, emotions, and desires.

No. 2: Stereotypes

It is increasingly clear that nature and nurture both play a role in how we grow up to be women and what we think a woman should or shouldn't do.

At work, both positive and negative stereotypes about women abound, in the minds of our colleagues as well as in our own minds. These stereotypes, although much more subtle than they used to be, still exist: for example, the conflicting stereotypes about what makes a woman seem feminine and what makes someone seem authoritative.

It is particularly important for women to recognize and manage these stereotypes during transition points: entering the work force, or reentering it;

reaching for more responsibility; and hoping to make it past a senior level to the very top. That's because whenever we are making a change, we come under closer scrutiny, and behaviors we may have previously gotten rewarded for are not necessarily the behaviors that will get us rewards now.

No. 3: Negative self-beliefs

For members of any minority group, it's easy to internalize stereotypes into negative self-beliefs. Women are no exception.

Beliefs, like "a good woman is modest," can be so deeply seeded that we don't even know we believe them, let alone recognize the way they influence our actions and decisions.

Recognizing those beliefs in ourselves, and learning how to manage them, helps us take charge of our lives. And, as we all know but as we all always forget, changing how we see the world, and how we behave in it, is the only way to get someone else to change how they behave toward us.

Fortunately, with a new belief system (which I call Me, Inc.), some new tools, and some new skills (the how-to part of pitching like a girl), you can take all these influences that might be holding you back and convert them into a power source that will help to move you forward.

And no matter how slowly you read, I bet you got through this in less than three minutes!

Now, for you pinks, just keep on reading. And for you hard-charging blues, full speed ahead on how to put all this information to work by learning how to pitch like a girl, starting with chapter 4 on page 93. (But PS: Remember, you promised to read chapter 3 . . . soon.)

Ronna Lichtenberg

CHAPTER 3
what's in your head that's not in his

PART 1: BRAIN SEX: OUR WIRING, OURSELVES

Our "wiring"—the way our brains and hormones work—underlie a woman's (and a man's) automatic pitching preferences: how we talk, when we talk, what we like to look at, whom we like to look at, what we are looking for when we're hoping for a reaction, and what we expect from others when they're listening to us. Wiring isn't destiny, but it is the starting place from which we create our destinies. The more we know about our wiring and how it creates both potential pitching advantages and pitfalls, the more control and choices we'll have.

For me, starting to look at brain sex preferences and abilities was like starting to look realistically at how my body processes food. I thought my body should do what I wanted it to, which was to let me binge on sugar and stay at what I considered the ideal weight, which happened to be what I weighed as a sophomore in college. I'd eat what tasted good, and my body would respond by seizing the calories it didn't need right that moment and storing them in the handiest container, which happened to be my thighs. I would then hate my thighs, my body, and myself—and eat more sugar, and my body would find new containers. I'd rant, rave, feel sorry for myself, and in general do everything except come to terms with reality.

When I started to accept the reality of how our bodies were designed millennia ago to live on minimal amounts of food that our ancestors had spent a lot of energy acquiring, the fight I was having with myself seemed pretty stupid. I now accept that my body responds to food precisely as it was built to. In fact, it is very clever. For example, it knows that I am older and that it isn't really necessary to the survival of the species for me to get enough calories to reproduce, so it is going to ask for even fewer calories than it asked for before. That's brilliant. Irritating, but brilliant.

So here I am, understanding that the challenge is to learn how to live happily in a primal body in a fast food world. No matter how much I hate it, no matter how much I wish my body handled calories another way, no matter how much I would like to trade my body's metabolism for someone else's, this is the way it is.

Which brings me back to brain sex. On average, men's and women's brains are not the same. In order to *be* who we are, we need to *accept* who we are; we need to accept the reality of how women's and men's brains work, not how we wish our brains worked, or how we believe men's brains could work if they just put a little effort into it. Understanding brain sex is crucial because the business world we live in, and the institutions we work for, were designed by male brains to work for men.

Men's and women's brains were engineered, in part, to handle quite different tasks, and that engineering is expressed in us still. The brains we now use to pitch were built to cope with life long ago when a day's work involved hunting and foraging for blackberries, not sending text messages with them. Yes, men and women are more alike than different. But the differences in how we take in the world and mentally process and communicate what we take in, make a difference in how we get things done. One of the reasons we need to pitch is to make it easier to bridge those differences: to translate what is obvious to us to what is understandable to someone else.

Ronna Lichtenberg

Brain sex differences are as basic as gender identity, that which makes us think we are male or female. You can find experts who disagree, who feel that culture is everything, but recent studies seem to show that gender identity is in the brain. That is, we relate to the world as men and women not because we did or didn't get a Barbie for Christmas, but because of biology.

For example, look at the results of one study conducted by a urologist at the Johns Hopkins Children's Center in Baltimore. A group of twenty-seven children were born with a strange congenital condition: they had normal male chromosomes (X and Y) and normal testicles. Because they had testicles, it indicated that they'd been exposed to testosterone in the womb. But even though they did have testicles, they didn't have penises.

Parents were presented with a tough decision. Given the absence of a penis, should they castrate the children—that is, remove their testicles—and raise them as girls? Or should they raise them as boys who didn't have penises? The parents of twenty-five of the babies decided on castration. The parents of the other two babies decided to go ahead and raise them as boys.

Despite what can only be described as a determined attempt to reassign gender for twenty-five of the children, all of them played like boys—rough and tumble. Fourteen of them said that they actually were boys; one as early as five years old. In other words, their parents wanted them to be girls, but mostly the children "knew" they weren't. The two who were raised as boys were reported to be "less psychologically maladjusted," which kind of amazed me given how brutal children can be to others who look different in any way. No matter what the body looked like, they were still boys. Is it possible that it's easier to be a boy with no penis than to be a girl with a boy's brain? It seems that the answer, at least sometimes, is yes. Brain sex rules.

Now, I want to make it clear that I know that looking at this subject can be tricky and that there are people who find the very idea objectionable. There's good reason for that. Scientific studies in the past were useful primarily as "proof" that everyone similar to the scientist—white, European, and male—had a brain that was superior to everyone who didn't. Bad science was used as

What's in Your Head That's Not in His

an excuse to deny educational and occupational opportunities to women, African-Americans, and immigrants. Please hear me: I'm not saying that different is better. Different is just different.

I'm also not saying that studies that address the average man and the average woman are true for any specific woman: Of the statements that follow, some may be true for you and some may not. There may be a woman for whom none of the statements about how men and women differ are true—maybe she is taller than Dikembe Mutombo, likes to solve complicated math problems in her head, prefers one-night stands to relationships, would rather be taken out and shot than talk about her feelings, and believes to the bone that winning is not an important thing, it is the only thing.

Even if nothing in this chapter rings true for you, given the law of averages, it will be true for someone you know. As authors Anne Moir, Ph.D., and David Jessel say in *Brain Sex,* an early classic on the topic, "What we are, how we behave, how we think and feel, is governed not by the heart, but by the brain. The brain itself is influenced, in structure and operation, by the hormones. If brain structure and hormones are different in men and women, it should not surprise us that men and women behave in different ways." By looking at the brain, we have a better chance of understanding our minds, "their" minds, and the natural skills and talents we have to work with as we pursue our goals.

THE TOP EIGHT BRAIN SEX DIFFERENCES AND WHAT THEY MEAN FOR YOU

In the following pages, I am going to take you through the brain sex differences that are most important for you to know as you live your work life. There are others I won't cover that have a big impact on relationships outside of work. If you would like to know more about the topic, and the possible implications for your personal relationships, take a look at the selected bibliography in the back, where I've listed well over a dozen books and relevant articles that should get you started.

Ronna Lichtenberg

1. Women's brains are built to multitask

Our Pitching Advantage:

❖ Will consider more variables

❖ More likely to anticipate downsides

❖ Can offer more options

❖ Can appear to be more flexible

Our Pitching Challenge:

❖ Can appear unfocussed

❖ Discussion of options can be time-consuming

It is well known that women can and do multitask with great ease, sometimes too much so. Long ago, we were always doing a zillion things at once: tending our own and others' children, gathering food and preparing it.

Men, as hunters, needed to pay deep attention to the one critter that would become dinner. Our brains are still operating on the same wiring.

Sally Shaywitz, M.D., and Bennett Shaywitz, M.D., both professors at Yale University, have been doing some really fascinating work on gender differences in the brain. Using magnetic resonance imaging (MRI), Drs. Shaywitz and Shaywitz asked their test subjects to do a rhyming task while researchers made detailed images of the subjects' brains. When men did the task, a small center called the inferior frontal gyrus lit up in the left side of the brain. When women did the task, the same region lit up in both the left and the right hemispheres.

One side versus both sides; focus versus multifocus.

In another study, researchers at the Indiana University School of Medicine used functional MRIs to measure high-speed changes in neural flow while subjects were performing a task, in this case listening. They found that as men listened, the majority of them showed exclusive activity on the left side of the brain, in the temporal lobe, which is associated with listening and speech. The majority of the

What's in Your Head That's Not in His

women showed activity in the temporal lobe in both sides of the brain, although predominately on the left. One side versus both sides; focus versus multifocus.

No wonder women are sometimes accused of not thinking in straight lines. We're not. We're working in different parts of our brains at once. The outcome of this kind of processing is what Helen Fisher, Ph.D., noted anthropologist and author of *The First Sex,* calls "web thinking" and what other writers on women's leadership styles refer to as our ability to see interconnectedness.

You might think this multiple-processing wastes energy, but it appears to be very efficient. In overall size, men's brains are on average 15 percent larger than women's, although our brains seem to be the same size when scaled for body size. If size does matter in this case, it isn't clear how; men and women score the same on IQ tests. Ruben Gur, Ph.D., professor of neuropsychiatry at the University of Pennsylvania, even argues that women's brains "must be more efficient since they are able to do more with a smaller volume of brain."

2. Talking is a great shared activity for women

Our Pitching Advantage:

❖ Lots of verbal pitches (but not all)

❖ If pitching someone else who likes to talk, great opportunity for bonding

❖ Can find out a lot about prospects

❖ Potential for powerful networking, especially with other women

Our Pitching Challenge:

❖ May be perceived as not getting to the point

❖ May overwhelm listener

❖ May not enjoy/may feel excluded from male bonding activities, like duck hunting and fishing, where talking is really not the point

❖ Easy to talk past the close

Ronna Lichtenberg

Women are better at talking, which is a big advantage in pitching—and a big disadvantage if the listener thinks we talk too much.

Women use speech, as opposed to activity, to process thinking. That's why if we have a lot to do, which of course we always do, we are likely to list all of it out loud in what can seem to a man as completely random order, mentioning all the options and possibilities. A guy is more likely to say, "I've got some things to do," and then disappear.

The theory is that in women's brains, areas of the cerebral cortex that are linked to language, judgment, and memory are packed with more nerve cells than in men's brains, which allows us to process this kind of information more effectively. More neurons in the left side of the cerebral cortex allow us, for example, to recognize tonal differences in language and music. Maybe that's why other researchers have found women's voices to be more variable, more musical, and more expressive than men's.

Whatever the reason, on average, women produce more words in a given period, make fewer speech errors (such as using the wrong word), and perform better in the ability to discriminate speech sounds (such as consonants and vowels) than men do.

Women's sentences on average are longer, and women are more likely to use standard grammatical structure and correct pronunciation. Women can even repeat tongue twisters more fluently and accurately than men.

As we'll see, talking is particularly important to women because it's the way we try to connect, particularly through self-disclosing. Men also value talking, but it seems to be in the context of an activity (like golf, or better yet, sex).

3. Women and men don't keep score the same way

For women, winning occurs in a context that includes personal and relationship considerations. For men, winning means someone wins and someone loses.

It's not that women don't love to win. We do. We love to win—in sports, in

Our Pitching Advantage:

❖ Has appeal beyond the narrow bottom line

❖ Finds high value in relationships

❖ Can define success to include life outside work

❖ Ability to connect to others via shared interests and commitments (like the bond between working moms)

Our Pitching Challenge:

❖ May not go after specific victories as aggressively

❖ Sends signals that are confusing to others who define achievement in classic male terms

❖ Relationship added-value (even with clients) is often not recognized by employers/companies

teams, in Las Vegas, and in the lottery. But often the way we define winning in our work lives is more multifaceted and complex than the way men do. We want to win our way: The game continues, we maintain good working relationships, and we still have room in our lives for something other than work. That complicates our ability to get what we want when what we want is broader than, say, the next promotion.

Of course, a lot of women want more money, or a promotion, or to be CEO someday. You only have to look at Venus and Serena Williams, who are often forced to play against each other, to know that women are completely capable of putting relationships aside for the sake of competition. But I've heard a lot more women than men worry about the human cost of those potential wins— that it will be hard on a friend to report to them if they get promoted, or that their team will suffer if they leave for a terrific new job, or that they will need to be away overnight more often when their children might need them.

Ronna Lichtenberg

Of course, there are a lot of reasons why each individual woman feels as she does about achievement, including how she was raised and educated, whether she's the oldest in her family, how close she was to her daddy, if she's able to share household responsibilities with a mate, and whether she feels she's been lucky or not in life. But one of the powerful reasons we look at winning the way we do is that our brains and our hormones tilt more toward supporting connection than competition. That's why a woman's definition of success can be more complex, and in some ways more difficult to achieve, than a man's.

The Testosterone Made Him Do It

Clinical studies show that testosterone increases aggression, competition, self-assertion, and self-reliance. If you want to have a single-minded, sustained focus on competition and you want to be willing to do whatever it takes to achieve power and rank, including not caring so very much about the impact on others, then what you want is to have a lot of testosterone in your body and the ability for your body to employ that testosterone to maximum advantage.

Women do have testosterone, and you may even have a lot of it for a woman—studies show that those of us who work for pay tend to have higher testosterone levels than women who don't work outside the home. But none of us have as much as the guys do; in adults, men average ten times as much testosterone as women. The research on testosterone is extensive and seems strong: From very early ages, higher testosterone levels fuel the desire for power and rank as well as aggressiveness.

For example, in one test, children were rewarded if they could persuade their friends to eat a particularly nasty-tasting cracker. Girls and boys both went for the reward, but not the same way. Boys lied, threatened, and challenged their victim. Girls apologized about the task ("It's their idea, not mine"), avoided direct lies, and attempted to persuade their victims to eat the cracker instead of trying to overpower them into doing it. Girls would even volunteer to share the cracker to get the desired result.

Males are more aggressive than females in pretty much every mammalian species. Take a look at aggression extremes. Men commit more crimes in general, more violent crimes specifically, and more murders. Women can be violent, too, most often at home with those we purportedly love. We can be savage in defense of our children, which is why Rudyard Kipling said, "The female of the species is more deadly than the male." But men are more likely to kill over disputes related to power and rank. Two-thirds of the homicides by men do not even occur during a crime but simply when there is a social conflict in which one man feels the other "dissed" him.

Obviously I don't mean to suggest that most men are hormonal homicidal maniacs, but it is important for women to understand that men have a biological incentive to compete, to be aggressive in that competition, and to care deeply about rank. The desire for power and rank, and the ability to focus aggression on achieving those goals, runs so deep that one study showed that levels of testosterone in men go up or down depending on whether they win at sports—not just when they're playing sports, mind you, but also when they're just rooting for "their" team from a big, fat, soft chair in front of the television.

Maybe that's why men seem more willing to "pay" more for rank. Rising in the hierarchy matters so much to men that they are more prepared to make sacrifices to do it, whether those sacrifices be time, pleasure, health, safety, or attending their kid's ballet recital. The cost to men of achievement is well known: exhaustion, unbalanced lives, alimony to the first and maybe the second wife. But even though an increasing percentage of men seem to question the return they get on paying for rank in these ways, there are still quite a few driven to achieve it. I'd be surprised if you couldn't name a few of these would-be alpha males that you're working with right now.

Why do men care so much about rank? According to everything I've read, one of the main reasons they care so much is *us*. Rank, status, money, titles and the like all add up to power, the power to attract women.

I just saw an engagement announcement for fifty-four-year-old Billy Joel and an astonishingly pretty twenty-two-year-old. I'm sure she loves him, but if he were bankrupt . . . well, you get my point.

Ronna Lichtenberg

Studies show that a woman continues to value power and rank as indications of a potential mate's ability to provide for her children, and to provide well. Dr. Fisher, in *The First Sex,* explains that "women in tribal societies, be they Zulus, Aleut Eskimos, or Mbuti Pygmies, are more interested in marrying 'big men,' individuals with rank. American women polled in both the 1930s and the 1980s considered a potential mate's financial prospects about twice as important as men did." No wonder men assign greater value to all things that indicate rank. I once had a male subordinate come to me in all seriousness, objecting because he had counted the ceiling tiles in his office and didn't have as many as one of his colleagues did. It seems less ridiculous to me now than it did then, especially when I consider the basic biological imperative behind it.

In fact, maybe we women should take it as a compliment that when asked what made them happiest, more men than women simply cited achievement. In the abstract, maybe it is a compliment to us as women that all that walking on the fence, look at me stuff is done in order to get our attention and our applause. On the other hand, in real life, working with someone with that single-minded focus can be a real drag—especially when they believe that our lack of that single-minded focus means that we aren't as good as they are, not as deserving, and incapable of top leadership because of it.

The Estrogen Connection

Men and women both have estrogen, and you can tell that a man named it because the word *estrogen* comes from the Greek word for "frenzy." Our estrogen levels are higher, though, and since estrogen serves to lower aggression, competition, self-assertion, and self-reliance, we are more likely to value connection and be concerned about actions that create the potential for disconnection.

That means that even though men and women are the same in what the shrinks call internal competitiveness, the desire to meet personal goals and display excellence, men score much higher in what's called external competitiveness, the willingness to elbow others aside to get ahead. Women, instead, tend to fuse success at work with a sense of relationship. The statement "I'm happiest when I can succeed at something that will also make other people happy" was endorsed by 50 percent of women but only 15 percent of men.

Women are just more likely to define winning as including a network of human connections. Think of it this way, says Edie Weiner, a highly regarded futurist: "If a man has a bumper sticker that says, 'He who dies with the most toys wins,' a woman's would say, 'She who dies with the most friends wins.'"

The Route to Winning

Not only are men more aggressive, but they are also more prone to direct aggression—like pushing, hitting, and punching. Women tend to be more indirect or relational (think of little girls on a playground excluding someone who didn't "play nice"). This direct aggression of men influences how men communicate and how they react to the way women communicate.

Men, for example, are more apt to attack with words, and they take coworkers more seriously when they argue back. Boys are more "egocentric" in their speech—they are more likely to brag, dare one another, taunt, threaten, override the other person's attempt to speak, and ignore the other person's suggestion, says Simon Baron-Cohen, Ph.D., professor of psychology and psychiatry at the University of Cambridge and codirector of its Autism Research Centre. They are also less willing to give up the floor to the other speaker.

Men interrupt more, too. Bill and Pam Farrel, in their book *Why Men and Women Act the Way They Do,* report that men are responsible for no less than 98 percent of all the interruptions that occur in everyday conversations (I am personally responsible for the other 2 percent).

Aggression makes a difference in how the sexes use humor, too. Male humor tends to involve more teasing and pretend hostility. For example, I once had a boss who thought intentionally mispronouncing my first name was the funniest thing on the planet since the whoopee cushion. And this from a man whose nickname was "Wickie."

Differing expressions of aggression start young. Michael Lewis, Ph.D., director of the Institute for the Study of Child Development at the Robert Wood

Ronna Lichtenberg

Johnson Medical School in New Jersey, has documented behavioral differences in children as young as one year old. In one study, Dr. Lewis placed toddler boys and girls behind a barrier, blocking them from reaching their mothers.

The boys and girls used very different strategies to get past the barrier. The boys tried to climb over the barrier. As Dr. Lewis described the process, the boy baby "is going to knock it down. He's gonna push on it. He's going to try to go around the side." And the girls? According to Dr. Lewis, the girls' strategy was to get help from another person. Remember when I said difference wasn't better or worse, it was just different? In this case, the girls got out from behind the barrier faster than the boys did. How? They showed distress, and their moms came and picked them up.

Adding it all up, male hormones make it easy to focus on personal victory. Female hormones make it easier to calculate victory for all the persons involved.

4. Women are bombarded with nonverbal cues

Our Pitching Advantage:

❖ Easier to see how pitch is being received and modify as necessary
❖ More information about potential likes and dislikes
❖ Easier to read another person's style (learning and emotional) and make adjustments

Our Pitching Challenge:

❖ Can be distracted by too many signals
❖ May overreact to signs of initial resistance: may see/hear them as "louder" than they are meant to be
❖ Can find it difficult to keep on course in the absence of signals (the impassive listener)

What's in Your Head That's Not in His

Women and men have different sensory abilities, which means that we get more nonverbal cues and pick up more reactions when we pitch than men can. Joanne Davis, advertising entrepreneur, says she can't even count the number of times she left a meeting in which ad agencies were presenting to a would-be client and heard a female agency employee say to a male teammate, "Wow, did you see that reaction?" and noticed that the guy didn't have a clue about what the woman was talking about.

Once again, this brain-based ability can be an incredible advantage—after all, what is better than knowing if what you are proposing is appealing or not? But receiving all this information can be distracting.

The fact is that most of what we communicate when we are communicating face to face is nonverbal. We all know that intuitively, which is why everyone still works so hard to have important meetings in person. Studies show that nonverbal signals account for between 60 and 80 percent of the impact of a message. What the message sounds like accounts for 20 to 30 percent. And the words themselves count for only 7 to 10 percent, which is something to remember next time you are slavishly rewriting a presentation at 3:00 A.M. in order to get every word right instead of sleeping so you will look more relaxed and feel more in control.

Women Are Better at Reading Facial Expressions

There is a study called Profile of Nonverbal Sensitivity that measures how sensitive someone is to nonverbal cues of emotion by testing how good the subject is at identifying the emotions of an actor. Women are more accurate than men at identifying nonverbal cues across the world, but why? Once again, it appears we process some of these tasks in different brain parts.

For example, Erik Everhart, Ph.D., assistant professor of psychology at East Carolina University, and his colleagues at the University at Buffalo found that boys and girls ages eight through eleven use different parts of their brains to recognize faces and expressions. They speculate that these differences may

Ronna Lichtenberg

help girls detect fine changes in facial expressions, so therefore they are better at sensing people's moods. Reading someone's mouth or eyes requires finer discrimination than does judging emotions in the entire face.

Dr. Ruben Gur and Raquel Gur, M.D., Ph.D., partners in neurobiology at the University of Pennsylvania, did another series of tests that involved studying photographs of faces. Both sexes were equally adept at noticing when someone else was happy. Women could easily read sadness in someone's face, whether male or female, with about 90-percent accuracy.

It was different with men. They were more accurate in reading unhappiness in another man's face than in a woman's. In fact, they were right about other men about 90 percent of the time, but when they looked at women's faces, they were right only about 70 percent of the time. And, said Dr. Ruben Gur, "a woman's face had to be really sad for men to see it. The subtle expressions went right by them." Which tells me that if we're waiting for a guy at work to notice we're mildly unhappy about something, it could be a very long wait.

5. Women have an easier time accessing, processing, and talking about emotions

Our Pitching Advantage:

❖ Bringing passion to a pitch
❖ Can establish emotional connection quickly

Our Pitching Challenge:

❖ May press for emotional reactions from people who can't/won't give them
❖ Potential to be really hurt by lack of connection, even at a casual level (lack of a hello)

Try the Toothbrush Test

Barbara and Allan Pease, in their book *Why Men Don't Listen and Women Can't Read Maps*, say that most women can brush their teeth while walking and talking on several topics. Women can make up and down strokes with the toothbrush at the same time as they polish a table using a circular motion with the other hand. Go try it. If it works, find a man and give him a toothbrush and a chamois cloth (so he will think he is polishing, not dusting, because if he thinks you're asking him to dust, he probably won't play).

See if he can polish and brush at the same time; most men can't. When men brush their teeth, their monotrack brain forces them to focus entirely on the single task of brushing their teeth. Watch a man brush his teeth. Can you imagine him applying a top coat of nail polish, making a grocery list, and waking a child up at the same time?

It is considered a bad thing to be "too emotional" in business. This is a big issue for working women because there seems to be worldwide consensus that women are more emotional than men—after a Gallup Poll was conducted in twenty-two societies, the pollsters declared that "more than any other trait, this one elicits the greatest consensus around the world as more applicable to women than men." A 1995 Prodigy poll reported that 65 percent of the men questioned were of the opinion that women are too emotional.

Having been accused myself of being "too emotional" on a regular basis, I think it's important to understand how brain differences may explain why women seem more emotional than men and how to use our emotional differences to our advantage.

For starters, research suggests that men and women process emotion in different places in their brains. Canadian research scientist Sandra Witelson, Ph.D., did a study that involved showing emotionally charged images to different hemispheres of the brain. That might seem hard to do, but it isn't—all

Ronna Lichtenberg

you have to do is first show images to the right eye and play sounds in the right ear, which gives you access to the left hemisphere of the brain. Then you show images to the left eye and play sounds in the left ear, which gives you access to the right hemisphere of the brain.

While male and female subjects looked at and heard these emotionally charged images, Dr. Witelson did MRI scans of their brains. She found that men processed emotion in two areas of the right hemisphere of the brain and women processed emotion in both hemispheres.

Why is this a big deal? Well, because emotion is positioned in the right brain of a man, it can operate separately from other brain functions. A man can use the left side of his brain to argue logic and leave the right side of his brain, and emotion, completely out of it.

Because emotion operates in both hemispheres of a woman's brain at the same time, we can process emotion and logic at the same time. This has huge implications for pitching because we tend to want to process emotion simultaneously with reason, and many guys are uncomfortable with that. As Tom Hanks exasperatedly said as the male coach of a World War II all-woman baseball team in the movie *A League of Their Own,* "There's no crying in baseball!"

We think it is perfectly natural—and for us, it is—to have an emotional response, say in a meeting, at the same time we are doing some kind of mental analytical calculation. We think and we feel all at once. Men are more likely to think, then to feel.

Women are also more ready to listen to emotional content from others as well as to process their own. When asked to judge when someone might have said something potentially hurtful, girls do better than boys, starting at age seven. A woman can use an average of six listening expressions in a ten-second period in order to reflect and then feed back personal emotions. If you look at a woman who is really engaged in listening to someone describe an emotional situation, her face will look almost as if the situation described were happening to her, not just being described to her.

Men are less likely to signal they are listening, which at least some researchers believe also has a biological basis—the job of a male warrior when listening was to remain impassive so he wouldn't betray emotions. Who knows? But although you feel frustration when you think a guy isn't listening to you in a meeting, it may have nothing to do with you, and he may *be* listening. You just aren't going to get the feedback from him that indicates he is listening that you can expect from a woman.

6. Women prefer people to symbols

Our Pitching Advantage:

- ❖ See human side of issues; critical for further selling-in
- ❖ Grounded in reality and nitty-gritty of human concerns
- ❖ Less likely to speak/write in "code"
- ❖ Potential to effectively use power of stories

Our Pitching Challenge:

- ❖ May still have some degree of discomfort with math
- ❖ Men we pitch to likely to be more impressed with models and code than with stories/human interest

Much of the work that has been done on brain sex shows that men are better at spatial relationships, such as having the ability to see an object in space and react quickly. Perhaps that's because of their ability to move information within each hemisphere of the brain.

Men get high marks for skills like map reading and playing ball because they can more easily imagine, alter, and rotate an object in their mind's eye. Men can learn a route in fewer trials, just from looking at a map, and correctly recall more details about direction and distance. Women tend to direct via landmarks. If Joe says, "Turn left on Ashland," Jane is more likely to say, "You have to turn before the cinder block firehouse." Often women

Ronna Lichtenberg

have to turn a map upside down if they change directions instead of being able to visualize the changed direction in their heads, as guys can.

The increased spatial ability may be why boys still have an edge in math, although changes in how we teach math to girls are closing the gap. In a study published in *Science* magazine in 1995, University of Chicago researchers analyzed thirty-two years of scores and found that in math and science, boys in the top 10 percent outnumbered girls three to one. In the top 1 percent, there were seven boys for every girl. In some mechanical-vocational tests, such as electronics and auto repair, there were no girls in the top 3 percent.

Michael Gurian, Ph.D., cofounder of The Gurian Institute, points out that boys, especially in upper grades, also tend to show a preference for symbolic texts, diagrams, and graphs. They like the coded quality better than girls, who prefer written texts. Boys also seem to find jargon and coded language more interesting. Whether it's language from sports trivia, the law, or the military, boys tend to work out codes among themselves and to rely on coded language to communicate.

Dr. Baron-Cohen has taken this basic finding—that men are better spatially and women verbally—and developed it one step further. In *The Essential Difference,* he argues that there are two types of brains. One is the empathizing

Math + Anxiety = Less Money

The financial impact of math anxiety is profound, according to the 1997 Dreyfus Gender Investment Comparison Survey conducted by the National Center for Women and Retirement Research. The study found that women whose parents or teachers encouraged them academically when they were young and who were comfortable with math during school were more confident about their finances. Women who were uncomfortable with math during high school and who had low self-esteem were three times more likely in midlife to worry about their present financial security, fear not having enough money in old age, and be more conservative in their investments.

brain, which is often female. Empathizing is the ability to feel an appropriate emotional reaction, triggered by another person's and done in order to understand another person, to predict their behavior and to connect or resonate with them emotionally. For convenience sake, he calls this brain type "E."

The other kind of brain, the "S," or systemizing brain, is often male; it's designed to analyze, explore, and construct a system. The systemizer intuitively figures out how things work or extracts the underlying rules that govern the behavior of a system. This is done in order to understand and predict the system or to invent a new one.

Systemizing and empathizing are two completely different processes, although we all have the ability to do both to different degrees. Because companies tend to hire people with similar brain types, a lot of cultures are oriented much more to one kind of mental process than the other. It makes a big difference in how effective your pitch is if you know, for example, that you are talking to a company full of strong systemizers, which you probably are if it is a company with a lot of engineers or actuaries or other technical types.

I've found the easiest way to "get" the difference is to find out how your own brain works, which is why I got permission to include the tests that appear in appendices 2 and 3. I strongly encourage you to take the tests, particularly if you feel that one reason you're not getting the attention and respect you deserve is that you don't quite fit in your current company.

Dr. Baron-Cohen's work provides scientific validation for my theories about pink, blue, and striped, which were simply based on personal observations and experience. But the translation is direct: Pinks have stronger empathizing skills, blues have stronger systemizing skills. Pink empathizing brains are sometimes found in men and blue systemizing brains are sometimes found in women. You can't assume you are dealing with a male or female brain just because you are looking at a man or woman, but on average you'll find these differences associated with sex.

This systems/empathy distinction comes up all the time. For example, I sat in on a meeting of a mixed group of professionals. One of the

Ronna Lichtenberg

senior women started talking about a recent experience her brother had. I understood her completely; she was explaining the world through a people point. The men in the room were completely lost. But I've also seen men in sales situations present materials that do not include a single reference to the would-be client. Often there are terrific charts and graphs and almost always something that speaks to the size of the organization. But people stories? Forget it. And forget that kind of pitch working with a woman, too.

7. Women are wired to choose from the sexual buffet

Our Pitching Advantage:

- Attractive women sometimes have an edge.
- Sex appeal is powerful and can be used effectively.

Our Pitching Challenge:

- Concerns about undesired attention.
- Potential for criticism for use of sexual attractiveness, whether intentional or not.
- Women who are "too" attractive may not be taken seriously.

Every woman who pitches to men spends some time thinking about men and sex. Maybe she's concerned that if a man is thinking about her sexually, he won't be able to really listen to her or take her seriously. Or she's worried that a specific man will mistake her interest in him and think she wants to get in his pants, when all she wants is to get into his pants pocket. Or she may be wondering just how much she can flaunt what she's got without being a distraction. Does she really want to be like the good-looking young women on *The Apprentice*, the Donald Trump business-reality television show, who won a contest both by using their brains and by pulling tight T-shirts over their bountiful chests only to experience the ultimate shame of being lectured on morality by a man of whom Leona Helmsley once said, "I wouldn't believe him if his tongue were notarized."

So let's just quickly look at biological basics that may affect the pitching process. Not all men want more sex than women want, and some women are happy to have sex without emotional entanglement. But male hormones, particularly testosterone, do drive sexual appetite. In recent years, gynecologists have even been experimenting with giving testosterone to perimenopausal women to help improve their libido. I know—I tried it and stopped. I didn't like thinking about sex as much as I did or having such a high level of desire. Not only did it seem to present a potential risk to my marriage, but it was distracting. It's one thing to sigh over how yummy Benicio Del Torro is in a movie. It's another to think that half the guys in a coffee shop kind of look like him. Testosterone is the reason why the answer to the question "Can't they think about anything else?" is "Yes, but with difficulty."

Now let's take this back to pitching. For starters, sex is a big distraction for men, which seems fair to me given that we are distracted by emotion. But it also means that the more we distract them the more their brain may be someplace other than on the place we want it to be during a pitch. That can be good—the pitching world is full of women who have learned how to use flirtation and sexually flavored interactions strategically—but it can also work against a woman. Making a decision about how to use sexual power with a man is such an important part of pitching that it really needs to be done consciously, not in an "Oops! Was that my bra strap that just slid down my shoulder?" manner. (By the way, I apologize for dwelling on straight sex so much—it's just that there hasn't been enough research on hormonal influences on lesbians for me to sound off on it.)

Men are also more turned on than women are by visual cues. They are wired to respond to the visual indicators of youth, health, and, of course, fertility. That's why the porn industry is, conservatively, a $4 billion a year business: Men like to look.

Technically, a woman doesn't even have to be responsive or even remotely

Ronna Lichtenberg

Whatcha Thinking?

Dr. Ruben Gur and his wife, Dr. Raquel Gur, both at the University of Pennsylvania, published a study in *Science* magazine that looked at how different parts of the brain are active in men and women at different times. The big differences were in regions that have to do with regulation of emotion. The formal conclusion:

Even when studied at rest, when these people were just lying on their backs and being scanned, men activate more primitive parts of the limbic system that do not have access to language, whereas women activate parts of the limbic system that are adjacent to language areas.

And what does this mean? It means that men, left to their own devices for half an hour, are probably thinking with the primitive parts of their brain—which means they are thinking about sex or aggression. Women, left to their own devices, are firing up the parts of the brain dealing with language and thinking about how to deal with emotion.

So now you know not to offer men a penny for their thoughts when they're resting—it's a 50/50 chance the answer is either sex or aggression, and in either case, he's probably not going to want to talk about it.

interested for a man to become sexually aroused, as any New York subway rider knows.

Added to the willingness to ignore disinterest, men also interpret "courting gestures" differently than we do. As University of Texas psychologist David Buss, Ph.D., put it, "When in doubt, men seem to infer sexual interest." How many times has a woman sat down to a quick salad and brushed back her hair to keep it out of the carrots only to have a guy across the room say to his buddy, "Hey, look at that. She's really into me"? Managing sexual energy adroitly during pitching changes with time. The younger and prettier you are, the more you need to do it, as I'll discuss in chapter 10.

8. Relationship stressors have more impact on women

Our Pitching Advantage:

❖ Motivates desire to deepen and strengthen existing relationships.

❖ Indirect approaches to resolving conflict can leave door open to future exchanges.

Our Pitching Challenge:

❖ Can be problematic in closing, which often involves a brief relationship stressor.

❖ One reason why money discussions can be so hard.

❖ Creates potential for "victim head" (why does this *always* happen to me?).

I think one of the reasons women do more relationship calculus (as in, "Let's see, if I say this, she is likely to think that") is that we take a harder hit from people-induced pain and it takes us longer to forget those old hurts. When we bring painful memories along with us when we pitch, even just unconsciously in our heads and hearts, we're likely to get the same kinds of results one gets after talking about one's failed marriage on a first date—not good.

Women also have the ability to remember stressors better than men, too—what someone said that hurt our feelings, how we felt when they said it, how their face looked, the whole ugly thing. Better connections between the two halves of the brain give women the ability to associate a specific event with its emotional impact so that women's memories are more vivid, and thus, well . . . more memorable.

Women also have more memory storage. Women have a bigger hippocampus, the part of the brain that handles memory. On top of that, estrogen increases the number of synapses between nerve cells in the

Ronna Lichtenberg

hippocampus. (The more synapses you have, the more information can be processed. It's like buying more memory for your computer.)

It is even possible that emotional pain is literally stored more deeply in women's brains, which is why one study showed that men were more likely to forget about a fight quickly—within instants, or hours—and women to remember it for much longer. Maybe that's one reason why men and women handle rivalries and conflicts differently, because our scars can be deeper and take longer to heal.

Women, more than men, tend to distance themselves from rivals. After a tough meeting, the guys will feel comfortable going out for a drink; a woman is more likely to bail. I've noticed that pink women, for whom business is in general more personal, are particularly prone to want distance after a tough session. Losing that relationship recovery opportunity, though, means losing a prime opportunity to reestablish connection and get ready to pitch again.

THE FINAL WORD ON BRAIN SEX

In an interview on WETA public television, Martha Denckla, M.D., a neurologist at the Kennedy Krieger Institute at the Johns Hopkins School of Medicine, said something I really loved: "I call myself an optimistic fatalist, which means [when it comes to brain sex differences] you've got a basic blueprint, you can kind of move the furniture around and maybe make some adjustments in the architecture of the interior walls. But . . . the basic blueprint is not something that we are going to actually change."

She went on to say something I loved even more. "The reason we want to study these differences minutely is in order to be able to liberate people. It all comes down to helping people use whatever his or her brain may be (that is, male or female) to the best advantage."

Understanding your brain, and your blueprint, means that you know what you need to do to pump up the abilities that are not your natural strengths, that are not the things you are good at and lean on. One of the major contributions of feminism over the past couple of decades is to encourage girls to work on spatial skills, do their math, and take a few hits on team sports. One of the major confusions associated with feminism, I think unfairly, is the belief that what women want is either to be men or to be like them.

We aren't men. And thank goodness! Part of our job as women is to learn to value our natural strengths and to become so comfortable with them, and so good at knowing how to share them, that others who are unlike us learn to value them as well.

As your comfort increases, it will mean coming to terms with men and what can seem like overwhelming male advantage and dominance. Understanding the basic male brain sex blueprint, and working with it instead of against it, puts you on the path to having control instead of feeling like a victim. To use a systemizing analogy, it's knowing, "Oh, if I push *that* button, his brain won't work," instead of thinking, "I just told him six things that I know are critical to the future of the business and that jerk didn't hear a single thing I said."

Over lunch with a blue woman one day, I was talking about brain sex differences and launched into a litany of all of women's advantages and at the end she said, hopefully, "We're better, right?" Nope, we're not. We have skills that are better at some things, sometimes. So do they.

Whatever your spiritual beliefs of however or by whomever in the universe we were designed, we are much more powerful and better off as a species because of our differences. Our work lives and our individual lives should be the same. Letting others be who they are is part of being who you are. It opens the door to getting more of what you want, which, because you are a woman, includes the joy and passion and power of finding ways to create value from truly working together.

PART 2: PERCEIVED LIMITATIONS: THE STEREOTYPES THAT SHAPE US

The stereotypes our culture has about women, both positive and negative, also have a powerful effect on how we think about ourselves and others: nur-

Ronna Lichtenberg

ture matters at least as much as nature. Because stereotypes shape expectations and set limitations; they can, if you let them, hold you back. The weight of other people's beliefs about you sometimes feels like an anchor around your leg: the weight of "their" prospective approval or disapproval can cost you time, energy, and opportunity. That is our enemy.

As with any enemy, it's smart to be clear about what you're up against. There are lots of stereotypes about women; we're only going to look at the six biggies that seem to have the strongest impact on our ability to go after what we want in the marketplace. Then we're going to look at how those stereotypes keep us from thriving in our career and turn them into advantages.

WHEN STEREOTYPES CLASH

Have you ever felt that no mater what you do, it's wrong? That may be because you are up against the businesswoman's dilemma: What you've been told about how to be a good woman is completely at odds with what you're told about how to be good in business.

I've seen it a million times. Cindy's boss tells her that she lacks "presence." Maybe she didn't verbally push her way into meetings, or she didn't boast, or she seemed too concerned about someone's reaction. In other words, the advice Cindy gets is that she somehow should act like a man, which is how people in business (in general) are supposed to act. But on the same day, her friend Mindy gets criticized for not being nice because she didn't say hello or stay late to help on a project that wasn't even hers. Mindy, in other words, gets grief for *not* acting like a woman.

Whichever way you go—acting like a woman or acting like a man—you make yourself open to criticism. If you always act like a woman, others will like you, but you may make less money and feel like no one really listens to you or takes you quite as seriously as you would like. On the other hand, if you are a woman and you always act like a guy, you may or may not make more money, but you will almost certainly be less liked.

What's in Your Head That's Not in His

do you really have to be in male drag every day?

It's kind of like that '80s movie classic *Victor/Victoria* starring Julie Andrews. In the movie, Victoria was a soprano with a failing career. A friend convinced her that the only way to succeed was by pretending to be Victor. But there was one more layer to the plan: Victor would be a drag queen, pretending to be a woman. Still with me? Victoria would pretend to be Victor, who would pretend to be Victoria.

When audiences believed Victoria was a guy, all the things that had seemed not so exciting before—like Victoria's ability to shatter a glass when she hit a high C—seemed incredibly exciting. Victor/Victoria became a big success. Victoria, starved for success, loved having money for room service and excessively sequined costumes. Eventually, though, she decided that the success wasn't worth it: It was really hard work to pretend to be someone else all the time, and living a lie cost her too much. The movie ends with a different Victor playing Victoria and Victoria being just Victoria. (I'm not going to say more because if you haven't seen it, you should go right out and rent it.)

Which brings us to the core question: Is there a way to be a woman in a business world created by men, for men, and still feel, and act, like a woman? My answer is yes, but it takes hard work and savvy about who you are, what your style options are, and how to juggle all of it.

"ACT LIKE A LADY"

Let me start with an extreme example of how we learn to act like women: the journey of a transgendered person. One night while channel surfing, I came across a documentary about a town that has built something of an industry around a local surgeon who specializes in gender reassignment. The surgeon has developed special facial surgery techniques to use with individuals who were born boys but who want to live their lives as women. In "before" photos,

Ronna Lichtenberg

most of the guys looked big and burly; this was not a dainty crowd. Post-hormone treatment and post-surgery, most of the patients looked not only like women, but like great-looking women.

Immediately after surgery, though, patients looked like they'd been hit by a train: bruised, heavily bandaged, painfully swollen. But even with that level of trauma, the surgery itself didn't seem to be as challenging as everything else patients had to do to appear to be women—to talk like women, walk like women, sit like women, even catch like women (they practiced with silk scarves, not baseballs, by the way). In various classes, professionals taught the "rules" of femininity: Raise your voice at the end of a sentence; throw from your elbow, not your shoulder; and, that all-time favorite, for goodness sake, keep your knees together.

Following is a list of some of the rules most of us were taught about how to be good girls—the stereotypes that were certainly in our ears, and may well remain, to some degree, in our heads and our hearts. Remember as you read this list that these stereotypes are an influence, not an absolute. It matters that you are conscious of them, primarily so that you can work with them and turn them to your advantage, as Jennifer Allyn, a director in the Center for an Inclusive Workplace at PricewaterhouseCoopers points out. "The trickiest thing around stereotypes is that they are so insidious because they often include both sides of a given point." I would add that not only do stereotypes include both sides of a given point ("women are too bitchy, too aggressive" versus "women are weak and pushovers"), but they can also be positive, which makes us want to believe them.

Stereotype 1: A good woman always puts other people's needs first.

In workshops, after I've asked women to think about what they would choose to have in their lives if they could, I ask them why they don't, or can't, have what they want. Often, women tell me that they can't have something they want because it would be a problem for someone else.

What's in Your Head That's Not in His

Beth, for example, was feeling overwhelmed, and with good reason. Her company was in the middle of a merger, and, like everyone else in the workshop, she reported that the normal deluge of e-mails and meetings had swelled into an ungovernable tide. Wistfully, she said that she thought she could get more done, faster, if she could shut her office door once in a while. I asked her why she couldn't, thinking that perhaps there was an official "open door" policy. She looked at me, horrified. Of course she couldn't close her door. What would people think? What if someone needed her?

Wanting to help Beth realize she had a choice, I went on to suggest that she consider a "closed door strategy"; she could, for example, tell people that three times a week she was going to close her door for an hour at 2:00 P.M. so that she could power through a pile of material, and that unless it was an emergency, she'd prefer not to be disturbed. No, no, no, she shook her head. She absolutely could not do that. I moved on, because she looked as if she were about to break into tears. As I left the workshop, I saw a male colleague sitting with her, trying to help her work it through. Beth was still shaking her head.

Beth was stuck because she could not fathom putting herself first, even when putting herself first was the only way she could take good enough care of herself that she'd have enough energy to take care of everybody else.

Many of us have this expectation—the expectation that, as women, we are supposed to care for other people's needs, including their emotional needs, without hesitation and often without financial reward.

Is Caring Valued or Just Expected?

Even though taking care of people is "valuable," in the workplace, it often isn't valued. My rule of thumb is that acquiring relationships, which is "male," is always valued more than keeping relationships going, which is "female." In other words, people who can bring in business are highly prized and paid accordingly, much more than those who keep client relationships alive.

Even though fancy consultants can prove that employee and customer loyalty drive profits, it is a rare organization that has financial metrics in place that

Ronna Lichtenberg

Challenging Stereotype 1

This stereotype holds true for so many of us: We want to be able to take care of other people, and we want the good feeling that comes from putting them first. When we're told (incorrectly, I believe) that we can only get what we want by resisting that impulse, it leaves us with a choice that no one wants to make: to either stop caring about other people, which feels unnatural, or to financially suffer for doing so. The truth is that you don't have to make that choice, and in the pitching process you will learn how to create value for yourself from valuing others.

value the "helping" or support functions that create those loyalties. It's hard to put a dollar value on caring even when you know caring creates dollars.

The feminist perspective is that caring about people at work is financially devalued simply because women are the ones who do it. There's an interesting book called *Disappearing Acts: Gender, Power and Relational Practice at Work* by Simmons School of Management professor Joyce K. Fletcher, Ph.D., that makes these arguments in a compelling way.

At the risk of oversimplifying a complex and nuanced piece of research: Basically, Dr. Fletcher shadowed six women engineers as they went about their day, noting time they spent on various tasks. Her detailed notes included all the work she calls "relational practice": resolving conflict and disconnection, sharing information, facilitating connection, etc. She then went over her notes with the engineers and talked with them about what they did and why. For example, why did one of them stay so late to help out with someone else's report, or why did another pick up a soldering iron herself to fix a mechanical problem? Not because she thought she'd be rewarded, but because she felt like she should "do it."

Dr. Fletcher found that the work it takes to take care of someone else often isn't even considered work. Organizations and employers tend to define work as task and not define or reward the relationship work it takes to get someone else to do

65

What's in Your Head That's Not in His

a task, or just to get things to run smoothly. Further, the women engineers themselves didn't feel entirely good about the work they did taking care of others. Even though they thought they should do it, they also worried that they would look, or feel, like suckers for what they did. I've heard this too: "No one notices what I do around here." And they're right. Their male colleagues either didn't notice the efforts or expected that the women would do them as a matter of course.

Stereotype 2: A good woman is modest.

Even though we aren't culturally always in agreement about what modesty means—some people think it means women should veil their faces and others think it means a woman should be able, as one singer did, to consider herself clothed because she was wearing a strategically placed ashtray—there is still some basic cultural agreement that women are supposed to be modest.

And one of the things a modest woman doesn't do is self-promote.

This social expectation that women shouldn't self-promote is both deeply ingrained and deeply debilitating for any woman who wants to get her ideas across, to make change in the world, to work, to achieve.

There has been a lot of industrial organization research done that proves what most of us intuitively suspect: that people who self-promote during interviews get hired more often than people who don't, and that the ability to self-promote is an important skill to have all the way up the organizational ladder. But historically, men have been much better at it than women. One reason, which we talked about earlier in this chapter, is that a bloodstream full of testosterone makes any kind of aggression, including self-aggrandizement, easier.

But there's another reason: Women who self-promote run the risk of being punished in some way for doing it.

The "Who Does She Think *She* Is?" Factor

Laurie Rudman, Ph.D., a Rutgers psychologist, has published some really fascinating studies on the "backlash" against self-promoting women. In one study, people interviewed a self-promoting man and a self-promoting woman

Ronna Lichtenberg

under conditions in which the interviewer thought that if the person interviewed did well, he or she would too.

The findings surprised me. When they thought it was to their advantage, male interviewers chose the self-promoting man 50 percent of the time and the self-promoting woman 50 percent of the time. When they believed it was to their benefit, men went for perceived competence, regardless of gender. That's the good news.

The bad news is that female interviewers *never* chose the self-promoting woman as their partner, even when they thought she was more competent. What's with this?

When women appear to boast or self-promote, people think it is inappropriate. Men and women both want to be consistent with their "own" gender rules, and it is a common thing to "police" others who fail to fit those roles. That's why it's reasonable to worry that women won't like us if we self-promote: Some of them won't.

You're a Woman, so That's Yucky

As embarrassing as it is to say, I've not only seen women criticize other women for self-promotion, but I've done it myself, and not all that long ago (but I swear I will never, ever do it again). An acquaintance sent me an e-mail that

---

Challenging Stereotype 2

Recently, there has been a lot of self-help advice that tells women to self-promote like guys do. That's reasonable, given that it's proven to be such an effective strategy for men. But it may be that you're better off finding a comfort zone, a way to talk about yourself that doesn't feel like you are elevating your position at someone else's expense. Is it really possible to find a way to say good things about yourself without having other women hate you and men resent you? Yes. It comes from understanding the value of your offering to others, which we'll talk about in chapter 7.

What's in Your Head That's Not in His

on the surface was about garnering support for a major public policy issue, but it was really an attempt to promote her book. The e-mail kind of bugged me, and I couldn't figure out why; the book was good, and it deserved my support.

Trying to figure out my reaction, I forwarded the e-mail without comment to a friend and then called her to ask what she thought of it. She said she thought that it was really yucky. When I asked her why, she said that part of it was because it was so awkwardly self-promotional—the author wasn't straightforward about what she was doing. It would have been better to just say, "Hey, I have a new book out—buy it," but because she was clearly uncomfortable trying to self-promote, she tried to disguise it. But my friend also said that part of her yuck response was because the e-mail came from a woman and a woman should have known better than to handle it that way.

When I looked deep inside, I realized that, like my friend, I had different standards for a woman self-promoting herself than I did for a man. My reaction, as ashamed of it as I now am, is not atypical. We expect other women to be "nice." Self-promotion is clearly not considered "nice."

The seemingly universal *yuck* is probably why the vast majority of women I've met have difficulty doing anything that smacks of self-promotion, for fear of eliciting it. Over and over again, I have seen fabulous women who can't say anything good about themselves, let alone anything fabulous. Women, for example, like Sheila Wellington, who is currently a clinical professor of management at the Stern School of Business at New York University.

In her influential book for women, *Be Your Own Mentor: Strategies from Top Women on the Secrets of Success,* one of Sheila's key points is that every woman needs to "blow your own horn." But if you ask her, as I did, she will admit that she hates the idea of self-promoting, that she's not very good at it. In fact, Sheila had to get help writing her résumé because she found it so hard to say nice things about herself, just as the rest of us do. Because she was brave enough to share her own challenge, one of the parting gifts she got from friends when she left Catalyst was a little silver trumpet. On it was an engraving that read, BLOW YOUR OWN HORN, just as a loving reminder.

Ronna Lichtenberg

Stereotype 3: A good woman is feminine.

There are a lot of places in this book where I talk to pink women because there are some elements of pitching that can be particularly daunting for pinks. But the challenge of managing cultural expectations around femininity can be incredibly frustrating for blue women. In fact, the challenge of managing this issue can become a career maker or career breaker for blues.

Femininity is in the eye of the beholder. What you and I think of as feminine may be completely different, even though we all think we know who is feminine and who isn't.

We all bring our ideas about femininity to work, and that's when things get really complicated. For example, in a high-profile case that went to the Supreme Court more than twenty years ago *(Price Waterhouse v. Hopkins),* a woman's candidacy for partnership was put on hold because of her perceived lack of femininity. Despite playing a significant role in securing major contracts, Ann Hopkins was told that in order to improve her chances for partnership, she needed to "walk more femininely, talk more femininely, dress more femininely, wear makeup, have her hair styled, and wear jewelry." (Price Waterhouse, by the way, went on to put major emphasis on diversity through its Center for an Inclusive Workplace.)

Even though this case taught employers that it is very expensive to talk about femininity in a formal performance review, it doesn't mean that people don't think about it, and react to it, and make judgments about us because of it. There is a classic story that when Jeff Zucker was executive producer of the *Today* show, he coached Katie Couric on femininity. According to Katie, "Jeff taught me that if you have a respectful tone, that if you are—dare I say—ladylike, you can ask tough questions without coming across as a witch." I just saw Katie in action, doing an interview with disgraced former *New York Times* journalist Jayson Blair about his new book. She asked him questions so tough they were almost wince-making; for example, why we should believe anything he has to say given that he has admitted to so many lies. But at the same time,

The complexity of expectations around "feminine" behavior speaks to the issue both pink and blue women face, but in different ways. In a culture change, for example, after a merger, one of the things that changes is favored styles—that is, just because an individual style worked well in the past doesn't mean it still will. The challenge is how you do, or don't, express your femininity when asking for what you want. If you are a blue woman and want to focus on task and are uncomfortable with standard feminine "markers" like high heels and lip gloss, how do you avoid being stereotyped as too male? We'll look at how to balance superficial feminine "markers" with deeper relationship enhancing behaviors in chapter 10.

with her long blondish hair and extremely shiny pink lip gloss, Katie simultaneously came across as sweetly feminine and—dare we say it?—ladylike.

In the business world, one enterprising consultant has even turned coaching "insufficiently feminine" execs into a thriving business. Jean Hollands, president and CEO of a California-based executive coaching firm, started (and has received a lot of publicity for) a program to coach women she calls "bully broads," which is a nice way of saying *bitch,* which, theoretically, one would have to be a bully broad to say.

Hollands says that 85 percent of her graduates are promoted within a year, after learning to speak slowly, smile more often, and avoid confrontation—in other words, to be more feminine.

Stereotype 4: A good woman is not bossy.

Along with being feminine, modest, and other-oriented, a good woman also makes it a habit to defer to male authority. I vividly remember my father taking me aside one day, clearly to impart an important secret. "No one likes a domineering woman," he said. The specific domineering woman my dad had in mind was my maternal grandmother. My grandmother helped run the family business—a bar in such a rough part of town that she sometimes had to reinforce good attitude by cracking a drunk over the head with her rolling pin. She was also pretty tough on the help, who were mostly family members. Everyone called her Mom to her face. Behind her back, they called her Bossy.

Bossy. When you hear that, do you think of a guy? Probably not. Culturally we are still not quite comfortable with powerful women and with how powerful women are supposed to behave.

What about When She *Is* the Boss?

There is a ton of research on stereotypes of women in power, reaching back for decades. Alice Eagly, Ph.D., while at Purdue University, did an important study that demonstrated that women in leadership positions were devalued when their leadership was carried out in stereotypically masculine styles, particularly when this style was autocratic or directive. To translate, women who acted like powerful men pissed people off. When women leaders occupied male-dominated roles and when the evaluators were men, women were devalued even more. Which is just the fancy academic way of saying that the men hated being bossed by women. What a surprise, huh?

We Assume Good Things about Powerful Men but Not Powerful Women

We're used to men being in charge. In fact, a basic American cultural assumption is that male authority is good. Marie Wilson, head of the White House Project, an organization that advances women's leadership in all sectors, including the presidency, told me about a huge piece of research the Project did not too long ago. It showed focus groups thirty-second television ads of twenty-five men and women, all of whom had run for governor in the past. The focus group members responded to the ads nonverbally, by dialing up (for positive) or down (for negative) on a device that registered their responses.

Marie was watching as they dialed and saw what happened as commercials for both male and female candidates were aired. "The minute a woman came up on the screen—participants dialed down, or just dialed across." In other words, if it was a woman, the best response she could start with was neutral. "A man coming up on the screen—they dialed up immediately." That is, a man could start out with a positive. A woman couldn't.

After the dial test, focus group participants also projected competence for the men and not for the women. This is consistent with other research that shows that people will say they feel good about female authority, but if you press for reactions underneath, you'll find that most folks still prefer men in high-authority roles and women in low-authority roles.

This is complicated and controversial stuff, so let me bring it back to the everyday world. Consider the following scenario: You're on a plane, and suddenly it feels like something is going wrong—maybe there's a drop, or the lights start blinking, or the turbulence is so intense that the flight attendant disappears with a paper bag. The pilot comes on the intercom to explain what's hap-

Challenging Stereotype 4

The key challenge for women pioneers in business was that in many situations it seemed, and reasonably so, that the only way they could present themselves as an authority was to adopt as many male markers as possible in how they dressed, spoke, and moved.

Thanks to them, to powerful academics and authors, and to male leaders and colleagues who have and who are making the effort to understand and value women's contributions, women now have more freedom to explore and adopt alternate methods of wielding and expressing authority. We are going to look in the chapters on pitching at the moments you may still want to use a "blue" marker, but also how to cultivate a broader range of power sources for your pitch.

Ronna Lichtenberg

pening. Imagine it's a male voice—it sounds deep, confident, maybe a little Southern (you know the drawl). How would you feel? Now imagine the pilot's voice is a woman's—it sounds not so deep, confident, maybe a little Southern. Is there a difference in your comfort level? Do you need a moment to decide the woman pilot's voice is okay?

Maybe if you're in an authority position, you've had direct experience with people needing to reset their expectations. It certainly happened a lot when I was a corporate exec. People would come in to meet a senior vice president, I would stand up to my full 5' 2" (okay, maybe 5' 1"), and I could see in their eyes a pause while they tried to quickly install a new program that said, "Oops, this short person in a skirt is actually 'the man.'"

Is Female Leadership Powerful?

If you see power as meaning one person is in the "up" position and the other is "down"—the classic male model of power—women don't look like born powerhouses.

But research that's been done over the past decade on the leadership styles of women proves that women just achieve power in a different way. Pioneers in this area, like Judy Rosener, Ph.D., and Sally Hegelson, argued in the '90s that, for a woman, authority and power come from connection to the people around them rather than distance from those below.

Not always, though. What seems to be happening is that women are starting to feel comfortable using both styles. For example, most successful women use a blend of both masculine and feminine styles, reported a 2003 study of Fortune 500 companies by Mary Fontaine, Ph.D., of HayGroup.

The study found that highly successful women did sometimes use directive and authoritative (commonly masculine) styles. They used male styles when it made sense. But highly successful women also lead by being more nurturing and inclusive, which are traditional feminine styles. In contrast, less successful women executives didn't use feminine styles and relied predominantly on mas-

What's in Your Head That's Not in His

culine leadership styles. And, by the way, these executives were associated with the weakest organizational climates.

You Manipulative Witch

Even as our culture is learning about positive styles of women's leadership, stereotypes remain about negative styles, including manipulation, or misuse of our "womanly wiles." In the movie *My Big Fat Greek Wedding,* Toula, an unmarried, first-generation Greek-American woman who lived with her parents and worked for her dad in the family restaurant, wanted to change her life by taking some computer courses at a community college. Toula's dad didn't think going to school was a good idea at all, since his idea was that Toula should marry a nice Greek boy and continue to work in the restaurant. He also thought that as head of the family, his word was law. Toula appealed to her mom for support, and Mom, Toula, and an aunt conspired to convince Dad that Toula going to computer school was *his* idea. The three women proceeded to do just that, in a great scene, which made for the kind of delicious comedy you only get when comedy speaks to something true in the human condition.

The belief that women are manipulative dates back to the Old Testament. Samson, renowned for his superhuman strength, was in love with Delilah. His enemies offered Delilah what sounds like biblical big bucks (eleven hundred pieces of silver from each one) if she would find out the source of Samson's strength and tell them. She accepted the offer and started asking Samson why exactly it was that he was so strong. Not being entirely stupid, Samson gave her the wrong answer three times. Here is where the womanly wiles come in. Delilah started saying to Samson, on a daily basis—allow me to loosely translate from the Bible—"Oh sweetie, I love you so much, how come you won't answer this one teensy-weensy question?" Eventually, Samson, whose "soul was vexed unto death" by Delilah's daily questioning, told her the truth. He was strong because he'd never cut his hair. Once he told her, she immediately cut off his hair, Samson lost his strength, and life went downhill from there.

Ronna Lichtenberg

I think this story speaks to the main reason women are accused of being manipulative: men's fear of the sexual power we have over them. Yes, they have the advantage of larger size and brute force, but they have the disadvantage of really wanting us to have sex with them. (Yes, women can be worked over by manipulative men, too, for exactly the same reason, but it doesn't seem to be as deeply an ingrained fear or as big a cultural stereotype.)

And, they are prone to think that we want to have sex with them, too, even when we don't. That's why the poor guy in the next cube you barely notice may think you have power over him, and are manipulating him, if you just look at him when he asks you a question. He thinks you know your perfume changes his pulse, and that you are wearing it in order to make him malleable, and that everything about you that he finds delectable is a conscious ploy to exercise power over him. (And, in fairness, I should add that every once in a while there are women who do work their sexuality consciously to create advantage. We'll talk about fairness in flirting in chapter 10.)

Stereotype 5: A good woman should wait to be asked.

Are women supposed to wait to be asked? There seems to be a cultural expectation that we should. In their book *Women Don't Ask,* Linda Babcock, Ph.D., and Sara Laschever say that men ask for what they want twice as often as women do and initiate negotiation four times more. Yet, a study of candidates for public office, by Howard University political scientist Richard Seltzer, Ph.D., found that women win just as often as men do when they run. But women are less likely than men to self-identify—that is, to decide to run for office on their own rather than at the invitation of their party. Women candidates wait to be asked.

Women want to be asked in other arenas. Socially, women still are often the ones waiting to be asked for a date or to be given an engagement ring. In business, women wait to be picked for a project, singled out for a promotion, offered a raise. In short, the times when asking is seen as taking the initiative, it's seen as male.

Material Girls

The opposite cultural stereotype, responsibility for responding to an offer, is female. Take buying versus selling, for example. According to the Center for Policy Alternatives, women make 80 percent of the purchases made in the United States. We sign 80 percent of the checks, too. And we're not just buying the small stuff, either. Women have sole or joint ownership of 87 percent of homes and carry 76 million credit cards. Buying is a culturally acceptable way for women to be powerful.

No wonder buying is fun. As Sara, a junior media major at Hunter College, says, "I *love* to shop. Shopping feels good. You get to look at pretty things, you get to buy pretty things. On top of that, someone trying to sell you something has to act interested in you. It's their job to make you feel good. Even when you know they're just trying to butter you up, it still feels good." Sara's comment is as classically female as a single strand of pearls. She wants "pretty things" and she likes other people to make her "feel good," even if she thinks they're not being sincere.

On top of that, when we are buying, we don't have to take care of someone else's emotional needs. In fact, when we are buying, sellers are supposed to take care of our needs and pay attention to how we feel for a change. Buying is a socially condoned way women can ask for care.

Maybe that's why one of the first signs I'll see that a woman is really unhappy at work is that she'll start shopping more and saying, "I'm buying all this stuff and I don't know why." In my workshops, when I ask women what

Challenging Stereotype 5

It is possible that if you are passive and wait for others to take care of you, it will happen. Giving them a clue, though, seems to me a better way to take care of yourself and them at the same time. That's why we'll talk about getting clear on what you want in chapter 5.

Ronna Lichtenberg

gives them energy, the answer is often shopping, accompanied by a big laugh. Buying is a quick emotional fix, short lived and as all-American as Twinkies.

Stereotype 6: Nice girls don't do money.

In a program called Women and Money, sponsored by the National Endowment for Financial Education and AARP, participants looked at major issues such as how well women are doing saving for retirement. The answer is that women are doing better, but not well enough yet. Because we live longer, we are twice as likely as men to live in a nursing home and twice as likely to live our retirement years in poverty. On top of that, we are more likely to work for small employers or nonprofits and have breaks in our employment to do things like raise kids or take care of our aging parents, which makes for less feed for our nest eggs.

Given that, you might think that parents would be more concerned about raising financially savvy girls than even financially savvy boys. But you'd be wrong. The Dreyfus Gender Investment Comparison Survey found that parents encourage their sons to start earning money at a far younger age (thirteen) than they do girls (sixteen to eighteen) and that twice as many boys as girls are encouraged by their parents to save money.

As one of the Women and Money conference participants said, "Girls are trained to be financially dependent and expect the knight in shining armor to take care of them. They are taught to seek safety and security rather than becoming risk-takers, and that has an impact on their decision-making in finances and investments. Girls don't do money. So when they become women, they don't do money either."

Before you yell at me about including a comment on knights in shining armor, consider the reality show where women almost completely exposed themselves in order to win the right to marry a millionaire, who was later exposed as . . . a thousandaire?

In a 2003 survey conducted by the American Institute of Certified

What's in Your Head That's Not in His

Challenging Stereotype 6

This stereotype can keep women from aggressively (and I use that word intentionally) seeking the education they need to be financially successful in their careers. If you're not comfortable thinking and talking about money, and you don't learn something about how money works, you are less likely to attract and hold onto the money you need and want to have. That's why we are going to look at money in both chapters 7 and 9, so you will find ways of thinking about it that make you more comfortable and more confident about your ability to get what you want when at least part of what you want—if not all of what you want—from work is financial reward.

Public Accountants, only 30 percent of the women polled described themselves as "confident" or as a "risk-taker" when it comes to managing their finances.

Yes, women are getting much better in this regard, and yes, women's investment clubs do better than men's, and yes, affluent women and affluent men tend to invest in similar ways. But in my consulting practice, I still work with groups marketing to women, and there are a lot of women left in the world who have gotten the message that "managing money is not my job." It *is* your job and it's part of running your career as CEO of Me, Inc. which we'll cover in the next chapter.

YES, BUT IN MY COMMUNITY . . .

The stereotypes we just talked about are widespread in American culture. Some of them, however, may not be true for you. Each of us receives different messages about who women are and how they should behave. What one Caribbean woman living in New York heard growing up may be quite different

Ronna Lichtenberg

from the stereotypes confronted by a Chinese woman living in California or a farmer's daughter from Iowa.

Research shows, for example, that African-American women are less likely than Anglo-American women to perceive a conflict between femininity and power. And some friends have told me that money was not discussed at all in their house, whereas in my house we could talk about how much we spent, but not how much we made.

You may want to take a moment to explore your culture's big stereotypes about women. If you can't list them off the top of your head, refer to the scenarios below to help you with that exploration. In the selected bibliography at

Exploring Cultural Stereotypes

Spend a little time thinking about the stereotypes that you have confronted throughout your own life—those that you have challenged and those that may still have some power over your freedom to make choices.

1. My parents told me that girls should . . .

2. My friends and I talked disparagingly about girls/women who . . .

3. Growing up, I was told that it was . . . to go after what I want.

4. I believe that women should respect . . .

5. In my house, it was . . . for women to talk about money.

6. In my culture, a feminine woman always . . .

7. In my culture, a feminine woman never . . .

8. Growing up, I was taught that powerful women were . . .

9. When women share their professional or personal accomplishments, it is considered . . .

10. Women who decide to stay at home and take care of their husband and children are . . .

11. Women who decide to pursue a professional career after having a child are . . .

the end of the book, you will also find some recommendations for a few books that look at diversity beyond gender, which may be helpful in understanding particular stereotypes that are relevant for you.

PART 3: GETTING BEYOND THE BELIEFS THAT HOLD US BACK

Everything we've just covered in the sections on brain sex and cultural stereotypes boils down to this: Your challenge is that you are wired and taught to make everything personal and to take everything personally. For most women, winning exists within a broad context of relationship and involves what I call "an equal energy exchange"—for value to flow back and forth evenly between people. But the traditional way of understanding business is that it is based on the ability to establish dominance: Winning means that you must be aggressive in order to establish advantage over someone else.

That's why it feels so hard—because it feels like you can't have both: that you can't be who you are, operating from a female context, and get what you want, operating in a male world.

You can, and you will learn how.

But first you are going to "unlearn" the old beliefs, such as those that follow, that might be holding you back. Then you are going to learn more about new beliefs, attitudes, and ways of understanding yourself that will help you to move forward.

"I don't deserve to have what I want because I'm afraid that it's bad to want it."

It used to surprise me when women sat in my office and finally managed to confess what they wanted out of work, and life, and then burst into tears when I asked them why they couldn't have it. There was a big wire wastebasket in my office; one woman cried so much she filled up the entire thing with used tissues. The reason she couldn't have what she wanted was that she was afraid

Ronna Lichtenberg

she was bad to want what she did, which, by the way, was to have a job where she could have some fun once in a while. Her fear was all wrapped up in ancient family Calvinist stuff about how work should be work, for goodness sake.

Fear, especially that subterranean kind that lives unexamined in the dark, dusty recesses of your mind, is much more likely to keep you from living a successful life than the most evil boss, client, colleague, or banker.

For me, fear is a chronic disease. It never goes away. Sometimes it's really a booger and sometimes it's not so bad. Since I am confessing, I will tell you that I am afraid a lot of the time. I am afraid of what people will think. I am afraid that if they really knew me, they wouldn't like me, let alone love me. Writing this book has stirred up all my old familiar fears and exciting new ones, including one right this second: that telling you that I'm afraid means you won't listen to anything else I have to say. Oops! There's another fear right on the tail of the first one . . . that you will somehow use my fear against me. I am afraid that this book won't help you and that will be my fault; that I am unworthy; that I am a fraud.

But writing this book has put one fear completely and utterly to rest: I am no longer afraid that I am alone in my fears because I am certain that I am not.

This morning I decided to write down fears I had heard from other women. Here are just the ones I could remember, from two days when I was mostly in my office and not involved in any big meetings or sessions.

❖ "I don't have any accomplishments." This one from a dermatologist who's regularly quoted as an expert in the national media.

❖ "Yes, I have six possible job offers. But what if they all fall apart?" This one from a job-hunting business executive who's been ranked tops in her field.

❖ "Maybe I'll get cut after the merger and never find anything as good; I'm pretty expensive." This one from an experienced HR exec who counsels people on how to handle change.

✤ "My daughter is afraid to go for an interview because she doesn't know what to say when they ask her if she has any skills." This concern regarding a recent college grad who's done well academically, in sports, and in a series of volunteer and summer jobs.

✤ "What if they don't like me?" This from a young administrator about going to a purse-making class sponsored by a local retailer.

✤ "I'm afraid that if I tell him my idea, he'll just steal it." This one from a high-level city bureaucrat.

✤ "I'm just kidding myself. Why should anybody hire me to do this?" This one from a freelancer trying to build a business.

✤ "I'm scared that if I ask for what I'm worth, they won't give it to me." This one from a business owner who just submitted a proposal in response to a request.

✤ "I fooled them again." This from a seasoned corporate trainer, explaining why her class had gone well that day.

Isn't it amazing how ridiculous fear seems when it belongs to some other terrific woman?

Flying home from a speech, I sat next to a woman in career crisis. (The flight kept getting delayed, and there's no place that inspires strong feelings like economy class in a plane on the tarmac.) Cheryl is a thirty-two-year-old mother of an eighteen-month-old boy. Her boss had just offered her a promotion, which she was about to turn down. I asked her to write down for me why she was going to tell him thanks, but no thanks.

Here's her list, which she now calls the "I Can't" Factor:

✤ I'll have to leave my comfort zone.

✤ How will the current businesses I've built grow without me?

✤ Will I lose all the relationships I've developed?

Ronna Lichtenberg

- Is the company setting me up for failure so that I too will be pushed out, just like a past executive was?

- Is the company promoting me because it's the most convenient or easiest solution?

- Will the company give me the resources to build current and new businesses?

- Will my sales force be supportive?

- Will I be convincing with new contacts because of the age/experience factor?

- What happens if I fail? My current job will not be there.

- Can I instill trust with new accounts and management?

- Do I have faith in myself?

- If the last person failed, why would I be successful?

(By the way, after looking at her list, Cheryl decided to accept.)

Letting go of fear is a life's work; in the coming chapters we'll work on practical suggestions. For now, let me just share what I try to do with fear.

My experience is that fear is a great teacher. It tells me what I want. If I am about to try something new and I get so frightened that my body reacts, it means that whatever that new thing is, it is worth exploring. It's become a joke in our house. When I say to Jimmy about some possible new venture, "Just thinking about this makes me so scared I want to throw up," he says, "Hurray!" And he's right.

Think of fear as a traffic light. Do you see it flashing red? Now I invite you to take another look. Consider the possibility that the fear light isn't flashing red. If you really look at it, you'll be able to see that your fear light is flashing green. When you accept that fear can mean "go" instead of "stop," you're on your way to a better life.

The other thing I do is what I now know officially is biologically good for me: I share my fears with friends. When I hear my fears from someone else . . . well, they're just not so bad.

Take, for example, my book fears. Jean Otte, who founded and heads a terrific company called Women Unlimited, which supports the success of corporate women, was working on her first book about the same time I started this one. I admire Jean. She's smart and savvy and brave. Given that, even though I know better, I figured that Jean, who to me is such an obvious expert, must have felt completely confident about her book project, as opposed to me, who was still in the book writing phase called "I am going to have to give the advance back because there is no way I can possibly do this."

So after her book was done, I asked her how she felt getting started, and she said, "I was so afraid; I was in terror. I recognized that I had to write this book. And I had to write about my journey, not about other people's. I had to write about what I thought was a good thing. Or what I thought was a bad thing. Or what had happened to me. And to me—and I still feel this way, I truly do, even at this moment—to me it's like standing naked and letting everybody see my cellulite. Because when I am all dressed up, I look pretty good. But with a book, people can really *inspect* you in a different way. They can read it two, three times, reread the same statement . . . it's all there for them sift through and then pick apart. And right now, as it's going to print, I know that it's gonna be tough for me to live through what people will say."

Jean and I agreed that what will happen with her project is what always happens with something new: some people will love it, some people won't. (It's now out, titled *Changing the Corporate Landscape;* count me on the list of people who love it.) And sharing the fear, and laughing at it, is an excellent way to drive it out of those dark corners, at least for a while.

"I really hate that I'm expected to change. They're the jerks. Let them change."

Anger can be a good, powerful, and righteous thing. Every one of us who works owes a debt to the angry women who filed lawsuits over being pinched on the

Ronna Lichtenberg

fanny and in the pocketbook. There are times when even I would say that pitching is not the answer and pounding someone over the head is: when you are asked to do something wrong, when you are subjected to abuse, when power over you is used inappropriately.

But for many of us, the challenge is not the big deal, "If they ask me to do that I throw the keys on the desk and walk out" issue. The challenge is the everyday anger of being left out, feeling dissed, and butting up against the invisible doors that seem closed to us.

The key is figuring out what you do with the anger, especially given the social stereotypes that may have inhibited your ability to even feel it, or express it. ("No, I'm not angry. The fact that I had a dozen Krispy Kremes/four Cosmopolitans/a Xanax/a shopping frenzy has nothing to do with it!")

There is only one response to feeling angry that is unacceptable (next to violence)—and that is to lapse into what I call "victim head." I hate victim head. Victim head is the devil's tool because it makes you think that someone else is in charge, that someone else is driving your life. And that makes you feel like you are off the hook. All you have to do is hate them, which often isn't hard to do, and blame them, which is really easy to do, and sit back in the comfort of feeling like "Hey, I did what I could." If you give in to victim head, "they"—whomever they are—win. You hand them the victory. And "they" do not deserve it.

You may now be thinking, "Okay, Miss Thing. You don't want me to sue. You don't want me to shout. You don't want me to sulk. What do you want, you uppity witch?" I want the same thing for you that I want for myself. I want you to start thinking about how to use your anger to your advantage, just as I wanted you to start thinking about doing the same thing with fear.

Anger may be a little easier than fear because there is a great model to learn from: sports. Donna Lopiano, Ph.D., head of the Women's Sports Foundation, compares it to athletic performance. "You have only one choice in anger, which is to prove them wrong. As an athlete, that anger sharpens your focus and allows you to zero in. That's the sign of greatness. They gather all of this energy and it makes them better, because they zero in on the ball, bar, or net, or whatever it is that they are trying to do."

The trick, which you'll learn in these pages, is how to take that fine multi-tracked brain of yours and focus it on priorities, prospects, and pitching so that every time you are out there, you can use the anger as a tool to improve your performance.

"If I just try hard enough, someone will notice and I'll be taken care of."

It is entirely possible that if you try hard enough, put in monster hours, and make inhuman efforts on a consistent basis, someone at work will notice and reward you for it. The belief I want you to abandon is the belief that you can count on that happening. No matter what, you will need to work hard and to produce results in order to do well. It's the passive part—waiting for someone to notice—that can still hold women back.

It is politically incorrect to say that there are women who have rescue fantasies, but the truth is that there are still women who have them. More than once, when I'm working with a woman on what she really wants, she will say, wistfully, something about how nice it would be to have someone take care of her. Maybe we all have rescue fantasies, including men.

The reason I'm bringing it up, though, is that the notion of being taken care of if we're good runs deep for many women. And I'm wondering if that's one reason why women work so hard to be perfect: because if we are really, really good, maybe someone will love us, take care of us, and never abandon us.

"I'm afraid that if I ask for what I want, it will make someone else feel bad."

My assistant, Jessica, is truly one of the bright stars in the galaxy. If you go directly to the acknowledgments, you can find me in full gush about her. One of the things that is a challenge for Jess, as it is for a lot of us, is what she calls the "feel bad" syndrome.

Ronna Lichtenberg

The feel bad syndrome is the calculation we do in advance that if we do what we want, it will cause a relationship rift. So we think we should do what someone else wants, but then we feel a little cheated.

That concern about someone else feeling bad is one reason why women worry about getting promoted, getting a raise, getting anything good. It's also the reason why it is sometimes so hard for women to set boundaries and to protect themselves from people who take up too much time and energy at work.

One of the workshops I've been asked to do a lot is called Work/Life Balance, the title of which, truth be told, kind of bugs me. I always feel like, "What? I have to choose between work and life?" Anyway, I think of the workshop as being about ways to boost your personal productivity, including your energy.

When we brainstorm about big energy drains, what makes women feel tired or resentful, the thing that tops the list is the "energy vampire," that person who just comes in, affixes himself to your neck, and sucks you dry. (As a quick aside, want to know who the energy vampire is in your life? Close your eyes. Imagine you have caller ID on your phone and you just saw that person's name or number on the screen. How do you feel? If you feel like running away, there's your very own little Count or Countess Dracula.)

I bring this up now because when you have an energy vampire in your life, you have to start saying some "nos." Nicely, but no. As in, "I'm sorry, now is not a good time for me to talk." Or . . . "I'm sorry, maybe there is someone better to help you with this." Or . . . "I can stay later on Thursday night, but Wednesday night I have to leave for school."

Sounds easy, right? So why don't you do it? You don't do it because of Jess's feel bad syndrome. You would feel bad if they would feel bad, and they would feel bad because you weren't making their needs a priority. And if they feel bad, they won't like you. Which makes you feel bad. But if you do it, when you don't really want to, they won't feel bad but you will because you'll feel like you've been used, which, by the way, you probably have. Got that?

Here's the cure for feel bad syndrome. If it is a real relationship, with the po-

What's in Your Head That's Not in His

tential for an equal energy exchange, saying, "You know, I feel bad about saying this to you, but it would be easier for me to do it this way/I'd rather not do it now/I can't really afford the time (or money)," is a way to get closer. Saying what you need lets the other person rise to the challenge of caring for you, which is a good thing for you, and for them.

If they don't, well, then you know that this isn't someone who is going to be able to commit to you and your dreams.

"I just want to make everyone happy."

For whatever reasons, we look to others for validation. When we get a reaction, when we get an "uh-huh," when we get eye contact, or a nod from someone else, it feels really good. And when we don't get that? It can feel really bad.

This desire to not just make everyone happy, but to *see* that you've made them happy, and to have them somehow indicate their approval, is part of what makes pitching so hard.

Sometimes the most important thing I can say to a woman I'm working with is "This person is not going to give you any validation. He (or she) is not wired for that. They're blue, and that's that. You can stand on your head and you won't get a compliment. Don't eat your insides out waiting for it, and wanting it, because it isn't going to happen."

If you don't let go of the desire to make everyone happy, the unmet desire can sour and then curdle into a big toxic waste dump that breeds victim head. This is how it happens: You think, "I did a great job. Mr. Bucks didn't even notice, let alone say that I did a good job." From there you go directly to either "I hate Mr. Bucks. He's a complete and total pig who doesn't appreciate or deserve me" or "There's nothing I can do to get it right"—either of which is an express train to despair.

There is another possibility. Mr. Bucks doesn't give anybody emotional goodies, and you should just be looking for yours elsewhere.

Now consider my two cats. When they run outside, the only way they will come back is if I call them by shaking the can that holds their chewy treats.

Ronna Lichtenberg

They know that there are yummies in the can. They have trained me to reward them with yummies when they do what I want.

The cats have it down cold. If the can doesn't rattle, they know there ain't no yummies in there and so they don't break a sweat coming back inside. And it may be that your Mr. Bucks doesn't have any yummies either. Unlike my clever cats, though, you may still be breaking a sweat expecting them.

"It just feels icky to ask for money."

If I asked you why you weren't pitching for money—be it a raise, venture capital, funding for a project, or a contribution to your favorite charity—if you're like a lot of other women, you might just tell me that for reasons you aren't sure about, it just feels uncomfortable. It feels icky, so you don't do it.

The reason it feels icky is grounded both in how we're wired and what we're told. We are wired for relationship context, and we've received lots of messages about how asking for money is dirty, bad, and selfish.

I'm not going to convince you that those things aren't true because those feelings may be really deeply rooted and it would take more than one book to blast them out. But I am going to tell you what to do about them.

Accept that there is a part of you that may continue to struggle against these feelings for a long time, maybe forever. These feelings will ebb after you start pitching and realize that, among other things, others will respect you more when you pitch than when you wait. But those feelings can bob up again and push you into a destructive mental framework, which is that it's all about you, and therefore, you can't ask for all the reasons I've been telling you.

The right mental framework is what I call the "bank shot" framework. Have you ever played pool, or billiards? I've done it only a few times, but one of the things you learn is that sometimes you don't aim to hit a ball directly into the pocket; you try to get the cue ball to bounce off the interior side of the table and strike the ball you intend. It takes some skill, but sometimes it is the only way to get the job done. If you've never seen a bank shot, get someone to demonstrate it for you or rent *The Color of Money, The Hustler,* or some other movie about pool that I'm not cool enough to know about but that someone you work with will be. With the bank shot framework, you move your focus to them in order to get results that are also good for you. It helps take away that part of asking for yourself that's dirty.

There's something else that relates to the icky feeling: It can be more complicated for a woman to feel like she's gotten a good deal. The classic goal in negotiating is that both sides of a transaction walk away feeling like they've gotten the best deal possible. When a guy negotiates, it can be impersonal, and only about the money. In the world of guys, there is one currency, and it is cash or cash equivalents.

Women tend to negotiate simultaneously in two currencies, and they tend to feel a good deal is one that is good in both currencies. There is cash, or some resource that involves someone else's cash (like a bigger budget, or larger staff, or promotional dollars), and there is emotional currency. Often, women are negotiating for emotional currency as well. It makes sense. We are wired to experience thoughts and feelings at the same time. We are wired to notice others' thoughts and feelings and to talk about them. We are socially, if not financially, rewarded for taking care of other people. No wonder we are keeping track of who brought what emotional goody and what we gave in return.

The two currencies are not interchangeable, but they do impact each other. You will like me less, at least in the short term, if I ask you for cash or something that in some way costs you resources. That's because if I ask you for something, then you also have to think about what you have to give up to get it. No one has unlimited resources, although some people have to think about price more than others.

When it's about money (unlike emotions), the price of my request is pretty clear, as are the trade-offs you will have to make if you say yes to me. If you are the boss, giving me a big raise means you have to face someone else whom you've cut back in order to reward me. If you are the client, it means spending less on some other service or product.

As a woman, I am sensitive enough to know that if I ask you for less cash

90

Ronna Lichtenberg

currency, I can feel I have a "right" to ask for more connection currency. But here's how Marilyn Laurie, who had a spectacular career, starting as an environmentalist and rising to become, by the time she retired, the highest ranking woman in the history of AT&T (as executive vice president of brand strategy), looks at it: "For me, the completion is when I see in someone's eyes that they get it—they get my idea—and then my 'personal' cash register rings."

"What I really want is a sure thing."

I've talked a lot about the emotional risks of pitching: rejection, abandonment, death by overconsumption of Dove bars. There is often financial risk when you pitch, as well. It is the nature of investing, and investing in your career is the biggest investment you'll make in your lifetime; the more risk you take, the higher the potential return.

Women investors tend not to be so crazy about risk when it comes to investing, at least in a superficial way. I say a superficial way because women, for example, will avoid stocks in favor of locking up their money in something that produces much lower returns, thus increasing the risk that inflation will destroy the value of their savings. Before my mom passed away, we talked a lot about how she invested her retirement savings. Mom had a bedrock position: "I don't want to take any risk. I just want to get higher returns." Me too, but so far I haven't figured out how to do that.

That means that whenever we're pitching, we're doing it in a context that will at some point be impersonal, *and* is dangerous, in the sense that we could take a risk and have it not turn out. We can react to risk in a couple of ways. One is to hide under our pillow, which presents the possible risk of suffocation and the certain risk of suboptimizing our income. The second is to educate ourselves—to have the tools we need to decide whether any given risk is worth it. But first, we need to give ourselves the chance to take the risk.

Often, women who are in a job-hunting situation worry about whether they will take a particular opportunity if presented to them. If you know that you flat-out don't want a job, you should just say so and not waste anyone's time.

What's in Your Head That's Not in His

But if you aren't really sure, then your job is to get the offer. You can't evaluate risk and reward in the abstract. You can only do it with something real and specific. That's why in chapter 9, we are going to look at pricing yourself in the marketplace, because pricing is how you handle risk. For instance, they want you to take more risk? Well, you want more return.

MOVING BEYOND SELF-LIMITING BELIEFS

You can probably think of more self-limiting beliefs than the ones I've listed, and I hope you do. The way to find them is to look at the choices you are making about what you do, and what you don't do, and then to ask yourself, "What do I believe that justifies this choice?" Ask yourself that question a few times and see how honestly you can answer. Or trade off with a trusted friend and ask each other. If you stay with it, you will start getting down to the creepy crawlies about being simultaneously not enough (feeling like a fraud) and too much (being too emotional). You'll know it is a belief when you find that you can't articulate it the first time clearly, when you feel it, and know it, more than you can say it, and when your first instinct is to preface it by saying, "I know this is completely ridiculous, but . . ."

With this chapter, I've tried to show you the connection between how our biology sets the stage and how we react to negative stereotypes by forming beliefs about ourselves that aren't true. Those beliefs rattle around in our heads so long that it seems as if they must be true, because anything we've held onto for so long seems pretty reliable. They're not. I thought giving you a little map of self-limiting beliefs and where they came from could help you decide to put them aside and get onto a new belief system, which I call the "Me, Inc. mindset."

Ronna Lichtenberg

CHAPTER 4

the me, inc. mindset

One of the things I've learned from a lifetime of diets is that the best way to get rid of a bad habit is to have a new one to substitute for it. If I say to myself, "I am never going to have M&Ms again," for starters, even as I say it I know from extensive experience that it is a lie. And then I would think about M&Ms so much I would be like a kid cautioned not to put beans up her nose: I would be able to think only about the very thing I was not supposed to be thinking about. If, on the other hand, I say to myself, "Instead of a big bag of M&Ms, I can have either a teaspoon of peanut butter or a couple of squares of dark chocolate," then I have a shot at doing just that, thereby changing from a habit that is bad for me to one that is at least a little bit better for me. No, it doesn't always work, but mostly it does, which is enough to get improved results.

With that in mind, I am going to offer you a new way of thinking about yourself to replace the unproductive individual beliefs and mental habits we've just covered. If our brains really were like computers, I could tell you simply to uninstall your old beliefs and install new ones. But our brains are much more complex than computers, and our old individual beliefs are deeper, more pervasive, and more culturally reinforced than the new ones will be. Shifting to a new mindset, to the Me, Inc. point of view, is going to take some time and work.

The good news is that making even a little shift from self-limiting beliefs to

Me, Inc. beliefs will give you an increased sense of personal power. More than that, it will open your mind to new possibilities and new ways of dealing with challenges that may have stumped you before. So let's get started.

THE CEO OF ME, INC.

I still remember the first time I did a workshop using the Me, Inc. concept. I stood in front of the room and asked the women attending, all from various backgrounds, who they thought they were working for. One said the name of a company. Another said the name of her boss. I waited a while. Finally, one of them said, "I'm working for myself," to which I said, "Bingo!"

Whether you are an employee or an employer, you are the chief executive officer of Me, Inc. You are the one in charge of what you offer, how you offer it, where you offer it, and what you will accept for your offering. You go to work every day where you do because you choose to do that. You choose to do it because you've either thought about why it is the best deal and makes the most sense for you or because you haven't accepted responsibility for making the right decisions for yourself. If the latter is true and you are living your life on automatic pilot, whatever your career, whatever it feels like, the truth is that you are not a slave. You are free to leave.

What can be terrifying about accepting that you are the CEO of Me, Inc. is that there isn't someone else in charge.

I can tell when people really "get" the Me, Inc. concept because the first thing that comes up is fear. In that first workshop, one woman raised her hand and said, "Could I hire someone else?" She was seriously distressed when I told her she could not. Being CEO of your own Me, Inc. is big stuff. And we all want the best possible CEO for our own Me, Inc. It seems like we should be able to find someone smarter, wiser, stronger, just *better* than we are for this vitally important job.

When it comes to Me, Inc., though, there isn't anyone else for the job of CEO. You are in charge. And no matter how many doubts you harbor about it, no one is better suited for it than you are.

94

Ronna Lichtenberg

"ME, INC." IS NOT THE SAME AS "ME"

There are lots of ways that the personal side of business can be either a challenge or an advantage for women. As you learn more about pitching, you will learn specifics about how to make this relationship orientation an advantage more often.

It starts with understanding that who you are as a person and what you offer in the marketplace are not identical. Look at it this way: If I have a handbag for sale and you are considering buying it, the marketplace transaction is mostly about the handbag. I say mostly, because if we are talking about the handbag, even on-line, part of your purchase decision is a reaction to me. You're asking yourself: Do I trust her? Do I believe she really understands my needs? But mostly, your decision is about the bag, what it's worth to you, and why it is or isn't something you're going to buy. In some ways, if I am selling my talents, skills, and services, it is just like selling a handbag. It's about that "offering," and it's also about me.

A potential buyer—whether it be a client or an employer—has to decide if they need what I'm offering, want what I'm offering, and think it's worth the price I'm asking. But my time and energy is an offering, like a handbag, or an office tower, or a vacation time-share, or anything sold in the marketplace.

Accepting that Me, Inc. is not the same as Me will save you a lot of grief. It allows you to take a step back in situations that just feel overwhelmingly personal, or that violate long-held individual beliefs about what you are worth, and get some perspective.

Me, Inc. is not the you that exists outside the marketplace; it is not the core of you. Me, Inc. is only about your offerings in the marketplace. Marketplace judgments about value, about price, are not about your own personal worth. Your personal worth is far beyond the value of money.

ME, INC. HAS CLIENTS AND PROSPECTS

This is one that can be particularly helpful to women who work for someone else, specifically for women in big companies. Consider, for example, Willa, who was in a job involving business-to-business selling. One year shortly before Christmas, we were talking about her career and her future. Willa's issue was her boss, Dennis. She hated him. In fact, almost everyone Willa worked with hated Dennis. Most of the team had worked together before; their company had been spun out from an old one. But the investors backing the new company wanted an "outsider" as CEO, so they brought in Dennis.

Willa had a lot to say about Dennis, and most of it was bad. He didn't pay attention to her, he didn't listen to her ideas; in fact they barely spoke. There were other people who sucked up to Dennis, she told me with great disdain, but her preference was to ignore him. And, by the way, she added that the new company wasn't meeting its targets, and there was some nervousness about who Dennis was going to get rid of next since he'd just fired one of the original team's favorites.

After listening for a while, I asked Willa how she would be treating Dennis if he were her biggest client. She hesitated, and then said that she would probably have sent him a Christmas card, or maybe even a small gift. With some prompting, she admitted that she would know the names of his children and ask about them. That she would stop by his office, just to see what she could do for him. She admitted she would also ask if he wanted to get together to grab a cup of coffee once in awhile.

Then I asked her how big a client someone would have to be for her to give them this kind of attention. She said that if someone represented 60 percent of her revenue, she'd treat them like a big deal. Then I said, "Okay, Dennis represents 100 percent of your revenue; tell me what I'm missing here." Willa went very still, and then said, "Okay, I'll try to see him differently." She later reported that she did try to see him as a good client and not as a giant waste of good oxygen. She also said that it was a struggle to keep this mentality instead of joining her most unhappy colleagues for round after round of Dennis-bashing. I can't tell you that after that Willa loved Dennis, but I can tell you she got a promotion and relocated to the city where she wanted to work.

It is all too easy—I know, because I have done it more than once—to believe that a boss is there to take care of you. But to *make* them want to take care of you

Ronna Lichtenberg

is the same as convincing any other prospect or client to exchange value fairly with you: They have to believe that what you are offering makes a difference for them. The more you understand about your clients and prospects, which I'm going to start addressing in the next chapter, the brighter Me, Inc.'s business prospects.

MANAGE THE SAME BUSINESS BASICS

Just because your version of Me, Inc. isn't as big as Bill Gates's Microsoft doesn't mean that you don't have to think about many of the same business elements that Gates does.

You should, for example, have your own personal board of directors, people you trust to talk to about the business of Me, Inc. It is critical, and I use that word

The Big Business Picture

- ❖ Women hold 8 percent of the top-level jobs in major corporations.
- ❖ There are eight female CEOs in the Fortune 500 and a total of seventeen in the Fortune 1000.
- ❖ Women are only 15.7 percent of corporate officers in the Fortune 500 companies, up from 12.5 percent in 2000.
- ❖ Women hold 9.9 percent of total line corporate officer positions in the Fortune 500.
- ❖ Women hold 779 board seats (in 2003), or 13.6 percent of Fortune 500 seats, an increase from 12.4 percent in 2001.
- ❖ Bureau of Labor Statistics data indicate that women now represent 50.6 percent of the forty million employees in management, professional, and related occupations, up from 40.9 percent of managers and professionals in 1983.
- ❖ Women make up 36 percent of MBA students, 47 percent of medical students, and 49 percent of law students.

deliberately, that you have access to people who can help you think through the financial consequences of your decisions, including pricing your offering.

As we've seen, women are good at networking, and really good at forming personal connections. But Me, Inc. needs more than the feeling of connection. Me, Inc. needs a board that includes a few people you can really trust to tell you the truth, people who share your dream or your passion or your commitment, and people who know something about how the marketplace values the kind of work you do. The board doesn't have to be formal; it doesn't even need to meet at all, let alone regularly. It just needs to include people who support your offering and who have some business expertise—marketing, legal, accounting, financial—ideally, expertise in areas where you're not so expert.

Me, Inc. also needs some basic knowledge about sources and uses of funds—some idea of where the money comes from and how it is spent.

You need to know this for starters because Me, Inc. faces financial risk. Either you work for yourself, so you know you're at risk, or you work for an employer and might be at risk for all kinds of reasons you don't even know about. *There is no job security anywhere, for anyone, other than the security of keeping Me, Inc. competitive.* On top of that, any career change you might consider involves some kind of financial risk, be it a change in how you're compensated or how your pension is funded or downtime between jobs.

That's why you need to know where money is coming from and how much it costs to keep Me, Inc. running. A few months ago I had a talk with Joan, who was considering whether to volunteer for a severance package at her company. Joan had been at the company a long time and thought that she would qualify for at least six months of severance, which is a good thing.

When I questioned her, though, it turned out that Joan had never really put a budget together for herself. Like a lot of folks, she knew that she spent everything she made, but she didn't know where she spent it. She had no idea how long the severance could last if she needed it to last longer to give her the time she needed to get a great new job.

Ronna Lichtenberg

It has taken me a long time to understand, but now I deeply believe that the purpose of a budget is to give you freedom and choices. That's because the way you are already spending money represents your choices and priorities, whether you have made those decisions consciously or not. To change them, you have to first know what they are.

Me, Inc. deserves and needs a marketing plan too—an understanding of what your core offering is, who needs what you offer, and why it is different from others like it. I'm going to spend a lot of time teaching you how to figure all that out in chapters 7 and 8.

CHARGE A PREMIUM PRICE FOR THE OFFERING

This is where I think the Me, Inc. mindset has the most practical value: when it comes time to think and talk about money. That's because before you even get to money, you need to get your own head straight.

Every time you are in Me head instead of the Me, Inc. mindset, you are at risk of getting caught in the net of "not-good-enough" thinking. That kind of thinking offers a litany of mental reasons why you should be charging less than

The Small Business Picture

❖ Nearly half (48 percent) of all privately held businesses in the United States are owned 50 percent or more by women.

❖ Since 1997, women-owned firms have grown at nearly twice the rate of all firms (17 percent vs. 9 percent).

❖ Women-owned firms employ over nineteen million people nationwide.

❖ Women-owned businesses' expenditures on salaries and wages are an estimated $492 billion per year.

Center for Women's Business Research, 2004

someone else would for what you do because for some unclear reason you think you are worth less. That kind of thinking guarantees that you will get less than you should.

If you accept the possibility that Me, Inc. could conceivably charge a premium for its offering, or at least be in the top of market range for the services it offers, then you can put together a road map for how to make that possible.

For example, Me, Inc. might be able to charge more if you had a different kind of education, or a different experience, or if you were willing to work in a different location, or at different times. It may even be packaging: Think about how much brown rice costs when you buy it by the pound in a health food co-op compared to the price of brown rice in a fancy gourmet store in an elegant little bag with a gold ribbon tied around it and a few grains of fancy wild rice thrown in to keep you from going into complete sticker shock.

When you think about Me, Inc. pricing instead of Me pricing, it opens the door to the possibility that you could comfortably charge more, and get more, because you know exactly why your offering is worth more—and to whom it is worth more, as well.

It also gives you a way to toggle mentally out of a relationship perspective, out of responding to other people's feelings, reactions, and desires, long enough to get a fix on what is fair in the marketplace.

CONNECT WITH PEOPLE IN WAYS THAT BENEFIT BOTH PARTIES

Business can be dirty. It can be about abuse of power, dominance, shady tricks, and a mindset of being out to get, or at least to take advantage of, the other guy. It doesn't have to be that way, though, and you don't have to be that way to succeed.

In fact, with the right mindset, you can do good things for other people at the same time you get a fair return for yourself.

Pitching someone is a way of inviting them to connect with you on a shared

Ronna Lichtenberg

goal, even when it is a small one instead of a big one. Part of what you'll learn in later chapters is how pitching can be relationship enhancing as opposed to being destructive to relationships. Getting what you want can, and in some sense should, be about helping the other person get what they want, too.

CHANGE YOUR BELIEFS, CHANGE THE WORLD

Before we get into pitching specifics, I want to take a moment to share another way the work you do to pitch will pay off for others as well as for you.

The efforts you make on your own behalf—the investment you make in learning how to pitch—will create value not just for you, but for your friends, daughters, and sisters. It will pay off for women, and men, whom you will never meet. When you reach for that promotion, or make the call to get capital for your business, when you choose to change your life through a pitch, it will change other lives as well.

As the boxes on the previous pages show, women are making real progress in big companies, and even more progress in the smaller ones we own. Progress is great; parity would be even better.

There are a lot of things that need to happen for women to reach parity, however: new policies, an activist stance by CEOs, organization design and performance management systems that value women and diverse ways of getting jobs done.

All of these things require support from men as well as from women. That's why learning how to pitch not only gives you an advantage when it feels like you're playing on a playing field that isn't level, it helps you level the field itself.

CHAPTER 5

visioning: discover
what you really want

If you are really going to invest in Me, Inc. and *run* your career, as opposed to letting your career just happen to you, you need to start where every good CEO starts: with a vision for the business. After all, you cannot effectively sell your ideas and yourself to get what you want if you aren't really sure what you do (and don't) want.

Getting clear about what you really want, at work and in life, is the first step, and for some people the most crucial, in effective pitching.

"Hey, that's not so tough," you may be thinking. In fact, many of you probably believe you're already quite clear on the *want* part of the career equation. You know you're eager to land a new job or get a promotion at your current place of employment. You're convinced that a more flexible schedule would solve your career problems. You're yearning to launch your own business or to switch careers entirely. And, because who among us wouldn't like to make more money, you're probably looking for a raise as well.

But whatever it is you think you want may not tell the whole story. Do you really want to run your own business, or is your deeper desire to gain more control over your professional life, whether that happens in a company setting or an entrepreneurial venture? Would a bigger paycheck really erase your niggling dissatisfaction with your job, or do you need to be doing work that better satisfies your creative side or your more spiritual self? If it's a new job you're looking for, what are the specific qualities of the position that will make you happy? Are you setting narrow goals when you really need to be exploring bigger dreams for your life?

Because there may be many layers of wants, some of which we're unaware of . . . because we may think we want one outcome when we really want something else . . . because we too often don't allow ourselves to dream big enough . . . because we want a lot of things but aren't sure what we want most . . . the first step in learning how to pitch like a girl is visioning, the act of imagining in vivid detail what our ideal work life would really be like.

WHY DO YOU NEED VISIONING?

When a woman comes to me for career coaching, she may say she has a very specific reason for being in my office, such as, "I am here because I want a new job," or, "My company is about to go through a major downsizing and I want to preserve the job I have." Or she may say she wants to change course because she feels as if she's stagnating in her current position and wants to find a way to move more quickly up the corporate ladder. Or she's eager to land a plum assignment or important new client, or maybe even to switch fields entirely.

Sometimes, she can't really say why she wants to talk to me, other than she feels stuck and confused and isn't sure how to even get started because she's not sure what she wants. Either way—whether the particulars seem clear or they don't—it's important to be able to consider the "possible" future to make sure the practical next steps have a chance of taking you where you want to go.

Visioning is a way to discover your deepest desires. It is a way to give yourself permission to see what is really inside you and to dream bigger dreams than you have allowed yourself to believe are possible.

As women, we particularly need visioning because we have a tendency to editorialize and discount our dreams before we can get them out of our mouths. The discounting, which I'll talk more about in chapter 9, starts in our heads long before it even gets to our mouths. We can give anyone willing to listen a thousand reasons why we can't do whatever our hearts and minds tell us we really want: we're not talented enough, we don't have the right education or skills, we couldn't take the time away from our families, we wouldn't make enough money, we're afraid to put ourselves out there that way. That makes it hard to give ourselves permission to imagine the possibilities, particularly for pinks. Couldn't, shouldn't, won't.

So we limit ourselves and our dreams from the start, often without even realizing we're doing it. If we even allow ourselves to "want," which, as we know, many women don't, we give ourselves a definition of what we want that fits a preconceived notion of whom we think we're supposed to be. Since we believe we're the ones who have defined the want, we can't be disappointed when we get it, right?

Wrong. If you unwittingly lie to yourself and say, for example, "I really want a raise," and you do all your pitching around that idea when the truth is that you really want to express yourself professionally in a different way, you are spending all of this effort on pitching for something that ultimately won't satisfy you. You may get the raise, but you still won't be happy. You can come out ahead in the inning but lose the game.

The purpose of visioning, then, is to move yourself toward a bigger, deeper desire—a truer, more deeply satisfying win.

That's a scary proposition for most of us. *Yes* is almost always scarier than *no*. Think of it this way: If you confide in me about your biggest, most heartfelt dream and I tell you that maybe you are too bigheaded and you shouldn't aim so high, you may be a little pissed off. But you'll probably also find it kind of comforting to make the target less ambitious and a whole lot easier to reach. If, on the other hand, I say to you instead, "You are looking at that hill, which is fine, but you should really be looking at the peak of Mount Kilimanjaro because you are capable of climbing it," that's scary. It's scary because a big vision raises the possibility of a failure that feels like real failure. This is where the tummy-churning fear we talked about comes in.

Ronna Lichtenberg

If you open your heart to a vision and you admit to yourself that you would really like to take a shot at it, then you can lose something you really, deep-down-at-your-core want. We all learn to defend ourselves against desiring that bigger, deeper want because of how we'll feel if we don't get it. Fear, especially fear of being rejected and fear of being judged, makes us all want to hide under the bed. So we learn to make do with wanting a little less.

The only problem is we end up leading lesser lives as a result. There's not as much risk hiding under the bed, but there's not much room to grow either.

So live dangerously. Take a leap. Imagine the possibilities. The results are worth it, really worth it. I promise.

the power of an image

If you need proof that the simple act of visioning can lead to profound change for the better, let me introduce you to Etta Jacobs, one of the first women I ever led through a visioning exercise and whose entire life was transformed by the power of a single image.

Etta was a participant in a Me, Inc. workshop that I created for *O* magazine a few years ago. The idea was to take a diverse group of women and spend an entire day helping them to think about the way they earned their living in a focused way that would enable them to see the possibilities and hopefully lead to more fulfilling work. I developed a series of visioning exercises for the workshop that proved so powerful that I've been using them in workshops and career coaching sessions ever since.

At the time of the workshop, Etta, then forty-four, was working as the design director for a big textbook publishing company in New York City. She was quite verbal about her need for the seminar to be practical, and I worried that she'd have difficulty with the softer exercises, which included envisioning an ideal workday.

But to her surprise and mine, Etta drew a remarkably vivid picture of her perfect day. She imagined a morning where she was sitting on a screened porch, with the sun on her face and the breeze in her hair, drawing or writing. She was creative, focused, and totally in the zone. In her fantasy, Etta was making money on the side as a consultant but increasingly getting by on her artwork. Her description was so clear and compelling that all of the workshop participants, myself included, could smell the fresh air. But Etta, ever the pragmatist, insisted that her dream had to be deferred for at least ten years—after all, she had to make a living. (I've since learned that the "maybe later" syndrome is quite common when women are afraid to pursue goals, let alone dreams.) She left the workshop with a plan to do more of her artwork on the side, which might have been right for some people.

But it turned out that the seminar stirred up powerful feelings about the constraining nature of her corporate life and started dislodging Etta's resistance to change. A month after attending the workshop, while Etta was still trying to understand this intense wave of emotions, her phone rang. It was a headhunter calling to talk about an art director position in Cambridge, Massachusetts. Etta hadn't thought about moving from Manhattan, let alone living in another state entirely.

Yet six weeks later, that was exactly what Etta was doing. In fact, by then she was in a house with a porch, getting up at sunrise so she could sit with the sun on her face and the breeze in her hair, writing. Her new job was using all of her creative muscles, more than she knew she had. And because she is a morning person, she was reveling in her company's flexible hours. She was at work by 7:30 A.M. and home by 4:30 P.M. when she'd be enthusiastically greeted by Fraser, a chocolate Lab who lived in an apartment upstairs. Her average day now looked much like the ideal day she'd imagined just a few weeks earlier, only better.

"Even though I didn't recognize it," Etta told me some time later, "my job was no longer challenging, and there was no place to go. The only way up was via a particular corporate ladder I didn't want to climb." She kept dreaming about "someday," without a clear plan. "I was sleepwalking through my life and didn't know it," said Etta, who felt that she was finally living the life she was meant to have.

Ronna Lichtenberg

WHAT IS VISIONING, ANYWAY?

Visioning is a series of exercises that will help you figure out what you want in your personal and professional life. Not what you think you should want, not what other people think someone in your circumstances should want, but what really, deep down at your core, will fulfill you professionally and personally.

Don't worry—you can do this.

The exercises themselves, as you'll see in detail in a moment, are simple. First, you'll imagine your ideal workday, answering a series of questions that will allow you to visualize the qualities that would make it perfect for you. Next, you'll repeat the experience, only this time imagining your worst day. You'll follow that up with a comparison of the details of the two days. For some people, physical surroundings are really important, for some they are not. Some people want to work with a team, some people want to be alone.

When you compare your images of the best and worst days, you'll get a clearer idea of the elements of work that are really the most important to you. You'll end with a reality check—a look at what's holding you back from achieving your dream and what practical steps you can take to move forward toward what you really want.

Simple, really. Deceptively simple, given how life-changing the results can be.

Understand going in that the vision you come up with first may be out of focus. Ambiguity is okay. It's a step along the way. In my first vision of post-corporate life, I had the idea that I wanted to be able to go outside in the middle of the day, sit in the sunshine and sip coffee while I wrote. I had no idea about what I was writing, but I thought it would be fabulous if I could do that. The vision implied how important freedom was to me and helped me realize that writing somehow needed to be a more direct part of how I made my living. But my vision did not include writing a book, let alone three of them, and it didn't include becoming a contributing editor for a magazine I respect and admire. I really couldn't have dreamed that. All I could see was just a single image, a snapshot of a possible life.

A vision gives you something to move toward, not the specific goals. Setting goals and priorities is the step *after* visioning: You set milestones for yourself on how to get closer to your vision after you've imagined it.

consider working with a partner

You can vision alone, or you can vision with a partner. The advantage of working with a partner is that visioning then becomes an interactive process, a back and forth exchange. A partner can ask follow-up questions, reflect meaning back to you, and press you on the details that are murky. A partner will hear when you are telling yourself a lie much sooner than you will. Working with a partner with a different style from yours, a different skill set, or a different network will give you the best results because it will stretch your thinking. Partners are particularly helpful for blues, especially those who haven't lifted their heads up from work lately.

When I work with clients on visioning, for instance, I write their responses to the exercise questions on a big flip chart that works like giant Post-it notes that stick to the wall. I have them tell me their answers, rather than reading them, because what they tell me and what they have written down is always a little bit different and the difference somehow illuminates what their vision is really all about. I ask follow-up questions to further explore aspects of the vision that seem vague. We put a check mark next to results that seem fuzzy or scary and return to reexamine them until their meaning becomes clearer.

Ideally then, if you work with a partner on visioning, trade roles as the facilitator. Choose your partner with great care: You don't want someone you work with on a daily basis—the exercise is so intimate and revealing that visioning with a close colleague can be downright embarrassing. Your best friend usually isn't the right choice either, especially if she's in a different field and doesn't really understand your work life. Neither is a close family member or other loved one. Often the people closest to you have a vested interest in not wanting you to change. Deep down, they may not want you to get what you want because they love you just the way you are and if you

Ronna Lichtenberg

change, maybe it will mean they have to change. The people who love you will come around eventually, but it's better not to invite them into the process until later.

Instead, look to partner with someone whom you respect, who does something for a living that is not completely unlike what you do, and who is personally motivated to change their life for the better too, because you want this to be a fair exchange. Or you could partner with a small group. Saying your vision out loud in a small group also creates the possibility that someone will support you—or will know someone who can. But if the vision is in your head and your head alone, others can't help you because they don't know what you really want. Besides, saying it out loud is the beginning of making it real.

If working with another person isn't an option, you can be your own partner. Bring a tape recorder into your session, say your answers out loud, and play them back so you can hear them. Saying the answers that you have written out loud also triggers additional thoughts about how you feel about your ideal day and, ultimately, your true vision for yourself. You will notice more details, add content, and sharpen the image.

ground rules and caveats

To get the most out of visioning, you need to follow a few guidelines.

First, carve out a time and space in which you can be totally focused on your visioning exercises, with no distractions. Go into a room with pen and paper, maybe bring in a cup of coffee, shut the door, and that's it. You don't eat, listen to music, play with the cat, or check your e-mail.

None of the exercises should take more than half an hour to complete. It's best to do it in the time of day you're at your best. You can either do one exercise a day over a period of three or four days or do all of them in a single visioning session, which should last no more than two hours from start to finish. If you take longer, you might be overthinking it, trying to make it perfect. The vision does not have to be perfect. You just need to write down the answers that pop into your head.

Recognize going in that you may be embarrassed by some of your answers. Dreaming big is uncomfortable for most women, for all the biological and cultural reasons we've discussed. But remember Me, Inc. This is not selfish, wrong, bad, or disgusting. This is your job, and one of your most important ones. So do not censor yourself from the get-go. This is not the time or place to give a microphone to the editorial voice in your head that may rise up and tell you that you are not allowed to dream this specific dream.

Before you begin, take a minute to talk to that critical inner voice and make her go away for a while. Tell her that, generally speaking, you really appreciate her help but that you don't need her assistance at this particular moment. Say, "Look, Miss I'm-only-telling-you-this-for-your-own-good, I really value your opinion—but right this minute I'd like you to sit in this lovely chair while I wrap duct tape around your mouth to eliminate the chance you'll say something that frightens my dreams away." Invite her to chill for the next twenty or thirty minutes, and reassure her that there'll be plenty of work for her to do later (as if there's any chance that after the duct tape comes off she'd keep her mouth shut anyway).

You may find too as you go through the process that you have multiple visions of what is possible for you. Lots of women do. It's our fine multifocal brains working overtime. The process of looking at that is visioning too—to explore the different ways you could go. But for your first session, limit yourself to no more than two visions of your ideal day, and if you can push yourself to focus on only one, so much the better. With two visions, you'll still be able to pick out common themes and work with them. Envisioning six ideal days is just a way to avoid getting into the true spirit of the exercise, which is all about focusing on what really matters most to you.

YOUR IDEAL DAY

Okay, here we go. You're ready to tackle the first exercise: imagining your ideal workday.

Ronna Lichtenberg

To get the most out of this exercise, you need to include as much physical detail and sensory information as possible. (Use the questions below.) I call this process *visioning* for a reason: You're supposed to come away with a picture of what you want, not just a bunch of words on paper. Working only with words limits the part of the brain you're using to the logical and analytical part, and that part of the brain just can't help you as much with this task as the part that works with pictures can.

So in answer to the question of, say, where you are during your ideal day, you want to "see" the physical location as much as possible. You might say, "I am in a room with pale blue walls, at an oak table, and Sam and Allison are

Imagine Your Ideal Workday

Take a few minutes to imagine the best working day you could ever have. Then jot down your answers to the following questions:

- ❖ What time of the day is it?
- ❖ Where are you?
- ❖ What are you doing?
- ❖ Who are you working with?
- ❖ What about this work feels good?
- ❖ Who are you talking to for support?
- ❖ Who is paying you to do this job?
- ❖ How much are you getting paid?
- ❖ Why are they paying you instead of somebody else?

Now jot down a few thoughts about how this scenario is most like your current situation and then unlike your current situation. Ask yourself what about this vision most appeals to you. Finally, write down the three aspects of this scenario you would most like to make happen. Then—put the ideal workday aside. If you're breaking your visions effort into shorter time periods, this is a good place to stop.

there with me." One of my visioning clients had her day starting at 9:00 A.M., just after she'd gotten her kids off to school, sitting in her big glass-walled office, warm, with natural light flooding in, sitting on a couch reviewing reports from her staff in preparation for a meeting later in the day with senior level executives from a company with whom she regularly did business. In her fantasy, she was pulling down a cool $300,000 to $500,000 a year. Not too shabby.

The more detail you can provide—even details that seem outrageous and totally out of reach—the more you'll get out of the exercise.

If you have trouble getting started, try thinking about people who give you pangs of professional jealousy. Not just the people you're supposed to envy because they're way up the food chain, but the ones you really do. Noticing the people you envy can be a great signpost of what you really want. When I made my career transition from corporate executive to entrepreneur, I realized that I didn't really care anymore when someone I'd considered a competitor got a promotion. But when someone I knew or admired had written something wonderful—sharp stabs right to my jealous heart.

Record any physical responses you have to your answers—say, if your throat tightens up or you get a weird feeling in your tummy. These responses are additional pieces of information and data you can use to help you interpret and analyze your answers when you're done with the exercise. Often your "gut brain" is more in tune with the emotional, real you than the brain in your head.

Working on your vision may jar loose little images and thoughts. You should note them too, but keep visioning. In order to catch those thoughts and honor them, make sure you have little note cards with you, or take notes in your Palm or BlackBerry, or record them on your tape recorder. I use a little dictation device that a friend bought for me from Brookstone. It only captures twelve minutes of dictation at a time, but that is more than enough. What's important is to honor those images—they are your guides to a better future.

Ronna Lichtenberg

. . . and now, your nightmare

Follow the same guidelines for the second exercise in the visioning process, this time imagining your worst possible workday.

People usually find this exercise easier to imagine than the ideal day, maybe, sadly, because they've had more experience with bad days than good ones. So while this exercise can feel bad, or sobering, it can feel kind of good, too. This is your chance to vent. So let it all go, girlfriend. The bad, the ugly, the boring, the just plain irritating.

Often a woman's worst day is an extension of a day she's already had at her current job. In my experience, fluorescent lighting often plays a part in people's

Imagine Your Worst Possible Workday

Now imagine the worst working day you could ever have. Jot down your answers to the following questions:

- ❖ What time of the day is it?
- ❖ Where are you?
- ❖ What are you doing?
- ❖ Who are you working with?
- ❖ What about this work feels bad?
- ❖ Who are you talking to for support?
- ❖ Who is paying you to do this job?
- ❖ How much are you getting paid?
- ❖ Why are they paying you so little instead of somebody else?

Now jot down a few thoughts about how this scenario is most like your current situation and then most unlike your current situation. Ask yourself which three aspects of this scenario you would most like to avoid.

worst days. So do windowless and cramped offices, overbearing bosses, endless meetings, high-maintenance clients, needy or incompetent colleagues, subordinates who don't do what they're supposed to do, lengthy e-mails, and isolation. So do unnecessary fire drills, ungrateful teammates, and dinner out of a vending machine. So . . . let 'er rip.

what the answers reveal

Once you've completed the visions, you're ready to move on to the next step: comparing your ideal and worst days to see what the differences tell you about your vision and what's really important to you. In business lingo, we call this a gap analysis. (This is, by the way, a good thing to say if your boss comes in while doing this at work—"Hey, I was just working on a strategic gap analysis"—which could cover just about anything.)

Sometimes the conclusions are obvious. If there's a lot of detail in your best day about working alone, and a lot in your worst day about sitting in endless meetings, you know that having time to work by yourself, without interruption, is important to you. If your best day includes seeing trees and your worst day includes a long rant about being cooped up in an interior conference room, you see that somehow incorporating nature into your work and life really matters to you.

There is no right or wrong. I've had people describe their best day beginning with them all alone at 7:30 in the morning and people begin their worst day by saying it's 7:30 in the morning and I'm all alone. My best day is another person's worst day, and that's okay.

So when you compare the two versions, look at what comes up in both—even in mirror images. That's what matters to you. If the moment you notice a commonality the editorial voice starts screeching at you about why it's ridiculous to even think about it, that's what's important to you and what you're not giving yourself permission to do. That's the juicy part, the stuff that will truly change your life.

Mei's Decision

Lexi, a senior HR executive at a Fortune 50 company I'll call BigCo, told me the following story about how daily life gets easier after you pay attention to the bigger issue of what matters to you.

"I consistently coach women on primary and secondary choices. Most of us know that what happens is we suppress the primary choice, the primary thing in life, and we let all these other people push their secondary choices on us. Those secondary choices take over the primary choice, and the more we let that happen, the more unhappy we get. So I coach women around here to identify what their primary choice is and get it out where it's supposed to be, put it where it needs to be—first. Then it's magic and everything works itself around. All the secondary things fall into place. When I see women finally do that, it's always scary. But it's also just magical.

"For example, Mei, a woman in her thirties in IT, would get sent somewhere by her boss for three weeks and she'd get stuck there for six months. She had no life, no friends, and as she got older, work became less important. The desire to have a relationship became her number one desire. I watched her struggle with this for a year, and every time she came in here she would have tears in her eyes.

"I would ask, 'What does your soul want?' She would tell me and then go away, do whatever management wanted her to do, and six months later be back in here crying. Finally, about six weeks ago she made the decision that she was sort of at a crossroads. She made a stand. She said, 'I want to look for something else within BigCo. It doesn't matter to me anymore; I don't really care what happens. They could fire me.'

"People shouldn't have to get to that place, but she did. And as soon as she did, her boss released her. The next day her boss actually called someone else and got her a new job, and she's gonna be here in a different group.

"Now she's just lit up and she's a different person. It's really cool."

REALITY CHECK

Now comes what is for some women the toughest part of the visioning process: considering whether your vision is reasonable and possible to achieve.

The good news: Of the many dozens of people with whom I've run visioning sessions over the years, everyone's dream, to some extent or another, has been achievable—although not always, or even usually, in the way they originally imagined. One person's dream of artistic expression, for example, started with learning to play the piano and resulted in getting an apartment in New York City. Another's quest for more meaning at work ended with the decision to have another child. Following your vision will take you to unexpected places.

Start by asking yourself another deceptively simple question: What's holding me back? Why can't I have what I want?

Your style color may have a lot to do with your answer. A blue, for instance, will usually talk about their inhibitors as outside factors that are function related. Often the obstacle has to do with money, especially for blue men, since we've seen how they're wired and reinforced for marketplace achievement. A classic blue response is "I can't have what I want because the market for that job doesn't pay enough for me to support my family properly."

A pink will more typically experience the obstacles as internal, often based on the relationships in their life. One common sticking point has to do with conflicts between our work vision and the personal relationships that matter most to us. The sentence "I can't have what I want because it would be selfish," right out of the self-limiting beliefs sound track, comes up a lot. Pinks with children will say, "My children need me—I can't put that much energy into a vision for work and take care of my kids properly at the same time." Women who are not romantically involved at the moment, and very much want to be, will say that they fear pursuing their professional vision will drain the energy it would take to find and nourish a relationship.

As anyone and everyone involved in the tricky balancing act that is the essence of a modern woman's life knows, there isn't an easy answer to these conflicts. I've found it is sometimes helpful to create a double-vision process that acknowledges the importance of both desires and develops concrete steps to pursue each. So the woman without the relationship of her heart, for instance, works to devise a plan that makes room for romantic connection, with a structure that allows her to meet men and spend time seeing where prospective relationships take her. That vision is about making sure that work doesn't become a place to hide from life. (Besides, there are men at airports, in meetings, in restaurants, everywhere. Once you make room, often all it takes to get rolling is to choose to lift your head up and smile instead of burying it in your laptop.)

Knocking down the internal glass ceiling that makes many women feel ashamed or embarrassed about their desires is even more challenging. It is during the discussion of these internal obstacles when seemingly successful women get upset. What seems to happen, though, is that once you verbalize the belief that holds you back, it melts; like the Wicked Witch in *The Wizard of Oz*, it will, temporarily at least, dissolve into green goo. Sometimes, you need to hack through what seem to be really practical reasons to find the internal obstacle lurking underneath.

developing a transition strategy

Once you know the obstacles that are stopping you, you need to develop a practical strategy to overcome them and get closer to your dream. You don't need to resolve all the issues at once—that's too overwhelming. But you can and should end your visioning session by coming up with no more than three specific steps, even if they're baby steps, that you can take in the right direction to see where they lead you. Even one baby step is fine. You just need to get moving.

Maybe you need to do course work in a different specialty. Maybe you need a different type of credential or professional experience. Maybe you need to go into therapy or do some spiritual work. Sometimes the first step is as simple as thinking, "Oh, that voice in my head that tells me I can't do this is ridiculous. I just need to ignore it and carry on." We'll look at the action steps in more detail in chapter 7.

After you've decided on your first step, achieving that step becomes your goal. If your vision is to be a writer and the next step is to actually start writing, the specific goal might be to publish an article in your company newsletter. You come up with a specific activity that can push you toward your goal. Make the activity "bite sized," something you could actually fit in once a week or so.

Some aspects of your vision may not be achievable in the way it first comes to you. If that's the case, it's important to examine your vision and figure out whether you can do something about it, other than waiting for lucky lightning to strike.

I once did a visioning process with a woman who was a hotshot achiever in sales but who wanted to do work with a higher spiritual content. As we discussed her vision, she admitted, with no small degree of embarrassment, that what she really wanted was a fantasy rescue. She said she wanted to find some guy with a lot of money who would take care of her financially so that she wouldn't have to worry about supporting herself anymore and she could just pursue the spiritual work she wanted without ever thinking about money again. We went back and examined that desire, laughed, and acknowledged that would be a wonderful development. But, in the meantime, what was she going to do to move her vision forward? We respected and honored the feeling but didn't let it keep us from the practical business at hand, which was coming up with steps that would allow her to do work that satisfied her soul and made her feel "taken care of" at the same time as filling her pocketbook.

KNOWING IT'S RIGHT

Do not worry if, after coming to the end of your visioning session, you are still not clear on what you really want. Remember, the vision doesn't have to be perfect.

Sometimes it's hard to come up with an idea of what you want because you're expecting the gift of vision to come with the edges perfectly taped, fluffy

Ronna Lichtenberg

ribbon perfectly tied, seams lined up, in pretty paper that's right for the occasion. Instead what you've got is the I'm-late-running-out-the-door, slightly crumpled, at-least-it's-not-newspaper-even-though-it-has-handprints-on-it-and-a-corner-poking-out version. That's okay. In fact, it's better than okay, because the high probability is that if it's not messy, it's not real.

Reality is always messy.

A vision is like a terrific book, or something new that you learn, or falling in love: You'll know it has power when suddenly you start noticing things in a new way. A notice stuck to a bulletin board about just the right language course pops up right after you decide your vision is to try teaching overseas. You meet someone who turns out to know someone else who is interested in piloting a new kind of exercise program when your vision was to open your own fitness studio. Serendipity starts to happen.

How do you know if it's the right vision? If it is, opportunities will start to pop up. Maybe not right on target with your vision, at least not as you understand it, but they will be opportunities nonetheless. Possibly really scary opportunities, opportunities that speak to all your self-doubt about whether you can actually do this.

Fear is a great sign that you've got the right vision.

And now is the time to share with people who love you. Even if the vision poses some risk for them, you'll be able to tell if they think it has power. My guide is to start with girlfriends—if nothing else, it's the right response to stress. And a real girlfriend will be able to say, "You know, I can see you as a . . . ," just as readily as she can say, "You know, the right shade of red just might work."

the proof is in the "no"

Most companies, and most women, love to think of new things to do. Possibilities are exciting, even if a little scary sometimes. With a little support, almost everyone can come up with possible paths. That part is relatively easy.

The moment I know a client—whether it's a company or a person—is ready to get serious comes when I ask, "What are you going to stop doing that you're doing now?" A client who is serious works to answer the question. A client who isn't really ready to commit to the hard work of change, can't, or won't, come up with an answer.

To make room for the new, you need to let go of the old. There is an old proverb that you can't ride two horses with one ass. Committing means you choose one thing over another.

I'm on a big tear about this one because the visioning process will just add to your stress instead of decreasing it if you just pile on more to a To Do list that is already too long.

In chapter 7, we're going to start looking at the specifics of how you find the time to do the work of living your vision. But for now, just start to notice the people around you who have work lives that are, at least in part, what you want. Do they have tactful, or maybe not so tactful, ways of setting limits and boundaries? I bet they do.

You can't say yes without knowing when you need to say—or at least think—no.

REVISITING YOUR VISION

As time passes, you may need to pick up your visioning pencil again. There are lots of reasons why a vision that was once right for you isn't anymore: your life circumstances and your priorities change, you move toward your vision and find the reality not totally to your liking, or you're just one of those people who likes a lot of stimulation and excitement and change in your life. (I just got back from Renaissance Weekend—one of those think-big-thoughts/networking-in-disguise things—where I met a classic of this type: a guy who got an M.D., a Ph.D., and a law degree and somewhere along the line decided to be an astronaut, too.)

It doesn't make sense to revisit your vision too often—trying to do it on, say, a monthly basis would be kind of like pulling up a tender young plant to see

Bonus Exercise: Envision the Future

Step 1: Write a curriculum vitae (CV) in fifteen or fewer lines. The CV should not be a résumé-like list of achievements, but something more conversational that you might give to someone who is introducing you as a speaker at some business event. To make it as simple as possible, pretend the person who is going to read it out loud will have never seen it before and will be really nervous reading it.

Step 2: Repeat the exercise, only this time write the CV as if it were ten to fifteen years from now.

Step 3: Ask yourself what specifically would you have to do or change to get from the first CV to the second.

Step 4: Now look back over your ideal day exercise and compare it to your second CV. Is the CV you imagined for your future self in sync with your description of your best day? If not, why not? How would you rewrite your ideal day or your CV to more accurately reflect what you really want?

Goal: To come up with a vision that is truer and more detailed than the one you originally devised.

how the roots are doing. But if it's been a year or two, and you are feeling like something isn't quite right, I encourage you to try it again. It doesn't mean you got it wrong the first time, it just means you are working to make it be "more right" for right now. Which is a good thing.

MAKE ROOM FOR YOUR SPIRITUAL SIDE

While this book is meant to be mostly a practical guide, there is, as with all of my work now, a spiritual component—what I sometimes laughingly refer to as ooga-booga moments. Visioning is the place where I personally experience the most opportunity for spiritual work and partnership.

I don't experience visioning so much as "God's plan," but as more of a conversation that involves helping other people be open to the small spiritual voices that are inside.

For that reason, I don't take money when I conduct visioning sessions. I've thought hard about this one because I wanted to make sure it wasn't about self-limiting beliefs. But in this specific situation, money feels like it would interfere with my ability to connect into that small voice—and it introduces another agenda, which is my obsession about making sure a client gets her money's worth, which I'm concerned could lead me to drive for a conclusion too quickly. So I refuse a fee, keep it pure, and confine my visioning sessions to people with whom I have felt some sort of connection; I offer my visioning skills as a gift of sorts. It has turned out, as these things often do, that these sessions have given me back much more than I give, including much of what I've learned and am sharing with you in this book.

When you are visioning and you are someone who holds spiritual beliefs that are important to you, do whatever you can to make sure that you are in touch with whatever you know and experience as the spirit, the universal energy, Divine Love. Pray first. Meditate. Find a place of quiet and calm, internally and externally. When you're looking for a partner, try to choose someone who knows how to find her (or his) center as well. The work you do in this heart space will be transformational.

Pieces of the vision, the clues you are looking for, come from the quiet and not the noise. Be patient with the silence. Sit with it for a while and the answers will start to come.

CHAPTER 6
identifying prospects

Once your vision is in focus, one immediate goal should be clear: You need to find people who can help advance your dream and support you in getting what you want. Identifying and cultivating these prospects is the next step in becoming an effective pitcher.

Understand this from the get-go: You are going to have to kiss a lot of frogs before you find a prince—or, in this case, the many princes and princesses who can help you along your way. This very useful analogy comes from my friend Janet Clarke, a high-powered entrepreneur who has done a whole lot of frog kissing in her professional life, with the commensurate career successes to show for it. Among other things, Janet was an executive vice president at Young & Rubicam, the giant ad agency, and now sits on the board of directors for four companies, including Cox Communications, a Fortune 500 company, and Forbes.com. My corollary to Janet's rule: A lot of frogs are going to pee on you before you're done, too. But finding the royalty who can help make your vision a reality is worth having to take a few extra showers from time to time.

Of course, tons of people already pass through your life and your work on a daily basis. You don't have a choice about many of these interactions, especially if you work in a big company. What matters most, though, are the people choices you make in the part of your day that's volitional—whom you choose to call, to e-mail, to engage in conversation, arrange a meeting or just share a cup of coffee with. How consciously and purposefully you make those choices is a key factor in your ultimate success. Making those choices wisely is the difference between being a powerful pitcher and a powerless one.

WHOM ARE YOU LOOKING FOR, ANYWAY?

Like lip gloss, lipsticks, and lip creams, prospects come in many varieties. Smart pitchers try to cultivate relationships with all different kinds, to varying degrees, at different times in their lives.

The direct prospect is the easiest to recognize and represents a straight path from where you are now to what you want. She's the person in charge of hiring if you're looking for a new job, or the well-heeled venture capitalist who specializes in your field if you're looking for backing for a new business venture. He's the potential buyer for your sale, the key decision-maker on your deal, the one who says yes or no, and that's final.

Then there are the indirect prospects, who aren't always as obvious but can be every bit as important. They may be people who can provide political support for you within an organization—they might be willing to put in a good word for you with people you want on your side, and their word matters. Or they may be in a position to provide intellectual capital—they can either give you information that's vital to your success or know how and where to get it. A classic example: When you're new in a job, a key prospect might be a senior manager's administrative assistant, who's been around for thirty years and knows not just how everything and everyone in the place works, but the "dish" that's deeper than a Chicago-style pizza. People who can help you gain access to decision-makers are key prospects too. Because in any pitching situation there is always someone in a position to ultimately say yes or no, and often it takes a little maneuvering to get to that person. You don't always have a straight shot.

One of my favorite pitching stories, for example, has to do with writer-director Sofia Coppola's determined efforts to nab comedian Bill Murray for the lead role in her film *Lost In Translation*. Coppola had written the part expressly with the notoriously elusive Murray in mind, but could not get the actor to speak with her, let alone commit to do the movie. Calls to his 800 number—Murray is known in Hollywood as brilliant but somewhat of an odd duck—went unreturned for months, as did more routine methods of connecting, such as calling his agent. Coppola ditched her attempts at the direct approach and spent the next five months convincing anyone she knew who knew Murray—and she happened to know a few of his closest screenwriter and director friends—to convince the actor to read her script and take the part—or at least to consider meeting with her. As Coppola told the *New York Times Magazine* in an interview last year, "Stalking Bill became my life's work."

Eventually the effort paid off—and paid off big. Murray agreed to a dinner, then to the movie itself. The result was a runaway indie hit, with Oscar nominations for Murray as best actor, Coppola for direction and original screenplay (which she won), and a Best Picture nod too. But without cultivating those indirect prospects—the mutual friends and friends of friends who helped Coppola land that first meeting with Murray—none of it would have happened.

not for business only

Most women I know already practice cultivating different kinds of prospects in their personal lives. And if you don't, you should.

Smart moms, for example, make it their business to get to know their child's teacher on a more personal basis, putting some time and effort into understanding who she really is and what she needs, making small talk, and offering assistance. In my book, that constitutes courting a direct prospect—that is, cultivating a relationship with the person who can help you achieve the goal of having your child succeed in school. In a bid for intellectual capital, those same moms also seek out parents with older kids, so they learn how the school system works and who the best teachers are. And if they're really smart, they'll make sure to chat up the secretary in the school office, so they get inside information about the place and easier access to the principal, if problems arise. That's a twofer: gaining intellectual capital and cultivating a gatekeeper at the same time.

Another great demonstration of how cultivating a gatekeeper can benefit you in your personal life is fictional, but nonetheless powerful. Fans of *Sex and the City* will no doubt recall the time when Samantha, a high-powered publicist who underwent treatment for breast cancer during the show's final season, attempted to book a chemotherapy appointment with one of New York's top oncologists. Told by the doctor's receptionist that she'd have to wait six months for an opening, Samantha, in inimitable Samantha style, asked bluntly, "Just who do you have to f--- to get an appointment around here?"

In the end, she didn't offer herself on a platter to anyone. As it turned out, the gatekeeper receptionist was a huge fan of Samantha's oh-so-hot young actor-model boyfriend. Upon learning this, Samantha promptly promised the receptionist a personal introduction to said heartthrob, who she promised would pay a visit to the doctor's office at his earliest opportunity. The receptionist rechecked her appointment book and found an early opening for Samantha the very next day. Pressing her advantage, Samantha then managed to secure an appointment as well for a nun she'd befriended in the waiting room.

Now that's what I call power pitching.

soft prospects

Not every relationship with a prospect has the potential for an immediate payoff. You also need softer prospects in your life, people who may not necessarily be able to help you in any specific way now, but whom you respect and admire and who may be helpful later.

I develop these kinds of soft prospects all the time. For instance, a year ago I was speaking at a conference for corporate women and met Linda, a former high-level executive at Microsoft who's currently doing consulting work in information technology. I was really interested in the work Linda was doing as

Ronna Lichtenberg

she described it to the audience and the quirky, cool, visionary way in which she understands the business world. So during a break in the conference, I introduced myself and engaged her in conversation. She turned out to be equally interested in me and my work since she was thinking about writing a business book herself. We exchanged e-mail addresses and have since established an online relationship that eliminates the distance between us (she lives in Seattle, I live in Manhattan). While there's no project we want to work on together now, I think it's highly probable that one day we'll find some joint endeavor that will be financially productive for both of us. In the meantime, if I have a technological question or she has one about writing, we're good resources for each other.

Linda is a good person to have in my life, even if we never find that mutually beneficial joint project, and I'd like to think I'm a good person for her to have in her life, too.

You need to keep yourself open to the possibilities. Remember that anyone with a shared interest or passion is a possible prospect, maybe not today but tomorrow or the next day. You do not have to see what could immediately come from a particular interaction to make the connection worthwhile. To wit: I recently went to a baby shower for a friend who works on Wall Street. One of the guests, a very senior woman on Wall Street whom I'd never met before, came up to me and said, "I've heard good things about you. I think we should get to know each other better, so let's get together and talk." So we scheduled a breakfast, with no specific agenda or goal in mind other than to establish an initial relationship and open up the possibilities for future interactions.

We chatted, enjoyed the food, got to know each other a little better. I have no idea whether any work will come from the encounter, but I know it was a breakfast worth having nonetheless.

Developing a prospect does not need an immediate payoff. You are planting seeds, not bringing home the harvest. Some will flourish financially, some won't, and both outcomes are okay if you are genuinely open to getting to know the person because of who she is, not just because of what she does.

slime-free networking

Networking got a bad name because too many people saw it as transactional: I'm going to use you/you're going to use me/let's hope I can get a better deal on this trade than you do. That approach can have kind of a "meat" market, last-call-at-a-singles-bar flavor, and fear of getting caught in that flavor is one reason many women work late at their computers instead of going to an event where they might actually meet someone who would be good to know. On the other hand, if you meet someone you might want to do business with and don't acknowledge that's what you want, even to yourself, you close off any possibility that something good could happen.

What to do? When you meet someone at a business function, whether it be an industry group or women's conference, that person is a prospect, and it's okay to think of them that way . . . it's even expected. If you meet them somewhere else and you're not sure if they would like to be seen as a prospect, you can do a quick qualifier and see how they respond. If you say, for example, "Oh, I sell beauty products" to someone who owns a beauty salon, and she says, "What do you think of these appetizers?" you know that she might want to be your friend but not on your call list.

be purposeful with your best prospects

At the other end of the spectrum are great prospects, with whom it is clear from the start that you have something in mind. You have to be clear with them about what you want, too.

Just after I moved from Texas to Washington, D.C., I had lunch at the Jockey Club with a man named True Davis, a former U.S. ambassador to Sweden and high-level pharmaceutical industry executive. True was a mover and a shaker, and it was a real coup that he was meeting with me. I didn't have a job, needed one desperately, and my mother, who had gone to high school with True, had suggested I call him for help. I did, and he graciously said yes. So I ended up going to lunch at the ritziest place at which I'd ever eaten, with

True, who at the time was by far the richest and most powerful man I'd ever met, a man with tons of connections. I hadn't done any homework on True, so all I really knew was that he was an important friend of Mommy's. And I hadn't thought through what I wanted, so I didn't ask him for anything.

What I got from this encounter was an excellent lunch.

What else could I have gotten? At the very least, I could have procured a few introductions and interviews that would have greatly advanced my job search. I could have said to True, "I'm interested in working on the Hill for Congressman So-and-So, whom I know you know. Would you be willing to give his office a call on my behalf?" Or, "I'd love to get an administrative position in one of those prestigious Dupont Circle associations that I know you belong to. How do you think I should approach them?" At the very most, who knows what more a specific request might have yielded? But I blew it because I hadn't done my homework, thought through what I wanted, and developed a powerful pitch around it. Which, by the way, he would have expected me to do and respected me for trying.

Even as recently as a few years ago, I still hadn't completely learned my lesson. Flying back to New York from a speaking engagement in Detroit, I noticed Ram Charan, legendary advisor to senior executives and boards of directors and business writer extraordinaire, sitting in the plane's first class cabin. I was very familiar with his work, which I find amazing; to be perfectly frank, I had a big business crush on Ram—he was, at the time, my idea of who I wanted to be professionally when I grew up.

Since I believed then, as I do now, that you should try to meet people who do things you admire, I worked up my courage and seized the moment when I saw him standing alone by the luggage carousel after the plane landed. I forced myself to make an introduction, gushed like a schoolgirl over his work, and asked for a meeting. To my amazement, he agreed.

So when I got back to my office, I called his assistant, Cynthia, a lovely woman who recognized my pink neediness and, despite her boss's very tight schedule, managed a 15-minute meeting wedged in between Ram's consulting sessions in New York. I arrived at the meeting, immediately offered my credentials (because by this time, at least I'd learned I have to credential myself with blues), and realized I had to make some kind of pitch. So I suggested we find some way to work together in the women's market. Ram looked vaguely alarmed, told me that wasn't really his sort of thing, and confessed that he had only agreed to see me because he thought I was someone else—some business muckety-muck's daughter. A gentleman through and through, Ram then graciously declined my idea. That was it. He did, however, send me a standard issue, unsigned Christmas card that year and has continued to do so every year since, which jazzes up my office.

As much as I appreciate the holiday card, if I'd taken the time to develop a more precise pitch, I might have had a shot at working with new and powerful clients. Maybe if I'd said, for example, "I do a lot of training around relationship management, which would be an excellent fit with the work you're doing on superior execution, and I think we could do X, Y, and Z together," I could have at least gotten a second conversation. Instead, I essentially burned a very high-value prospect.

The moral of these stories: Save pitching your best prospects until you have a specific purpose or goal in mind that you can clearly articulate, and until you have thoroughly done your homework, which includes thinking through the benefit of what working with you or otherwise supporting you would do for them. Keep reading—I'll show you how.

not the usual suspects

At this point, your goal should be to cultivate a diverse group of potential prospects rather than being bogged down by narrow definitions of who can help. So, your prospects might include not just your boss, but your boss's boss, his counterpart in the next department, and his executive assistant. Not just your colleagues, but your competitors as well. The speaker you admire at a conference and the senior manager you meet at a wedding or party. Anyone with shared interests is a possible prospect, even if you do not share the same immediate goals.

Ronna Lichtenberg

Consider this scenario: You're up for a plum assignment, along with several candidates in your company, and various decision-makers meet in the corner conference room to choose who gets the nod. Your boss is in the room and you know you can count on his support. But there are several others there, too, who don't have any reason to support you; in fact, they have reason to argue against you because they want their own person to get the job.

Those people are prospects, too.

So you need to start thinking about indirect ways to cultivate those relationships. At the most basic, you might simply engage them in an occasional conversation. Or perhaps you could provide a useful piece of intelligence now and again—"Hey, Tony, I thought you might like to know . . ." Tony still may not actively help you once he gets to that conference room, but he'll be far less inclined to actively argue against you, and he may be more easily swayed to accept you over the person he'd originally thought would be the better choice.

As for your competitors, think of it this way: If you are competing with someone, you both have the same goal, which implies you have a similar vision. If you view this person as a prospect, thinking about a way to carve out the territory so you can support them in their piece and they can support you in yours, you have turned a competitive relationship into a functional, value-producing one. Politics really do make strange bedfellows.

This is an area where men often have an edge because they do not take competition as personally as we do, nor do they retreat from conflict as often. After a big ball game, men have no problem going out for drinks with players from the other team. We, on the other hand, just want those girls from the other team to go away—they're bad girls and we don't want to play with them anymore. We see the relationship context; men see the competition. We see girls who wanted to beat us; win or lose, guys see other guys who like baseball the way they like baseball and that's what's most important.

If you can make the mental shift that allows you to see your competitors as both competitors *and* potential prospects, you put yourself in the right mindset to win.

FINDING YOUR PROSPECTS

Where do you find your best prospects? I'm tempted to say, in my best imitation of a spooky movie-about-aliens voice, they're everywhere. Because, as long as you're consciously looking, they are.

You find them through traditional routes—for example, at your current place of business, by networking in industry associations, professional societies, and similar groups—and through nontraditional routes, such as social gatherings and just plain happenstance and serendipity. You recognize them as the people who do what you want to do, people who know people who do what you want to do, people who will use what you do, and people who just know people or information that could be useful. Where you find them is less important than being open to who they are and purposeful about developing the relationship once you identify them.

That's a lot of prospects and a lot of places to look for them. In fact, the classic rule is that you have to talk to a hundred potential prospects to qualify ten as prime prospects and to find the one that will result in a sale. Which is why I recommend tweaking a traditional sales technique to help you identify and narrow the field to the people who may be most helpful to your vision right now.

developing a list of prime prospects

People in sales always want to work with a list—a list of people who buy X or who give money to Y or who work in Z. They'll pay good money for a list of, say, everyone in a particular zip code who drives a BMW and voted for President Bush in the last election, as if those names are the mother lode, the magic answer to landing the biggest deals.

But there is no generic list that you can subscribe to that will tell you who your best prospects are, because your prospects are unique to you. If you're looking for a marketing job, you can search the Internet and develop a list of companies with marketing departments and then send out 300 résumés, but

Ronna Lichtenberg

unless you've come up with 300 separate reasons why anyone at those companies should really be interested in hiring you, you're just flushing paper away. Generic lists are clumsy instruments at best when the task of advancing your vision calls for precision tools.

That's why the first action step toward making your vision real and developing a power pitch is to come up with a list of prime prospects who are unique *to you*. It's like reading *The South Beach Diet* or some other diet guide, then making your first trip to the supermarket with a new shopping list in hand. If the list has salad, veggies, fruit, and whatever else you're supposed to eat on the new diet, you've moved another step in the right direction. But if you read the book and go to the grocery store without a list, just

Create a Targeting History

The first step in developing your list of prospects is to think seriously about the kind of people who have been good prospects for you in the past.

Ask yourself the following questions and jot down your answers in a notebook:

- ❖ Who has hired me in the past?
- ❖ Why did they hire me?
- ❖ Who bought my services?
- ❖ Why did they do it?
- ❖ Who has said no to me, and why?
- ❖ How did I meet the people who said yes?
- ❖ Who told me about the people who said yes?
- ❖ What did I have in common with the people who said yes?
- ❖ How did I start the conversation with the people who said yes?
- ❖ Does this person have a history of supporting other people like me or with ideas like mine?

Then go back over your list to see the patterns and trends.

popping Ring Dings into your cart as usual, you haven't gotten any traction. (A recent convert to the South Beach diet plan, I have personally made the Ring Dings mistake more than once so I know whereof I speak.)

When you write down the names of people who can help and support you, you start to believe in and create the possibility of getting what you want. The exercise on the previous page will help get you started.

be honest about your results

In trying to discern the patterns among the names in your targeting history, be careful to look at what is really there as opposed to what you want to see—a common trap that I sometimes fall into myself.

In the early days of Clear Peak, for instance, I aspired to be a brilliant financial services strategy consultant. Although I'd had some of my greatest successes at Prudential while developing programs specifically for the women's market, my aim in the new business was to be gender neutral in the clients I served and the initiatives I devised.

As it turned out, however, the people who hired me were mainly women, who were more apt to appreciate my emphasis on building relationships with customers than men were. Moreover, these women typically wanted to tap my expertise in developing the women's market for their businesses. True, after they hired me for an initial project, they sometimes would hire me again for more generalized strategy work and provide referrals for similar consulting jobs, but that general strategy work never became the driver for my business.

Similarly, when I started writing business books, I wrote with the intention of advising both men and women, even though my publishers kept asking, "Are you *sure* you shouldn't be writing a book targeted more specifically for women?" I'd get all bent out of shape and insist I was writing for everyone. Then, after I'd written the books, I'd go to visit them at the bookstore and find my work in the women's section. It drove me crazy. It felt as if the market just kept saying, "No. No. No."

After a while, though, I finally realized that however much I wanted to see myself as a straight business consultant and writer who was providing valuable information for businesspeople of both sexes, guys were never really my primary prospects, at least not for great chunks of my business. With that single light-bulb-over-the-head insight, I was able to refocus my prospecting on the kind of people who were most interested in the work that I was doing and had a vested interest in supporting me and my vision. I started to hear "maybe" more often, and "yes." The answer "yes" begins to come when you're asking the right question to the right prospect.

Which led directly to more work and, better yet, to the kind of work that was more satisfying to my soul as well as my pocketbook. For example, it led to my deal for this book, my first ever aimed primarily at women.

Your ideal target market is the one that supports your dream because it supports theirs.

decide who you're gonna call

With a good idea of the type of people who have been good prospects for you in the past, you're ready to develop a list of current and future prospects who can support you in your vision and immediate goals.

So turn the page for another exercise: creating an inventory list of people who are in your life now or could be in your life later and who can help support your dreams.

understand the cost to the prospect

In going over your answers to the second exercise, be particularly careful to think through what each of your prospects would have to give up in order to do what you want to ask of them. Because there is always a cost to support. Maybe the prospect would have to forgo supporting someone else for a particular position or project you covet. Maybe they have to give up some of their time and they're particularly crunched at the moment. Maybe they'd have to use up a favor with someone else to help you. There's always something.

Before you make your approach, think hard about whether the price—whether it's emotional, financial, or both—is one your prospect can be reasonably asked to pay.

I'm always astonished at both the number and nerve of people who approach me for one kind of support or another without bothering to consider whether the request is reasonable from my point of view. Case in point: A gentleman who heard me speak at a conference in Atlanta sent me an e-mail, agreeing with a comment I'd made about the need to develop a list of prospects who could essentially serve as your own personal board of directors and letting me know that, as a result, he had scheduled a trip to New York to start building his board. He then proceeded to ask me to e-mail him the names and phone numbers of any Wall Street honchos I knew whom he could contact during his stay, to get his list up and running.

A Prospecting Inventory

Step 1: Write down the names of twelve people you know who you believe could somehow help you achieve your dreams.

Step 2: Go back over your list and for each person you've named, ask yourself the following questions:

❖ Why would this person support my vision?

❖ What would this person have to give up to support me? (What's their cost?)

❖ If I were this person, would I do it?

Step 3: Now write down the names of twelve people who would be your dream prospects, the ideal candidates to help advance your vision. Half of these people should be people you already know, half can be people you've never met.

Step 4: Now repeat the questions you asked yourself in step 2, plus one more:

❖ What do I need to do to make this connection?

Ronna Lichtenberg

The answer, of course, was no. *No.* Duh. Why in heaven's name would I provide that kind of information to a total stranger? Why would I bother people I really cared about for someone I didn't even know? No good reason I could think of.

This sort of approach gives pitching a bad name. When you think about being pitched this way yourself, the reasonable and appropriate response is "Ugh, leave me alone, I need to take a shower." It is not pitching like a girl because pitching like a girl means being sensitive to relationships. I am not pitching you like a girl if I don't intend for the experience be good for you, too.

Indeed, if you take away only one concept from this book, let it be this: *The best prospects care about what you're trying to do because the goal benefits them, too.* The best pitchers think through this benefit ahead of time and fashion their pitch around why supporting them is good for the people to whom they're pitching. (We'll talk a whole lot more about this kind of benefit thinking in the next chapter.)

DON'T BE BLINDED BY COLOR

While it is crucial to understand why your prospects will like your ideas, it is not essential that your prospects like *you*. It might be nice, but it is not necessary.

Which brings me to a mistake that pinks often make: focusing too much on their need to be liked and not enough on their prospect's need to benefit from the exchange. If someone comes to me with a great proposition that will somehow help me or my business, I will consider moving forward regardless of how I feel personally about the guy—that is, unless he's a total scum bucket and I can't bear to be in the same room with him. But feeling neutral toward him is okay.

I will not consider moving forward, however, on the basis of like alone. I need more—and remember, I'm pink! I need to believe the offering has real business value. But if the offerings are roughly the same (including cost), because I'm pink, the person I like most has the edge.

Of course we continue to identify people as prospects based at least in part on whether we like them and think they like us. Since pinks tend to like and feel comfortable with other pinks, someone may seem like a prospect to you primarily because she's pink. (Blues tend to favor other blues as prospects, too.) In your dealings with her, she comes across as warm, engaging, and interested in what you have to say, so you come away thinking, "There's lots of possibility there."

Maybe. Remember that while liking each other is a nice plus, it's not nearly as important as what's potentially mutually beneficial about the relationship. It may be that your best prospects are really blues, or a least a nice pink-blue blend, because this natural tendency to want to do business with people who are as much like us as possible is not the smartest way to go.

Style diversity makes for better decisions and is better for business. So you should not only be sure that your list of prospects includes pinks, blues, and stripes, but if you're so color sensitive you think in shades, you can even go for rose, navy, aquamarine, indigo, fuchsia . . . (just don't tell a blue guy you think of him as a lovely aquamarine).

but use your pink advantage

Women, particularly pink women, have a huge natural advantage in prospecting. Our innate ability to nurture relationships enables us to think clearly about why a prospect should want to play ball with us and focus on their needs. Once we wind up for the pitch, our superior sensory abilities allow us to pick up more cues about what's working and what isn't working in any encounter and to tweak our delivery more quickly in response to those cues than most men are able to do.

Our challenge is to understand these advantages and use them purposefully—to use more of who we are to get what we want. The challenge is also to get out there in the field and do it. Be visible. You can't find prospects, and prospects can't find you, if you're not out there where they can see you.

Ronna Lichtenberg

establishing your credentials

Colors matter too in how you present yourself to your prospects, particularly those you are meeting for the first time or otherwise don't know well. Smart pitchers do not use a one-size-fits-all introduction. *Tailor the way you present your credentials to the prospect, both in terms of the information you give and the manner in which you give it.*

Knowing the color of your prospect is key to smart credentialing. If you're dealing with a relationship-oriented pink, look first to establish some sort of bond, then present credentials that connect to the work she does, people you know in common, or a shared passion. This helps create an emotional connection as well as establishing who you are professionally. A classic opener with a pink prospect might begin with "Have you met so-and-so . . . ?" With a just-the-facts-ma'am blue, on the other hand, you immediately credential yourself with a list of achievements that relate to what they need done.

Consider this credentialing scene, recently played out by me at a first-meeting breakfast with Meredith, a senior officer at a big company. We knew almost nothing about each other, except that the women's group I network with was interested in Meredith as a potential new member.

We began talking about our hair. We both have curly hair that we seek to tame, so this conversation created an immediate bond over products we'd both tried and discarded. A bit later in the conversation I mentioned that I had attended a prestigious Harvard Business School program with a mutual acquaintance, who had just retired as chief investment officer of a major financial services firm. But because Meredith was pink, I mentioned the program only in passing and in connection with talking about someone else whom we both knew so it wouldn't feel like a direct brag but would help establish my professional standing without ever mentioning specific jobs or achievements.

By the time we were done with our meal, Meredith was totally able to "get" me—she understood who I was socially, emotionally, and professionally.

Had Meredith been Michael, and clearly blue, I would have introduced myself by saying, "Hello, I'm Ronna Lichtenberg. I'm a consultant specializing in helping men and women lead, sell, and develop profitable relationships. My clients have ranged from Merrill Lynch to Bellevue Hospital. I also write books and am a contributing editor for *O* magazine." End of story. A blue wants your title and a list of positions or achievements that will place you in the business world.

In any given business situation, if you can't detect the color of your prospect immediately, go blue. If you later find out they are pink, you can always shift your presentation. But if you go pink with a blue, you may have lost them forever.

INTRODUCE YOURSELF LIKE YOU MEAN IT

I first tried this next exercise in Phoenix, with a group of forty women at a workshop for the top women beauty salon executives in the country. I was there to help them learn how to be even more successful, and I wanted to start by having them practice selling themselves. Exceptionally well groomed, attractive, and well spoken, they made their livings being "out there" in some sense: educating salon owners, taking care of clients, representing product lines. My guess was, though, that they didn't see themselves in the same warm light I did.

So I asked each woman to stand up and introduce herself, using no more than four lines. It was clearly harder for some women than for others; some apologized for not being good at it, some had to refer to notes, some went on for sixteen lines instead of four. One mentioned a "husband who was her hero." Another told us the names of all three of her beloved cats.

At the end of the introductions, I asked them what their intentions were when they introduced themselves. After a moment, hands shot up around the room. "I wanted to be vulnerable so I could connect with the other women." "I wanted to get ideas about things I could do better." "I wanted to make everyone laugh." The intention, by and large, was to introduce themselves in a way that made it easy to form relationships with the other women in the room.

Then I asked them to stay at their tables of eight and introduce themselves

Making Introductions

Step 1: Write down four things about yourself that you would normally include in an introduction.

1. _____
2. _____
3. _____
4. _____

Step 2: Write down four things about yourself that you would include in an introduction if you were a man.

1. _____
2. _____
3. _____
4. _____

Step 3: Notice if there is any difference in either what you include on the list or how you talk about it. Be honest, not politically correct.

again. This time they would have exactly the same skills and business experience that they had before. It was just that this time, they would imagine themselves sitting there in boxer shorts and ties: This time, they would introduce themselves as if they were men.

The room exploded with a wild energy. As I walked around, I heard very different comments than I'd heard the first time through. "I started my division and tripled revenues within a year." "I launched a new program that completely revitalized my line." "I'm the youngest VP in the history of my company."

Once again, I asked about intentions. As "men," the intentions were about power: letting everyone know what a big guy they were (actually, there was more sexual innuendo than that, but this is a PG-rated book), wanting to assert dominance, wanting to prove how important they were.

This difference in intentions is particularly important at two points in pitching: when you introduce yourself and when you are trying to close. That's where I am going to ask you to really think about the style you want to use at these two stages in the pitching process. So try the exercise for yourself, and see whether your results are similar to the women's in Phoenix (and everywhere else I've tried it).

Even though I am asking you to consider a style shift when you credential, does that mean I am asking you to act like a man? No. It simply means that there are two places in a pitch where matching up styles (see more on syncing on page 232) can be vital. We're going to talk more about style syncing all throughout chapters 8, 9, 10, and 11, but remember this: If you don't start off right, the trip is much harder.

PLAYING CATCH

Pitching is never a one-way exercise, and neither is identifying the right players for the game. Your long-term objective is a great game of catch, in which the energy goes back and forth between you and people who are in a position to support your goals. I find that the best way to put the ball into play is to first offer your support to these people. Do something of value for them and see what comes back to you.

It's called reciprocity, a key point as described by Robert Cialdini, Ph.D., an Arizona State University professor who has done a lot of work on influence and persuasion, including an article in the *Harvard Business Review*. It is important to give what you want to receive. Reciprocity, according to Cialdini, transcends all cultural boundaries. Everyone knows that if you give something to somebody, they owe you, and that is how society works.

The key—and this is particularly true for women—is to *claim the gift*. You don't say, after coaching someone for twenty minutes, "No, it was nothing." You say, "You're welcome, and I am sure that in the same situation you would do the same for me." Notice the subtlety of this statement: It not only says

Ronna Lichtenberg

"thank you," but puts obligation back into the other person's court without saying, "You owe me one."

As Jennifer Allyn, a director in the Center for an Inclusive Workplace at PricewaterhouseCoopers, puts it, "I think women have this sense of being taken advantage of and 'I give, I give, I give, and then what do I get?' Part of it is we don't ask back." She illustrates with an example of gift-giving and reciprocity:

"The woman across the street from me, Tracy, had offered to take my daughter, Jordan, to school from time to time because she takes her kid. I have called on her to do it three times (before morning meetings) because I can then walk Jordan across the street before 8:00 and then she can get her to school for 8:30. I have suddenly realized that Tracy never asks me for anything and that I need to be more proactive and find out if there is something I can give her, because I want to be able to ask her since she has really helped me out in a pinch. I really need that backup because she is taking her kids to the same place, but it's not going to be fair if I have asked tons of times and she has never asked me for anything. Then I am going to start saying I can't ask again, it is too much, I'm too in debt and I don't want to be. I want it to be reciprocal." In this case, as in most, Tracy needs to "claim the gift" to make it possible for Jen to feel good, too.

When I meet someone with whom I'd like to do business in the future, because they're doing work that interests me and I have a good vibe about them, I often end up doing some kind of service for them as an opener, a way to see how it feels to engage with each other. That is often how my best business relationships start. I'm able to hook them up with some resource they need; maybe I'll draft a piece of writing or do a pro bono speech for their favorite charity. Or if their kid is looking for a job, maybe I'll be able to put them in touch with someone who might consider that son or daughter for a good entry-level position. Smart people learn early on that it is always good and right to put yourself out for someone else's family. It's a great way to start a game of catch.

The kind of people you want to support you probably have other people coming to them constantly, asking for stuff. As with a lot of folks who've been around for a while, people come to me all the time saying gimme, gimme, gimme. So when somebody comes along who offers me something of value instead of asking me to be the provider, my energy, heart, and motivation open up to them. With a single act of thoughtfulness, they put our relationship in another place.

While I was recently consulting to an insurance company on a marketing initiative, I heard a wonderful story about an agent named Joe and a prospect named Bill that demonstrates this point. Bill's net worth was roughly $200 million, which meant he needed a lot of complicated financial services and that he was a terrific prospect for Joe. In their first meeting, Joe got Bill to talk about himself and listened attentively while Bill told him stories from his World War II days. During this conversation, Bill mentioned that he had earned a Purple Heart but never received it, even after he'd called his congressman to complain. Clearly it bugged Bill.

Joe left that first meeting without ever having talked about financial planning, insurance, or estate planning; without having plugged in a PowerPoint presentation; without even leaving a fancy brochure. All he did was go back to his office, call his own congressman, and make arrangements for Bill to finally receive his Purple Heart.

Are you surprised to learn that Joe eventually got all of Bill's business? I bet you're not.

No matter who you are or where you are in your career, you always have something of value you can give. A piece of information, a heads-up phone call, a hand with a pet project, an unexpected act of kindness. Giving is powerful, and being in the power position takes away some of the discomfort women have with pitching. When you give, you are no longer a supplicant and some of the ickiness associated with pitching goes away.

the catch to playing catch

There is a fine line between offering support to a prospect in a positive, powerful way and being calculating and distasteful. Do not cross it.

The difference, as I will discuss in the next chapter, has to do with intention. If you offer a prospect the gift of support only to help ensure that they will help you get something you want, your gift has a little bill attached to it. The amount of that bill will almost always be more than the prospect would be willing to pay. Or, if you have a secret expectation, you are likely to receive a whole lot less than you bargained for. The entire exchange will have a bad feeling attached to it.

If you surprise someone with a bill when they thought it was free, they hate it just as much as I did the time my hotel left a bottle of water in my room, which I thought was free and they thought was four dollars. I felt ripped off— manipulated by the almost-invisible price tag. I didn't trust them and never went back. That's how everyone feels about invisible price tags, I think.

Keep it clean. Because once you prove to me that you don't really know how to play catch, once you display poor sportsmanship, I am moving on to another game.

prospecting mistakes

Here are a few other no-nos to keep in mind while prospecting:

❧ Don't assume a senior-level woman will support you just because she's a woman. Maybe she will and maybe she won't. Shared gender is not sufficient reason to expect a busy woman to help you. She's got stuff to do. You must think through why it would be worth her while to support you and make the benefit clear before you approach.

❧ If you offer no benefit to the prospect, *stay away.* Go find someone else to play ball with you. (We'll get to understanding how to think through the benefit you offer in the next chapter.)

❧ If you must forge ahead anyway, at least acknowledge your debt. This is one that guys often get right: When asking a professional favor, they will say frankly, "I owe you one." This single sentence goes a long way toward defusing the possible annoyance of the person you're querying.

❧ Don't automatically go for the easy prospect. Within any given organization, we all know that senior level person who is easy to chat with and whose door is always open. But the most approachable and accessible prospect is often not the best prospect because he is everybody else's prospect, too. Mr. Popularity does not have the time or mental energy to be uniquely in your corner, Janet Clarke says. That's why she prefers to zero in on a highly competent but somewhat difficult person within an organization. "That person is usually helping far fewer people, so when they need to step up for you, they really are, instead of simultaneously stepping up for thirty other people."

❧ Don't forget your boss is a prospect, too. Just because he hired you doesn't mean he shares your goal or your vision or can be counted on for support when and how you need it. Cultivate him the same way you would any other prospect, just as Willa did in the story on page 96.

❧ Don't neglect the people who can say no. We typically think of prospects as the people who can say yes in any given pitching situation. But it's also important to develop relationships with the people who might be inclined to say no or who would be able to block a yes. Think of your enemy as just a funky kind of prospect.

The bottom line is that we need to be prospecting every single day. If you're not prospecting with clean intentions, you're closing yourself off from the chance to your dream. After you get started, you will even find joy in it, despite the occasional shock of encountering green warty skin that gets slimier the closer you get instead of firming into a royal opportunity. Remember, you have a lot of frog-kissing to do before the prince shows up. It's best to start puckering up now.

CHAPTER 7
pre-pitch homework and heartwork

Every pitch needs two basic elements: a description of what you have to offer and an explanation of why what you have to offer will benefit your buyer. Most pitchers work hard on the first part but inadvertently neglect the second. We think we're doing our due diligence in thinking about the needs of the people we're pitching to. But we're really just wondering what our prospects think about us, which is not the same thing at all.

Becoming a more effective pitcher involves clearing away enough mental underbrush to pay full attention to the people we're pitching to and what they need from us. We need to shift our thinking from "What will they think about me?" to "What do I think will be good for them to know about me and what I can do?" Your pitch, at its core, should not be about you—why, after all, should they care about you?—but about what you can do to help them. *That* they care about greatly.

This is where pitching like a girl starts to get really powerful. Because we know all about nurturing relationships. We care about taking care of other people. We're good at it; it's what we do. In pitching situations then, we just need to apply the kind of benefit thinking about relationship that comes naturally to us in a smarter, more purposeful way.

When we can bring this kind of benefit thinking to pitching, when we start to understand that pitching is good for us *because* it is a way to be good for them, we really shine. (Don't worry: We'll get to what you should be getting back from this in the next couple of chapters. To paraphrase the famous quote from the movie *Field of Dreams,* "Build it, and they will pay.")

DO YOUR HOMEWORK

The first step in benefit thinking is to learn as much as you can about the prospects you're approaching. The more you understand about their business, their background, their goals, and their challenges, the more clearly you'll be able to articulate what they stand to gain by supporting you. People pay more for ideas, products, and services that fit their needs precisely. The more you know about those needs, the better a tailor you can be.

Sounds simple, right? And not exactly breakthrough advice, either—everybody knows you have to do your homework before you enter into any given professional interaction, whether it's a job interview, a bid for a new account, or a meeting to get funding for a key project. You learn this most fundamental step in business kindergarten.

Well, people may know they should do it, but most of them don't follow through. Maybe they're too busy, maybe they're lazy, maybe they're just clueless about what "homework" in this context really means. But by my estimation—and many of the top businesswomen I interviewed for this book agree—as many as 70 percent to 80 percent of pitchers don't do the basic prep work before they make first contact with their prospect. To step into the role of Mean Mrs. Lichtenberg for a moment . . . that means only 30 percent of you, at best, are doing your homework. Naughty! Now that you've said you're sorry, we can move on.

What's doing your homework? Start with an Internet search on both the prospect and the company and gather whatever official data and analyses you can. Google like a madwoman. Get the company's quarterly and annual reports. Read its recent press releases and news clips that shed light on the latest developments for the firm and the industry. If the company is public, find out its investment history and how the stock has fared lately. Get the bios of the principal players so you get a beat on their background, education, and experience. (I like to look at their pictures if those are online too—you can learn a lot from noticing how they dress, if they smile, if they're the only woman out of 750 men . . .) Researching the company's competitors is great, too. Know who the other major players in the industry are, as well as the key facts about them that matter to your prospect. Also pay particular attention to finding out what has gone wrong for your prospect lately. Ignore the crashes and mistakes at your own peril.

You should also make it your business to talk to contacts who know the prospect, the company, and the industry and who can therefore give you the inside scoop. Chat with the person who referred you to the prospect in the first place. Call members of professional organizations or clubs that you belong to and play six degrees of separation. You call the person you know and say, "I heard XYZ company is looking for a new marketing rep. Do you know anyone over there?" And the person might reply that she doesn't know anybody but she thinks that fellow member Suzy Q might, "so call her but don't use my name." The odds are, within a few phone calls you'll find someone who's knowledgeable about the situation at hand and is willing to share information and insights with you.

If you're pink, with your people-first approach and gravitational pull toward human interaction, you're likely to begin your homework with these conversations, eager to find allies who can fill the information vacuum. If you're blue, with your predilection for facts and figures, you'll probably start by looking for official sources of information. Both the pink and blue approaches are necessary and important parts of your homework. Which one you start with doesn't matter nearly as much as making sure that before you're done, you do both.

data are your friend

If you're dealing with blues, which you're going to be in the business world, a crucial part of your pre-pitch homework is to find relevant numbers to attach to your proposal. Numbers help establish your credentials, and numbers help explain the benefit you bring to the table. If you can translate what you want into moving some crucial number up or down—say, boosting sales from A to B or cutting costs from X to Y—so much the better.

Numbers are blue. Blues like numbers; data make them happy. Companies with a lot of blue systemizers eat numbers for breakfast, lunch, and snacks. But, as we've seen, there are still a lot of women who, if not mathphobic, may be a little math resistant. Talk numbers to a really pink mathphobe and she'll say, "I hate it. Don't make me go there. I'll get a rash."

Well, sorry, but even you have to go there. Even if you are pink, even if you are a really strong empathizer, and your systemizer score was 6 out of a possible 80 (as was mine), you need to go there.

It's a two-part process. First, you need to know *why* you care about the number, which often means finding the connection between the number and someone you care about in your life. Early in my corporate years, for instance, part of my bonus was based on company performance. When I really concentrated on how company performance translated into specifics for the family, like sending the kids to college, I became more interested in the numbers and got better at understanding them. Even a small shift in my department's results could have an impact on my family—whether or not we had to think hard about where we could take the family for a special dinner and how free everyone could feel in ordering.

The second part of the process is to take your relationship orientation and translate it back into numbers, so that the systemizers at your company feel comfortable, too. You have to do the translating work for them. The more you talk to them about numbers, the more they will talk back to you about them, and that means the more they will explain them and answer questions. (By the

Ronna Lichtenberg

way, I've found the smartest numbers people are the ones with the simplest explanations.)

I am a very pink girl, and I can always find numbers to support my goal. If I can, believe me, anyone can.

There are two types of numbers that you ought to be looking for: credentialing numbers, which help establish who you are in the business universe, and selling-point numbers, which are the relevant numbers about their business, particularly numbers about their business that you believe you can change for the better. *Every pitch needs both kinds.*

Basic credentialing numbers are important: It matters if you run a company with one hundred employees or a division with one thousand or can handle administrative work for nine divas at once. But credentialing numbers get better the more they tie to the business you're pitching. For a speaking engagement, for example, clients are more interested in the number of times I've addressed a company like theirs than whether I've talked to one hundred organizations.

Don't make them do the work of translating what your experience does for them—you do it. To use a résumé example, it's not that you spent three years at Whocares, Inc., it's that you made a direct contribution to saving them 20 percent.

But don't overwhelm your prospects with numbers, either. Death by statistics is usually a crime perpetrated only by blues. Everyone, though, needs to be cautious about using numbers strategically to make key points rather than simply littering a proposal with facts and figures. You may hope to dazzle your audience with the amount of research you've conducted, while you're probably just making their eyes glaze over and your key points lost in a sea of numbers. Focus instead on the three key figures that best establish your credentials and the three selling-point numbers that illustrate the business benefit to your prospect. Less is more, and you can always put in additional numbers later if necessary.

To find your most powerful credentialing numbers, as well as other key numbers you may use to power your pitch, try the exercise that follows.

Miss Wonderful

Step 1: Write down your five greatest professional accomplishments.

Step 2: Back up each of your claims with data or statistics of some kind.

Step 3: Go back over your list and choose the three most compelling and relevant accomplishments; cross off the other two.

Step 4: Review the statistics you developed for each of these accomplishments and choose the most compelling number for each one.

Step 5: Now imagine a specific situation in which you might be pitching a prospect: trying to get a new client, getting yourself assigned to a prestigious project, landing a new opportunity, or getting a promotion.

Step 6: List all of the potential benefits to your buyer that you can think of for supporting your goal. Each of the benefits must address the following question, from the buyer's perspective: What's in it for me and my company?

Step 7: Go back over your list and choose the three most compelling benefits.

Step 8: Back up each of these claims with data or statistics of some kind.

Step 9: Go back over your list and choose the single most compelling and relevant number for each one.

understand how they make money

The single most important number to get a grip on is what drives profitability for your prospect. In other words, you need to know how your prospect makes money.

Ask yourself, "What drives revenues for their business? What is their biggest expense? Where are they losing money?" Force yourself to look at the balance sheet and understand what it says, at least at the most basic level. If you've never read a balance sheet, find a class, the local small business association, or a business major and ask for help. If you did your Me, Inc. homework related to managing the same business basics as any other CEO (you *did* do that, didn't you?), it will look familiar.

Ronna Lichtenberg

When you have a feel for how your prospect makes and loses money, that knowledge changes the kind of conversation you can have with your boss, headhunters, potential employers, and prospective clients. You can say, for instance, "I know in the retail brokerage business, there's a lot of concern about the percentage of revenues coming from people over sixty. How are you dealing with that?" The more you show you know about them, the better.

Even in a nonprofit, money is an important driver, because the organization needs revenues to support itself and to fund its activities. In the PTA, it's the bake sale and other fundraisers; the Girl Scouts have their cookies (gotta love those Thin Mints); charities may have celebrity pitchers. No matter what kind of organization or person you're dealing with, money is always key.

You should also make it your business to know the competition's numbers. Not just rival businesses, but your own competitors. Any time you're pitching, you're up against somebody, hypothetically or in reality. If I'm your employer, for instance, I don't want to pay you above the market price for salary; your competitors are all the other people out there in your position—not just within your company, but within your industry or in other industries with your same skill sets. So in this example, the relevant numbers to know are the market rate for salaries among people in the position you seek and the high end of the range. Always think through what and whom you're up against.

FIGURE OUT THEIR PAIN POINT

Money is the most important number you can know, and the single most important piece of information you need to know is your prospect's pain point— that is, what makes it difficult for the prospect to get the results they need to get, difficult almost to the point of physical pain. Everyone in business has a pain point. Smart pitchers look to provide the medicine that makes the pain go away.

Since money and pain in business are invariably intertwined, start figuring out this pain point by asking yourself, "What does my prospect get paid to do?" Whenever I'm coaching someone who's having a problem with her boss,

I always start off by asking, "What does your boss get paid to do?" Most of the time, my clients don't have a clue. In a corporate job, your boss is one of your biggest prospects, and everyone in a corporate job has performance objectives, to which their compensation is directly or indirectly tied. Your boss's pain point is likely to be, at least in part, his compensation. So the central issue is, what could you pitch that would make it easier for your boss to meet his performance objectives and therefore to get the compensation he feels he deserves?

Instead, the client will invariably tell me what her boss *should* be interested in—namely, her pitch. I say, that's fine, but will your proposal help your boss meet one of her performance objectives? Is his salary or bonus dependent on accomplishing what you propose to do? I say, tell me where the big bucks are for your boss. If you can't tell me how your proposal connects to how your boss makes money, especially if your boss is a guy, you're in trouble.

Likewise, if you are selling a product, you have to be able to tell me how that product solves some problem I have. I'm interested in products that make my life better. If you can't explain that to me, move on.

Now, I'm going to quote Joanne Davis extensively in this section, for several reasons. The most compelling is that I've prospected with a lot of people and Joanne's one of the best. I'm not the only one who thinks so—*USA Today* listed her as one of the top five business developers in the country a few years ago.

Joanne's content expertise is in the advertising business; she grew up on the account executive side (as opposed to the creative side), ran an advertising agency, and now consults to clients on how to find agencies. Given the business she's in, much of what she does is connected to prospecting: agencies looking for companies, companies looking for agencies, and everyone looking for clients.

Anyway, during a recent search Joanne conducted to find a new ad agency for a fast-food chain, she was bombarded by e-mail pitches in which the subject line was "We're Hungry." The pitchers, no doubt, thought they were being terribly clever. Joanne thought, "What makes them think I care?"

A prospect doesn't want to hear about your need for food; the prospect wants to know if you can feed *her* when she's starving. An even better pitch would let her know you can feed her when she's starving *and* you will prepare a really great meal, avoiding her allergies and weird food issues while you're at it. The best pitch of all would let her know you'll feed her, the meal will be great, it will include of all her favorite foods, *and* you'll take care of cleaning up afterward. Now, that's a great pitch. But don't ask her to cook for you. You'd be amazed (I still am) at how many people get that wrong. They think about their needs instead of the prospect's needs, desires, and—yes—pain.

hidden pain points

In most business situations, there is an explicit agenda and an explicit pain point, for which you may be able to propose a specific, explicit benefit. But often there is an implicit pain point as well, which may have less to do with the business proposition at hand than it does with the prospect's personal issues. Everybody's got their stuff. Maybe your prospect is unconsciously looking for someone who will make them look better to their boss, or they're anxious to gain more visibility in the community, or they're hoping for help out of a tight spot, or looking for support with a political problem in the office.

If you can find this implicit pain point and ease the hurt, then you are really cooking.

Recently I was talking with a prospective client named Lea, who recounted an incident early in her career when her boss told her that a senior manager in their division hated her. The manager was a crusty old guy, and tensions between him and Lea quickly mounted—he got crustier with every exchange, and she countered with some serious professional attitude.

But Lea soon reconsidered her approach. After all, she thought, Mr. Crusty had the power to assign her to interesting projects and clients, and he weighed in on salary and promotion decisions. So Lea thought hard about what he really needed from her, and she *finally* realized it was admiration. The guy wanted to be liked and respected for his place in their little corner of the business world. So Lea began changing their dance by simply asking him questions, playing the role of the young

155

up-and-coming professional to his seasoned veteran. She didn't fawn; she just displayed real interest in what he had to say and the knowledge he had to impart.

She thought she'd hate it. Instead, she ended up feeling powerful and in control of the situation. And she and the older manager became professional friends and allies. She'd eased a personal pain point for him, and he became a "client" instead of a chronic pain in the ta-ta.

pay attention to the signals

If you listen, really listen, your prospect will provide clues about their pain point and about how best to proceed.

Joanne Davis, who professes shock at the number of people who "don't pick up signals even Helen Keller should see," provides some common examples about mistaking the signals. You have probably made all of these mistakes; I know I have. They all come down to thinking "Moi! Moi! Moi!" instead of "Me, Inc. has clients . . ." These come from another search Joanne conducted for an advertising agency to represent a major financial services company. An article about the search appeared in the *New York Times*, so many agencies became aware of the opportunity, and Joanne was flooded with approaches by agencies looking for business. Here's what happened.

Mistake No. 1: Pushing through a Busy Signal

Joanne got a call from a small agency saying, "We know you are very busy with this big search and we are too small for this job, but we thought this would be a good time to introduce ourselves." Nah, I don't think so. All the folks at the agency did with this phone call was prove to Joanne that they had no judgment or respect for her time. As Joanne explains, "Either they should have called and said, 'We know you are handling this search and probably think we're too small, but here's why we're not and why we should be considered.' Or, the agency should have waited a couple of weeks, sent a note congratulating us on the success of our big search and letting us know they would contact us in a month for consideration on other projects for which their firm would be more

Ronna Lichtenberg

suitable." Joanne notes Rule No. 1 of Successful Pitching: "You have to put yourself in the shoes of the recipient of your pitch."

Mistake No. 2: Being Lazy and/or Arrogant

A top, big-name agency sent an e-mail letting Joanne know they were also interested in competing for the account and asking her what they needed to do to be considered. No, she remembers thinking, it is *your* job to tell me why you should be considered. Joanne judged their approach to be lazy and arrogant because those at the agency assumed it was so well known that she should remember why it would be appropriate for the job. Remember what I said about translating? No prospect wants to do that, and in this case, that included Joanne. The e-mail the agency should have sent instead would have ticked off three key reasons to throw its name in the ring—say, "We already have experience and success working with complex financial service organizations from our dealings with X, Y, and Z companies; we are a fully integrated agency so we'll be able to service the client on all aspects of the account, including A, B and C; and we are a private, independent firm so we won't be distracted by holding company issues."

The specifics didn't matter as much as the demonstration of having given some thought to the benefit it might bring to the table.

Mistake No. 3: Being Disingenuous

Then there were the e-mails Joanne got from agencies proclaiming, "We love financial services! We would love to work on this account!" Joanne responds, "Who cares?" She wasn't looking for love; she was looking for an agency to create a brilliant ad campaign for a major client, someone who would add value to the project. If you're looking for love, try an online dating service, or someone related to you by blood, or someone with four feet and a wagging tail.

Mistake No. 4: Ignoring Instructions

Some of the pitchers were smart enough to call and say, "We read about your search; we want to participate; we want to send you whatever you need to convince you we are right for the job; we think you need boom, boom, and boom, but we respect you and the process, so can we chat for a couple of minutes to make sure of what you need?" Joanne remembers one in particular that she called back saying, "Okay, I'll give you a chance. Here are the three most important elements we're looking for. Please make your case responding to those specific points in a concise one-pager—it doesn't even have to be an attachment, you can just do it in an e-mail."

Instead, the agency came back with the longest e-mail Joanne had ever read, with attachments and bios and long ramblings about the firm's capabilities, plus a hyperlink to its Web site so she could check out their creative work. The next day a UPS box the size of Texas arrived with even more supporting material.

Rather than demonstrating how great it was, all that agency did was demonstrate it did not take direction well, and it was out of the running, just like that.

know when to back off

Business pain points create an acuity similar to physical pain. And like physical pain, they come in acute and chronic varieties. Most of what we've been discussing is chronic pain, but if your prospect is in acute pain, back off, unless your pitch speaks directly to that pain and will somehow ease it. If the person is in the middle of a business crisis or some other highly stressful professional situation and you cannot get them to the emergency room, leave them alone until they've recovered.

I will not pitch an idea for my next column to my editor at *O* magazine, for example, when she's in the middle of a hectic close on the current issue. I can tell just by the way she answers the phone that she's crunched; most women know these things. At that moment, I could say, very politely, "I know you're really busy right now, so I'll just take a few moments of your time, but can you listen to this great idea I have for my next piece?" Well, no. The two most probable outcomes here are that she'll say, "No, I don't have time now," or she'll say, "Okay," and will listen with half an ear. Either way, all I'll really have succeeded in doing is annoying her by not being respectful of her time crunch. And when she finally does really listen to my idea, she will undoubtedly be far less receptive than she would have been had I simply waited.

If you forge ahead when all signals suggest you shouldn't, you gain no current benefit and lose the opportunity to benefit later. You close the door.

Conversely, if you are overtly respectful of those signals, you stand to gain a lot more than you may originally have bargained for. Joanne Davis vividly remembers conducting another search for a major client who was hoping to spice up its advertising campaign. But beyond the creative aspects, they also wanted a full-service firm that could run direct marketing and direct response efforts and work with them on Internet and other media communications. As Joanne puts it, "We wanted to have our cake and eat it, too." She invited an agency she'd never worked with before to pitch because she'd heard they did brilliant and innovative campaigns and wanted to give them a shot. The agency, however, graciously declined the opportunity, letting Joanne know that while it could deliver on the creative side, direct marketing was not its strength so it was probably not the right agency for the job.

Joanne's reaction? She was impressed with their candor; impressed with their show of respect for her, the client, and themselves; impressed that they chose not to waste anyone's time on a project for which they were ill suited—so impressed that she can't wait to do business with them. "They respected my time and my professionalism, they respected my client's time, and they respected themselves," she says. "I'm chomping at the bit to find another opportunity that will be right for them."

Now that's benefit thinking.

pink danger alert

If women are so good at nurturing and putting the needs of others before their own, why do so many of us have trouble with this kind of benefit thinking in professional situations? Sometimes it's our resentment of men and the fatigue that goes along with that. We don't want to have to adapt to their business style and pay attention to their business needs. Why can't *they*, for once, adapt to us, be sensitive to *our* needs? We want the men we deal with in business to be empathetic and care about relationships. In a nutshell, we want men to be more like us.

Well, as Tony Soprano might say, fuhgeddaboutit. As a pink woman who, as you know, has engaged in missionary work on more than one occasion in her career, I'm here to report that attempts at conversion just don't work. They don't want to be like us any more than we want to be like them. So forget conversion and shift to benefit thinking. True benefit thinking means you have to see your prospect as "other," not as the same. You need to step back, observe, and do some analytical thinking about what the other person may want that is different from what you want. Here's where we have to fight our natural tendencies. Because when you're pink, you want to find common ground with the person you're dealing with, to minimize differences and the potential for conflict. We want to be on that groovy pink cloud, where we intuitively understand each other; we're holding hands and jumping rope together and feeling great. But you can't be on a pink cloud and practice benefit thinking.

You may give up feeling good and groovy in any given moment, but what you get back in the trade-off is worth it: some power and control in the professional situation at hand.

listen first

How else can you find out what your prospect really needs and wants? You do your homework, you get some ideas, you schedule a first meeting, and then— this is really important, my gab-happy pinks and data-spewing blues—you shut up and listen.

A classic pitching mistake is to go into an initial meeting prepared with a proposal before you've given the prospect a chance to clue you in to what they really want. You provide the answer before you've even asked the question. The risk is that you make it more difficult to have a relationship because you've already defined the terms. Some prospects will work only this way, but with others, you have more latitude.

Ronna Lichtenberg

You need to have a proposal ready if you need it, but you also need to be ready to play it more like a first meeting with a new doctor. Only in this case, you're the doctor. You conduct an intake interview, get the patient to give you a medical history, discuss what's on his mind, and tell you where it hurts. In business language, that means finding out what the prospect is working on and what the big issues are before him. If there's a specific project or aspect of the business you want to explore, ask leading questions: What have you tried so far? What typically works for you? What never works for you? What haven't you tried?

Your job at this point is to listen. When I was coaching top salesmen at one of the biggest financial services firms in the country, I noticed that the best of the bunch always went into an initial meeting with nothing more than a legal pad and a pen in hand (and a binder in their briefcase, just in case). That sends a very strong and confident signal. The message is this: I am here to find out what's on your mind and learn how best to serve.

In listening to the answers, pay close attention to the language your prospects use in describing their situation so you can reflect it back to them later. Everyone in a particular industry, profession, and company has a lingo reserved for insiders, so you want to learn the rudiments of their language. If you were planning a trip to Greece, you'd want to learn to say hello, good-bye, thank you, Can I have a discount? and Where's the bathroom? in Greek. The same concept applies when you're traveling in a strange business land.

Understand too that the true purpose of a first meeting is to get them to want a second meeting. Almost no one decides to do business with someone else on the basis of one meeting—they're not going to hire you in one meeting, they're not going to support your project in one meeting, they're not going to buy something from you in one meeting.

In fact, one of the most common mistakes we make when first putting together a pitch is listening for a yes from the buyer too soon. What we want to hear: "Yes, I like you; yes, you are wonderful; yes, I like your offer; yes, I'm prepared to move ahead with the deal." What you should be listening for instead: "Yes, I will share with you what I need."

FINDING THE PASSION

Once you have found out everything you can about your prospect's needs, you have one last bit of homework to do: You have to make sure that deep down inside yourself you know that you can deliver, and deliver with energy and enthusiasm for the task at hand.

Your ability to convey that assurance is crucial to your ultimate success.

I was reminded of this point at one of those rubber chicken charity benefit lunches, where I had the good fortune to sit next to Lily, an MTV producer who had a lot of great inside dish about reality shows. I was really curious about what makes some of them work when others are so awful, so I asked her. She replied, "We've found that when people are passionate about something, it works. It's believable. Passion is the differentiator."

How do you get passionate about your offering when part of your offering is you, the you about whom you may harbor some serious doubts? It seems to me there are three possibilities.

First, you pick the right parents, who think everything you do, starting with your first toothless smile, is divine.

Second, you have an intrinsic passion tied to a creative gift—art, math, sports—and see yourself as a vessel for the expression of that gift.

Third, for the majority of us, you focus on something about yourself that is a gift that can make a difference for someone else. This is the essence of pitching like a girl: bringing all of your talents and skills to bear for the benefit of your prospect while benefiting yourself at the same time.

conveying the passion

Why is it so hard for women, particularly pink women, to convey passion about their own skills and talents? Guys do it all the time, and no one seems to think any less of them.

Just think about Muhammad Ali, the classic passionate-about-himself guy. He came right out and said, "I am the king of the world. I am the greatest," and people were captivated and charmed. Of course, he really *was* the greatest, and he backed up his statements with results. Can you imagine a woman saying about herself the kinds of things Muhammad Ali said? Certainly not. And if she did, we'd hate her for it.

The key to successfully promoting your own skills and passion for a project, without coming across as one of those overbearing, aggressive, shamelessly self-promoting hussies we love to hate, involves making yet another mental shift. If it feels yucky to be passionate about yourself, don't try to go directly from yucky to wild enthusiasm. Instead, think about showing passion for the value of what you can bring to your prospect—in other words, apply benefit thinking to the emotion. You don't say, "I am passionate about what I do." You say instead, "I am passionately committed to resolving this issue for you, committed to making the boo-boo go away." And you don't state your passion starkly; simply infuse what you're saying with it. Otherwise you can seem to be a little . . . overwrought.

Two caveats: First, deeply blue prospects often don't care about whether you're passionate, no matter in what form you express those feelings. Deep blues need results, some tangible outcome that shows them what you mean—you're so passionate about what you do, say, that you work around the clock until the project gets done. The trick here is not to get hung up on the fact that they don't care.

Second, you must really feel the passion, believe what you are saying at your core. False passion is bad. Unless you are Meg Ryan in *When Harry Met Sally* and are faking an orgasm in a New York deli to prove a point, false passion doesn't work.

tooting for slinkys

To help women learn to apply benefit thinking and personal passion to their pitches, I developed a series of exercises that I use in workshops called Toot Your Own Horn. We start by crafting pitches for a product, any random product—a Slinky, a lipstick, chopsticks—then move on to pitching ourselves. The women are paired in teams, taking turns being the pitcher and the prospect, so they get immediate feedback on the power of their pitch.

Workshop participants typically have a lot of fun with the physical stuff, crafting their pitches around countless creative uses they'd devise for the product at hand. One woman who took on writing a pitch inspired by an ad for one of the national egg councils was exhausted by the number of uses she came up with for an egg: in addition to your basic scrambling, frying, and poaching, you could make an omelet for dinner or hard-boil the egg and put it in a salad, take it to work for a snack, color it for Easter, or use it as a Christmas decoration. By the end, she had come up with thirty-two different uses.

In addition to thinking about the benefits of their product, participants talk about the competitors to their products and the selling price. In the end, they learn not only how to put together the elements of a powerful pitch, but, more important, they learn that the process of selling itself can be comfortable. Once you figure out that the problems you have with pitching are not about the process of selling, you can apply those same techniques to promoting yourself and your dreams.

In workshops, I help this shift along with a second exercise that challenges participants to sell themselves as CEO of the company whose products they just touted. In the third and final exercise, they try selling a prospect on supporting them in their dream.

Immediately, with these last two exercises, problems become apparent. Participants find it difficult to articulate their value and cannot even bring themselves to talk about money. But the biggest single reason why many of the pitches they devise don't work is that the person on the receiving end could not answer the questions, What's in it for me? Why would I want to do this? It was easier to get them to consider buying an egg than to get them to consider supporting a dream—which makes sense. Supporting a dream "costs" a lot more.

Ronna Lichtenberg

Realization is more than half the battle. Once the lightbulb goes off over their heads, the women are able to go back and re-pitch their dreams far more successfully than they did the first time. And that is exactly what you will do, too, in the following exercise.

Tooting 101

Note: This exercise is best done with a partner, who can give you feedback on the effectiveness of your pitch. Work through the following steps.

1. Select a tangible item that you will pretend to sell. The object itself doesn't matter—it can be a tape dispenser, a hand cream, a toy.

2. Pretend you are selling this product to a prospect. List as many benefits for the item as you can think of. Be sure to address competitors' products and pricing.

3. Pitch to your partner. Have her make notes on what she found convincing and unconvincing about the pitch and give you feedback.

4. Now pretend you are selling yourself for the job of CEO of the company that makes the object you just pitched. Say, you're pitching yourself to a director for the job of president of Cool Socks, Inc. You're pretending it's your first meeting; your partner is a decision-maker.

5. Was there a difference in how you *felt* about the pitch? Were you more or less comfortable than pitching a product? Was there anything you avoided talking about, like money? Take a moment to write down your reactions.

6. Ask your partner for feedback. Ask her to tell you what was more or less compelling about this pitch than your "product" pitch. Have her tell you what she would have needed to hear/feel in order to say yes.

7. Now go to your own dream. Think about something that you need to realize it: more time, different reasons, a chance to try something new. Think about who could help you with this goal, and ask your partner to pretend to be that person.

8. Make the pitch, and then check in with yourself (as in step 5) and with your partner (as in step 6) for feedback.

9. Congratulate yourself! You've now said what you wanted to say out loud, and it wasn't so bad, right? From now on, it will only get easier and better.

DON'T WORRY, BE HAPPY

You've done your pre-pitch homework. Now comes some extra-credit heartwork: getting yourself into the right state of mind for the task at hand. This requires administering a good old-fashioned dose of positive thinking. You need to believe in what you are proposing and in your ability to deliver. You need to believe you deserve this shot and that you have as good a chance as anyone else of getting it.

Easier said than done, I know.

But consider this: Prospects don't want to hear from someone who is down. They don't care about your insecurities or your problems or your mood swings. They will enjoy your pitch much more if it comes with energy and enthusiasm; if you are not just passionate about what you have to offer them but downright happy, you will help your cause immeasurably. This is true, of course, in all aspects of life—pitching is no different.

So what do you do about your pitch if you are feeling like a fraud, down and insecure and swamped? Remember that you are not unique in feeling uniquely fraudulent, bad, and wrong. Now that you *know* why you feel this way you can let it go.

Try different techniques for moving away from self-limiting thoughts: one is to compartmentalize. Joanne Davis recommends, "You take the pity feeling, put it in a black box, and put the box away." Otherwise, she says, you will end up having a pity meeting. If you allow yourself to dwell on the bad stuff, you become what Joanne calls a "woe-sy me." No one will want to play with you if you are no fun.

Or you bury the feelings with activity. Stop thinking about not being prepared for the pitch and fixate on what you can do to prepare further. Send out lots of résumés, do more Internet research on companies you want to do business with, take a course to learn something new in your industry, volunteer to chair a committee within your professional organization. Then go to the health club, have a manicure, go to the movies, have dinner at your favorite restaurant with family or friends, take an Argentinean tango class.

Ronna Lichtenberg

Busy makes it easier. Busy takes your focus off the bad feelings and puts it onto something constructive.

These feelings have a lot in common with the monsters that dwell in children's closets. To help a child get to sleep, we firmly close the closet door, or we leave a light on, or we create happy, friendly monsters like the ones in the animated movie *Monsters, Inc.* to replace the nasty images.

Do not let the monsters in your closet come out. Our dreams are too sweet, too powerful, too compelling to allow them to be squashed by imaginary bogeymen. That's why we're going to do another exercise; this one will help you sell yourself to the toughest prospect of all: you.

Dear Me

This exercise will help you articulate why you really deserve the opportunity you're pitching for—and eventually even come to believe it.

Step 1: Write a two-page pitch letter to a potential buyer, pitching someone with a background similar to yours who "deserves" whatever it is that you're pitching for: a job, more money, resources, a project, an opportunity.

Step 2: Now write a second "Dear Me" letter to the same potential buyer, this time pitching yourself for the same opportunity.

Step 3: Think about why it is so much easier to pitch someone else, anyone else, even when their background is similar to your own. Are they deserving because they have a degree and you don't? Because they volunteered at a camp for kids with cancer? Because they've had some managerial experience? This part of the exercise helps identify your relative competitive strengths and weaknesses and teaches you what is most critical to your career development.

Step 4: Now write a third "Dear Me" letter explaining why you're even better than the person you pitched in the first letter. This exercise will help you pinpoint your most compelling competitive selling points and deal with anticipating and overcoming objections even before they've been raised.

Step 5: Eat a Tootsie Roll to reward yourself for sticking your neck out, and to remind yourself that horn-tooting can be sweet.

GETTING IN SHAPE FOR THE GAME

Many of the women I meet are exhausted—physically, emotionally, spiritually. We are trying to do everything, for everyone else. Trying to do it perfectly. Trying to do it all in one day.

When the opportunity to pitch comes, whether it's planned or, more likely, when it's a surprise, we're not going to have much fun, let alone be very effective, if it looks like pitching is just one more thing we have to do when we're too tired already from doing everything else.

As you've probably noticed, I interviewed a lot of top women executives for this book, and one of the things I asked them about was how they got enough energy to pitch. They all said the same thing: There isn't a whole lot you can do in the moment, except be as relaxed as possible. What you can, and must, do is learn how to keep your energy at a pretty high level, pretty much all the time. You have to make sure the needle on your energy tank isn't dipping into the red line that says "empty" too much of the time, let alone all of the time.

That's why now we're going to look at how you can make sure you have energy in your tank all the time, because you never know when you are going to need it.

But first, I want to tell you a story about how I learned I wasn't getting the whole energy thing right. As you read it, I'd like you to think about what in my story sounds like your life—you're going to use that information in a minute. The story is about a day I had in my corporate life when I still believed all the self-limiting things I asked you to let go of: that I needed to do everything for everybody; that I shouldn't ask for anything for myself; and that if I didn't do everything perfectly, I was a complete and total failure.

That particular day started about 3:00 A.M., as many of them did in those days. I woke up, in a panic. I woke up because I had "list head." List head:

the seemingly endless list of things that I hadn't gotten done that day, all of which were clamoring for attention in the middle of the night, making such a ruckus that I couldn't get back to sleep.

So I got up and went to do middle-of-the-night e-mail. Now, there are a couple of things that are scary about middle-of-the-night e-mails. One is how often you get an immediate response, most likely from another woman in the same time zone. The other is that everything seems so much more important in the middle of the night that there is a good chance that the recipient who is looking at it the next day is not going to be as impressed with your devotion as you are secretly, or maybe not so secretly, hoping he will be. He is going to be thinking, "Is she on drugs, or what?"

After about 90 minutes of e-mail, I went back to bed. And, of course, just as soon as I was finally, and deeply, asleep, the alarm went off. The alarm went off because I was supposed to get up and get on the exercise bike, which was the piece of equipment that had become a half-way house for clothes that weren't dirty enough to go in the laundry bin but not worth the effort to put in the closet.

Anyway, did I get up and exercise? Don't be ridiculous. Of course I didn't. I rolled over and snoozed until I had to jump up and start the day.

Now, my rule is that anything in my house that can't talk gets fed first, which meant the cats got their breakfast before anyone else. Then the kids. Then Jimmy. Did I get breakfast? Don't be silly. I got coffee. A big mug of coffee, to hold me through my commute of two subways, two trains, and a couple of longish walks.

By the time I got to work, I was stoked. I'd been working all through the commute, of course, so I was ready to roll when I walked in the door. It is possible that I ate lunch, but I don't remember it. I pretty much always gulped down something at my desk, so if you asked me an hour later if I'd eaten, I probably wouldn't have been able to tell you if I did, let alone what it was.

But the day seemed to be going pretty well until around 2:00 P.M. when all the lights started spasming on my phone. My assistant came in. There were two calls she knew I would want. One was from Amanda, my step-daughter. One from Bob, the chairman. I figured that it wasn't the school nurse calling, and that I could catch Amanda in a minute, so I had my assistant tell her I would get right back to her—not something a teenager wants to hear. I picked up Bob because, like all big shots, he had the attention span of a two-year-old. Actually, that is kind of an insult to two-year-olds, but you know what I mean.

He needed something tomorrow. Big surprise. When did he know about it? Don't ask. I didn't, because I knew it would just make me crazier.

Now we are at about 3:00 and I am starting to sink like a stone. It feels like I can't do anything right. In not too long I will have to race to get the commute home started. There's more to do than there was when I started in the morning. I started to despair.

By this point, I had figured out a technique for rough spots like this. It was my own special technique for drinking M&Ms. I'd rip off the top of a bag, chug them like a stein of beer, and immediately take a big gulp of coffee. I had found this turned the candy into a kind of easy to swallow sludge. It got me going like someone had just taken a big syringe of adrenaline and emptied it directly into my heart, like in the movie *Pulp Fiction* when the character played by John Travolta sticks Uma Thurman's OD'ing character with a giant syringe right in the chest. Big rush! And in a big rush, I got through the day, made it to the train, and made it home.

Walking through the front door is always exciting when you have a family, and that night was no exception. I thought of it as the "wall of need." Lots of things I was supposed to be doing; even more things I hadn't gotten done.

That night I was feeling like I was still in pretty good shape, because not only did I know what I was making for dinner, but I had the ingredients on hand. This, for me, was a major victory. I rattled around, shaking with fatigue and hunger, and eventually served a salad and pasta. The sauce was a red sauce, with walnuts and Gorgonzola. I sat there waiting for them to love it and to love me for making it. Amanda was the first to announce that it looked nasty, but the general consensus was that it looked, and tasted, like vomit. Even Jimmy, who wanted to be loyal, couldn't get it down.

And there I was, at the end of a day when I had tried my best and all I felt was my worst. Tired. Resentful. Heavy. Uninspired. I can remember thinking that this was not the way I wanted to live my life. It's not the way you want to live yours, either, and if you are like a lot of other women I've met, my day reminds you of days you've had, or are having now.

What I've learned since then is that it is the small choices we make every day—the choices about how we use our energy, and how we refuel ourselves—that make the difference in our ability to perform, including our ability to pitch. Yes, it's the small stuff that gets us. But it is also the small stuff that makes us: the choice to eat real food, or get to bed a little earlier, or take a moment for ourselves. We're going to look at the choices you make now.

put on your own oxygen mask first

My general rule of thumb is the more you give, the more you need to receive. If you're not taking any energy in, when it's time to give some to someone else, it isn't there. In my Work/Life Balance workshops, the first exercise is the one on page 172. It's designed to help you get a better handle on what gives you energy.

You know how flight attendants always remind you to put on your own oxygen mask first? Now, I think the reason they do is because it is so counterintuitive, especially if you have children, or someone else in your care. If you're taking care of someone, the impulse is to take care of them first, right? But just as in a situation where you actually do need an oxygen mask, there is nothing you can do for someone else if you haven't made sure that you are able to function.

With that in mind, try the exercise for yourself, either alone or with a partner. Then, when you're done, admire the lists you created. Be grateful for them. Pat yourself on the back for doing it; you've done a good and revolutionary thing to decide that what makes you feel good is worth paying attention to.

Put On Your Own Oxygen Mask First

You should be able to do this exercise in five minutes, ten if you have someone to talk to about it.

Get a piece of paper and make two columns. Title the first column "What gives me energy." Title the second "Who gives me energy." Under "What gives me energy," write down the things you do that give you a lift. It can be anything. Here are some answers I've heard:

- Listening to salsa music
- Taking a bubble bath with the door locked
- Sleep!
- Cleaning closets
- Running
- Washing the car
- A hot, hot, hot shower
- Whistling
- Shopping
- Sex
- Chocolate
- Going to church
- Smelling my children's hair

Ronna Lichtenberg

The more specific your answers, the more useful they will be later. Challenge yourself to find an unexpected answer.

Then, in the other column, write down the *people* who give you energy. Avoid categories, such as friend; some friends give you energy, some friends may not. Your list can include people from and outside of work. Examples:

- ❧ Your best friend
- ❧ The grade school friend you don't hear from often enough
- ❧ The coworker who makes you laugh
- ❧ Your kids, or grandkids
- ❧ Someone with whom you worship
- ❧ A buddy at the gym
- ❧ A security guard at work, who always flirts with you in a respectful kind of way
- ❧ A former boss

If you are writing the list from your heart, you'll notice a couple of things. Every name you put on the list makes you smile. You will feel warm inside. As soon as you think you "should" put someone or something on the list, it doesn't feel as good. Forget the "shoulds." Now put your paper aside—you'll need it again soon.

find the energy leaks

The next step is to figure out where you're losing energy. Take a moment to go back to imagine the start of your ideal day from chapter 5. Now make it even better. Maybe you somehow got eight hours of sleep the night before and you did twenty minutes of cardio that morning. On top of that, maybe you managed a real breakfast. Even the commute was okay and you listened to your favorite music the whole time. Plus, your best friend sent you an adorable card for no reason, things are going okay at work, and you have plans for after work that make your eyes sparkle.

Now it feels like some ill wind comes and starts messin' with your day. The day is full of little bumps and lumps: suddenly all that fine, zesty energy you had in the morning starts to leak out until by the end of the day you aren't feeling so great about your life, let alone yourself. What happened?

Time for another sleuthing exercise (below). You're going to find out what takes your energy away by looking at two things: what and who makes you tired and resentful.

There's a great quote attributed to Carrie Fisher that says, "Resentment is like drinking poison and waiting for the other person to die." But we all do it; we do things we don't really want to do, or choose to do, and then we're all annoyed with someone else for "making" us do it.

Find the Energy Leaks

Pick up another piece of paper, and make two columns again. The first one is titled "What I do that makes me tired and resentful"; the second is titled "Who makes me tired and resentful."

The first one is pretty obvious: What are you doing that wears you out? You don't have to make judgments on this point about how you have to do it so there's no use thinking about it and all that blah-blah in your head. Just write it down.

Then think seriously about the people who make you tired, the people who take more energy than they give. Those are the energy vampires we talked about on page 87.

There are no right or wrong answers here. One woman's energy blast is another woman's energy drain. For every woman who loves to clean closets there's another who hates it. People and things I've heard make women tired:

Ronna Lichtenberg

- Shopping
- Television, especially the news
- Conflict
- Chocolate
- Lack of sleep
- The list that is never done
- Housework
- Ex-mother-in-law
- Kids' homework
- Negative people at work
- Finding clean, folded clothes in the dirty laundry pile because, according to the person who put them there, "It was easier than hanging them up."

Women have also told me that often the same person is on both lists. Mom can be great for giving us energy, except on the days when she wants to talk and we can't and we feel guilty trying to cut the conversation short. Our honey is an energy drain when we are too tired to even breathe, let alone engage. Or there's a friend who can be terrific, but who lately seems to be in a place where she needs a lot, and can't, or won't, give us anything back.

Notice all of the energy drains. But pay particular attention to the ones that you feel guilty about noticing, because once you address those, life gets a lot better.

YOUR ENERGY ACTION PLAN

Now we're going to look at how you can bring more energy, more joy, more "you" to every day and every pitch. Take out your Palm, BlackBerry, Filofax, Day Runner, or Snoopy diary—you're going to need it—and do the exercise on page 176.

Let's see if we can stop, or limit, some of your energy leaks. Remember the power behind your vision is the power of choice, which means setting boundaries. I have found that this next exercise is really difficult for some women. I remember one woman who crossed her arms, legs, and everything but her eyes when I asked her to think about what she could stop doing. Her opinion was that she couldn't stop anything she was doing. Everything was essential.

If you feel that way, then I invite you to rethink your position with three things in mind.

The first is to take a moment and look at your energy-drain lists and ask yourself this question: "What on these lists do I have control over?" At first glance, it may look like the answer is nothing. For example, one woman said

Choose Your Energizer

Look at your schedule for tomorrow, or, at a maximum, for the next week. Think about all the things that aren't even written down but that you are planning to do.

And then make a choice. Ask yourself, "What's a fifteen-minute oxygen blast I can add to my day?" Look at your notes from the oxygen mask exercise on page 172. It doesn't have to be the whole list. What's one thing you could do tomorrow? Not because you have to but because you deserve something that fuels you every day. What can you choose to do to give yourself a lift? Is it . . .

- One walk around the block?
- One call to a friend?
- One bubble bath?

Then write it down on your schedule. Treat the choice to do something for yourself as if you were important. After all, you are—you're the CEO of Me, Inc. Right this minute, write it down on your agenda: the energy blast you're going to do on Monday at 2:00 P.M. or Sunday at 9:30 A.M. or whatever specific time suits you is . . .

to me in a workshop that her big energy drain was menopause. Well, you don't have control over menopause, but you do have control over how you deal with it. Exercise helps. Diet can help. Support groups help. Be honest with yourself—isn't there something on your lists you have control over?

The other thing to think about is the benefit you are getting out of the energy drain. It may be that doing everything makes you feel like a good person. "Look at me! It's only 1:30 on Saturday afternoon and I have already done six loads of laundry and carried them home on my head from the river with absolutely no help from anyone . . . how virtuous am I?" There are real psychic bennies to be had from doing too much, as we all know. Notice if you're hanging onto it because there's some way you're getting off on it.

Be honest with yourself, especially if you're doing it because you want it done *your* way. Sometimes control really matters to us. If you are choosing to do it because you want to be in control—then whatever you are doing should be giving you energy instead of costing it. Own it.

The third thing I want you to think about is one we've talked about before and we'll cover again. That is, are you "paying" too much in any given relationship? Do you feel complete dread when that sorry sack from down the hall comes to tell you everything that's wrong with the boss? Do you really owe her the time it takes for her to download all of her mental sludge onto your day? Do you really have to work during the entire commute home to cover for an always-needy colleague, or can you crank up Outkast on your iPod and rock? In the next exercise, we'll take a look at how you can find time for what you want by plugging up those energy drains.

My personal rule about energy leaks is that I try to choose it, lose it, or amuse it. If I'm doing it because I am being a control freak about the outcome, well, then it's my choice and I should be doing it with a full heart. If I can stop doing it by setting a boundary, say with an energy vampire or someone who just momentarily put on her Countess Dracula outfit, then my job is to do that. And if I really have no control, I try to have a good time while I'm doing it. That's why when I fly, which bugs me because I have a thing

> ## Choose to Stop an Energy Leak
>
> Go back to your notes from the energy leaks exercise on page 174. Cut out fifteen minutes of energy drain from your day tomorrow. What if you . . .
>
> - ❖ Cut short a conversation with an energy vampire?
> - ❖ Don't answer stupid e-mails?
> - ❖ Don't make the bed?
>
> This stuff is probably not in your schedule because other than boring, unnecessary meetings (something that comes up on a lot of lists!), we don't usually commit to energy leaks. Make a commitment now. Write this down: The energy leak I'm going to address is _____
>
> _____

about turbulence, you will often find me reading Danielle Steel or some bodice-ripper instead of something I am supposed to be reading. When the guy sitting next to me finds out I am a serious business person and looks quizzically at the cover of my book, which often features a couple in period dress in some kind of hot embrace, I think, "Hey . . . get over it. I get to choose." And that's the point.

honor your dream

The final step in your action plan is to try to bring your dream back from being lost somewhere in the future to have something that has meaning for you today.

Though we spent a lot of time on visioning, I'm not completely done with dreams. That's because when I talk to women about days that leave them with enough energy to ask for what they want and need and days that don't, one of the differences is whether the day has meaning beyond activity. Visioning is about your workday; dreams can be bigger, and outside the box. Because vi-

Ronna Lichtenberg

sions and dreams aren't always the same, it's good to check in on both. That's why I am asking you again to give yourself permission to dream, and to take a moment to write it down in the following exercise.

Be honest with what you want. In Des Moines, a woman said simply, "I want a monster truck. Not a play one, a real one." A woman in Chicago said, "I want to write a screenplay, while putting God first." In a surprise announcement in New York, one woman said, "I love my husband, but I want to have an affair, and I want to know if it 'counts' if it is with a woman." (My guess was that her husband would think that it did.)

Which brings me to the point of sharing your dreams. In New York, we talked to Mrs. Affair about her statement that she loved her husband, and the group offered some blush-making ideas for how to bring a little sizzle back to a marriage that was fizzling. The would-be-accordion player in Milwaukee prompted another woman to say, "I know a place you could play." (Just as an aside that proves that women worry about self-promoting: Not a single woman in the dozens of

Honor Your Dream

This exercise is really simple. Just write down any dream or goal you want. No dream is silly. Every dream has a little fire in it that could spark something wonderful. I've heard some wonderful dreams in my workshops. Here are just three I heard in Milwaukee:

- ❖ "I want to go back to the accordion so I can play in a German band and wear a frilly dress."
- ❖ "I really want to climb Mount Everest. I've always wanted to, but then I gave up because I had problems with my heart. It's just that . . . I really want to at least get to base camp."
- ❖ "I want to retire and not be in a big sweat about money."

Keep the list; you're going to use it in a minute.

corporate workshops I've done has ever said her dream was to be the CEO, or even a top officer, of her company.

Don't push your dreams away. You may not be able to have the whole thing now, but you can have a little bite on a regular basis. In fact, you actually already know how to cut your dream into bite-sized pieces and get started, and I'm going to prove that to you now.

To help you figure out whether your vision is achievable in some form and, if so, what practical action you can take now to advance it, take a step back for a moment and pretend that your best girlfriend or someone else you love has just told you that this is what *they* want. As in, "Leslie, I'm thinking I'd like to try selling clothes in a little shop because someday I want my own boutique." You know Leslie (i.e., you) wouldn't say, "What an idiot." She'd say, "Cool! Maybe you should stop by that store you like and see if they could use you once in a while." Then tell "her," your imaginary best friend, what her next move should be—what practical steps she should take next week to start moving toward her dream. It's a lot easier than telling yourself.

Then look at the advice you've given "her," this person you love, and pretend—if you have to pretend—that you love yourself enough to give yourself the gift of a dream. Look at the action step you just suggested to her, and then go back to your calendar. Is it something you could do tomorrow? Next week? In the next two weeks? If the answer is nothing in the next few weeks, start over. There is some concrete thing you *can* do in the next few weeks, even if it is just a phone call. Write it down in your schedule. I guarantee you this will make devising an action plan a whole lot easier. Women are wonderfully creative at dispensing practical advice and brainstorming solutions for the people they love best, but we're woefully challenged to do it for ourselves, for all the reasons I covered in chapter 3. So turn that "other-orientation" to your advantage and treat the CEO of Me, Inc. with a little respect!

Remember, even a tiny step fuels the heart. Remember also that pursuing a dream brings passion to everything else you do. Your "day job" will be better for it. Give yourself permission to start, and to start small.

Ronna Lichtenberg

check in with yourself

After you go through these exercises, what starts to happen is that you learn how to check in with yourself—to notice what gives you energy and what takes it away. More important, you learn how to make tiny adjustments that change the day and your life. I'm big on learning from other women and make it a point to look for women who seem to stay energized and optimistic on a regular basis.

Jennifer Buchholz, director of HR at GE Consumer Finance, is one of these women. She seems particularly good at staying happy and energized in a high-stress job, and I asked her for her secrets. She said, "I make sure that I'm in tune sort of constantly throughout the day, by checking in in the morning and at night just to see how I'm feeling and what's going on with me emotionally and just physically. Am I tired, am I not? Why? What did I eat that day? What kinds of things are happening? Am I keeping balance in all wheels of my life?" What's particularly savvy about Jenn is that she doesn't check in with herself just on the bad days, as many of us do. "Even when I'm happy I ask myself, Why am I feeling this way? What's going on that's giving me perfect balance of everything I need?" She added that, over a period of time, through trial and error, as she kept checking in over and over and readjusting accordingly, it became a habit.

And that's the goal: to make a habit out of noticing what it takes to keep your energy tank full, and to make sure you get it. This kind of refueling is important for everyone, but it is even more important when you're working outside your natural style.

If you're a pink in a systemizing culture that's run by blues, your workday is automatically going to "cost" you more than if it were a closer fit. You need more fuel to make up for everything you're putting out.

I'm not telling you to follow your bliss, and your natural style, out the door. There is good reason why you're where you are—most likely that you believe you can make more money there than you can anywhere else (which may or may not be true). But so long as you are there, recognize that you are going to need more nourishment than you'll get automatically—emotionally and spiritually. If you are working outside your style, you must not only notice what you need but also learn how to find small ways to give it to yourself.

It doesn't have to be a big deal. Mary, knowing she was riding on energy fumes, took off at 5:00 instead of 7:00 so she could get a dozen paint chips of sage green to find precisely the right one for the living room wall. Liz said sometimes she just goes to the bathroom so she can shut the door and take a few deep breaths. Deb got up ten minutes early so she could manage a few minutes in the park.

Does this sound selfish to you? No. And it shouldn't sound selfish (although it can) when the sweet voice in your head asks, "Can we take a break now?"

CHECK YOUR BELIEFS

Now that you are in good shape and your energy tank is full, before you actually wind up to pitch, take a moment to consider your beliefs. Do you believe that something good actually could happen? Too many times, I talk to a woman who is getting ready to pitch and she tells me why it won't possibly work. Usually it's a version of the self-limiting beliefs with an overlay of something that's true in the outside world: "I'm good, *but* there are a lot of really terrific people and the market is really terrible right now." It feels like if you keep yourself from believing that something good could happen, you won't be as disappointed when it doesn't. But the truth is, you'll still be disappointed and you will have denied yourself the chance to feel the energy, and to communicate the energy, that comes up when you believe that something good actually could happen.

Believing something good could happen is a revolutionary and radical act. I once sat next to a woman at a luncheon whose son was born seriously ill. The baby hovered between life and death for some time. The woman said the turning point came when she had a talk with him and said that it was his choice to fight to be here now or not: that she wanted him to stay, but that she knew that it wasn't up to her. Her next action step was quite profound. She told the baby's doctors that they couldn't start a conversation with her with bad news.

Ronna Lichtenberg

Her rule was that they must say something positive first, every time. At first the docs balked, because they didn't think there was any good news. But they did their best, and little by little, they found good news to report.

Her son lived, and is doing well. The doctors explained it as a miracle, and I believe that is true. I also believe that believing attracts miracles, and that it is worth the risk. When you intend to pitch, but secretly, or maybe not so secretly, believe that failure is inevitable, it's like trying to pitch with your upper arm bandaged against your body. You may manage something, but it won't be a powerful pitch.

check your assumptions

When you aren't at work, and you aren't doing business, and you're not with your family, you are with the people you choose to have in your life. Friends, neighbors you like, buddies, new acquaintances. Think about them for a minute. Think about what you like about them the most. Now think about what you like about yourself. I bet what you like about them is kind of the same. You both have a whacky sense of humor. Or you both share a passionate commitment to a certain approach to child-raising. Or you both love the thrill you get from extreme sports.

It's easier to be with people who are like you. But in business, we aren't, which is a good thing for all of us. It's all too human, though, when someone who isn't like us does or says something we don't like, to make an assumption about *their* intentions. "She just said that to make me look bad," or "He did that to suck up to the boss," or "Those people in IT always ask for more time than they need."

It can get much more complicated than that in diverse environments, where it's easier to fall into the trap of making assumptions about someone else based on what they look like, where they come from, and the personal choices they make about how to live their lives.

On top of that, we make assumptions about how they feel about us. When I first started at Prudential Securities, several people took me aside and said, "Watch out for Tank." One told me he hated women. Another told me he hated "creative types," which they assumed I was. Others told me they knew for a fact he hated Jews.

I could have believed it because of my assumptions about him. Tank is a tall, lanky, blue-eyed former military guy. Pressed and crisp, except for his slight drawl, he looked like the kind of guy who is known not to like the likes of me. But this time I decided not to assume everyone was right and went to see Tank to tell him what I'd heard. He looked me straight in the eye and asked what I thought. I told him I thought maybe it wasn't true and that I was willing to work on that assumption.

None of the things I'd heard about his biases turned out to be true. Tank became, and remains, one of my dearest friends. There have been lots of other times, though, when my assumptions got away from me. Those assumptions—assumptions of negative intent on the other person's part—turn out often to be true because we make them true.

That's one reason why concentrating on differences can be so powerful. *Style differences allow you to assume benign intent.* Style differences let you move from thinking "Her goal in life is to make me crazy because she hates me," to "She's a blue systemizer, and that's why it's hard for her to hear my fourteen great ideas all at once."

I know this seems like a ton of work. That's because it is a ton of work.

The way it works, though, is the more you do in advance, the less you have to do on the spot. The more you know about your prospect, and the more work you've done to put yourself in the right place, the more effective you will be. Make a big deal out of all this advance work, and in the moment you can sound like what you want is "no big deal," which dramatically increases your chances of getting what you want.

Now that you've done your homework about them, and your heartwork about you, we can start work on the pitch itself.

Ronna Lichtenberg

CHAPTER 8
crafting the pitch

You've done your prep work: You've come up with your vision and set goals; identified the key people who can help you achieve them; done your homework on those prospects, their business, and the value of your offering; and warmed up your mind, body, and spirit to get ready for the task at hand. You've been, in a sense, like an athlete in training, and now you are finally ready for the Big Game.

Pitching is how you will do well in the game, and to do well as a pitcher you have to craft, price, package, and unleash the right pitch at the right time—then close it well. Over the next 5 chapters, I'll cover exactly how to do just that.

In this chapter, we'll talk about the crafting part—that is, how to put your ideas on paper and hone your content to the essential points your prospect needs to hear to agree to play ball with you. The key to this phase of the game (just to torture that sports metaphor a little bit longer) is to first understand where the power in your pitch comes from so you can use that muscle to your best advantage.

The goal is to be able to deliver what your prospect needs to know in precisely the way they will be most receptive to the information. This in turn will greatly increase your chances of getting to yes—and an enthusiastic yes at that.

UNDERSTAND THE POWER SOURCES

There are three main sources of power in any pitch: the strength of your relationship with the prospect, the business appeal of your offering, and the leverage you can get from your professional role. Smart pitching requires that you call on all three.

Think of it this way. It's kind of like the intricate systems many women develop for their hair. First there is shampoo, but it has to be the right shampoo, depending on the day. Then there's conditioner, but it might be a conditioner that you can only use a tiny bit of or you'll look greasy. And then there's some kind of goo, or several kinds of goo, the exact combination of which you may have spent considerable time figuring out. Obviously you can't put the goo on before the conditioner, and if you mix the wrong goos, you can end up with something that looks like a fender, and . . . you know what I mean. Same thing goes for pitching ingredients.

To determine how much to rely on each of these sources of power and in which order to use them, you have to understand a little bit more about them.

Relationship power comes from the strength of the connection your prospect feels to you, and it helps determine the order of your pitch. So before you even begin a first draft, you need to calibrate your relationship to determine whether you have a connection to this person, or the potential for one, that would make them want to do business with you. If so, you want to incorporate that connection into your pitch, probably even lead with it.

You also need to think through your colors—your prospect's as well as your own. The pinker the person on the receiving end, the more attention you need to pay to relationships in your pitch, and the more important it is to make it clear that you care about them and their needs before you move to the content of your offering.

Recently, for example, I was developing a pitch for a sales training program with Rick, a blue partner. We worked hard on the business appeal of the program, focusing on the needs of the company, which had just gone through a major acquisition, and on putting together a competitive pricing structure. When we were done, I told Rick we couldn't send it to our prospect, Susan, that way. Susan is pink, and I knew that she would find the prospect of working with us infinitely more appealing if we demonstrated first that we understood her needs and were paying attention to them. So we started our pitch by acknowledging that we knew Susan was really under the gun as a result of the acquisition and we sensed that she wanted several options to consider about the best way to blend the two staff cultures. It was a small change really, but one I believed would strongly influence her decision. She needed to know that we cared, not just about getting her business, but about helping her personally. Susan's color did not change the content of our offering, but it mightily affected how we began our pitch and the order and tone of the material we presented.

Had Susan been Stuart, or Blue Susan instead of Pink Susan, Rick and I would have begun our presentation instead by going straight to the second source of pitching power: the business appeal of the offering. In this case, we probably would have gotten very quickly to numbers tied to the increased retention we believed would result from the training.

To figure out which aspects of the business content to emphasize in your pitch, you need to put yourself into the head of your prospect and imagine what they need to hear to find your offering appealing. Here's where a woman's wiring works to your advantage. We naturally pick up more signals from the people with whom we interact, which means we can take in more information about their likes and dislikes, their style, and their pain point. Then we can use that knowledge to adjust and highlight the parts of our pitch that speak most directly to their needs. All we need to do is be more deliberate about a process that comes naturally to us, to more consciously look for the signals that matter most and not allow ourselves to be distracted by the ones that don't.

The third source of power is the leverage you can get from role: yours or someone else's. You may be in a position where you have authority over someone and they are already predisposed to think that your ideas are good, and that your jokes are pretty funny, too. Or you may be in a position, as many women are, where you are working from the power of someone else's role: Mr. or Ms. Big. Or you may be pitching within your own organization and you've been there so long and done your job so effectively that you don't have to first establish who you are and why people should listen to you and want to do business with you. You already have a check in the credibility box.

When you derive power from your role, simply because of your title, your boss's title, or longevity within an organization, you don't have to pitch as hard. A softer sell is more effective, and less taxing on you. Pitching to subordinates is also one of the ways smart women yield authority in a "feminine" way.

If you are in a subordinate or junior spot, then you don't have role power. There are other sources of power you might have: special expertise; relationship power because of ties to another important area in the organization; sheer personal magnetism; or having been recognized by someone other than your boss as a person with future potential who should be developed. Even with these sources of power, investing the effort in a truly powerful pitch is going to pay off even more for you than for someone more established in her role and career.

CREATE A WORKING DRAFT

Every pitcher needs to write down important pitches, even if the actual delivery will be verbal. Putting your ideas on paper allows you to physically see what you've got, read it aloud, and hear how it will sound to others. Writing helps you refine your ideas and see where you need more detail or support, a change of tone, or sometimes even an entirely new approach.

In the best of all worlds, you will write the pitch, put it aside for a couple of days, and then come back to it with a fresh mind and eye. The more important the pitch, the more important it is to take time to mull and refine.

In fact, you should create three written versions of your pitch. On your first draft, you can indulge yourself, writing down everything that seems important about this pitch, everything you know about the appeal of the offering, and what you're hoping will result. Essentially, you do a mental data dump. In the next version, you're going to take this big, sloppy, out-of-shape version to the gym for slimming, strengthening, and toning. For your final version, you are going to boil your pitch down to its three essential elements—the three most powerful and compelling points you can make that will inspire them to buy whatever it is you're selling. And you're going to write them so tightly, *hone your message* so precisely, that all three points will fit on a single Post-it note.

Communications expert Mary Taylor, who is currently vice president of communications for AXA, a global financial services company, likens this boiling down process to the steps you'd take if you were creating an advertising campaign. Mary, who has done communications for a number of major companies in different industries over the course of a highly successful career, says that with virtually every pitch you write you have to start by asking yourself a few key questions: What are the product or service qualities we want to promote in this campaign? Do we have a competitive advantage? What are the main features that would compel someone to buy?

Most people, says Mary, want to show they've done their homework by making their pitch far too complicated, filling it with esoteric jargon that their prospects will neither understand nor be interested in. They think that because they know every detail about, say, the way a 401(k) program or a second-to-die life insurance policy works, the person on the receiving end should know those details, too. They want to dazzle the buyer with their knowledge, as if to say, "Look how smart and well prepared I am."

But, like the consumer who may buy a high-priced skin cream and doesn't really give a hoot about any of the ingredients in it, the recipients of a pitch don't usually want to know every in and out of the topic at hand.

They want to know just three basic pieces of information: the benefit to them if they buy from you, the Post-it note version of your offering, and why your offering is better than another competing product. That's it. In fact, that's it whether you're selling root beer, raising funds for a charity, or asking your boss for a raise.

Sure, you must be able to provide detailed backup and additional information, if you're asked for it. But keep the message of your pitch simple and clear, centered on what they need to know to make an informed decision.

getting down to the nitty-gritty

Got the picture? At the heart of every pitch are three basic elements: your best understanding of what your prospect needs, the in-a-nutshell version of what you're offering, and why what you're offering fulfills their need better than their alternatives. Whether you're pink, blue, striped, or polka-dotted, an empathizer or a systemizer, tall or short, blonde or brunette, employee or business owner, every pitch you make must be built around these fundamentals.

It's time to get going.

Start your draft with your best understanding of what your prospect needs and how your offering fulfills that need. Make sure to explain why you think they need it. Many pitchers mistakenly assume that their prospect will immediately recognize and understand the benefit. But just because you think what you've got to offer is good for them doesn't mean they will automatically see it that way, too.

Next, focus on the content of your offering—the relevant details that your prospect will find most appealing and that best meet their needs. Let what you've learned about brain sex be your guide in how you present this information.

Finally, make sure you include an explicit discussion of why your offering is better than the alternatives available to your prospect. No pitch exists in a vacuum; whomever you're dealing with always has other options. When you take the time to explore why you're the best one for the task at hand, you

Ronna Lichtenberg

demonstrate real caring about the relationship. You've taken the time to think through your prospect's needs and to see the situation from their perspective rather than your own. Sometimes the reason you're better than the alternatives may be as simple as what you're offering is more convenient. Sometimes people choose their bank because there's a branch with an ATM on the corner or to exercise at a particular gym because it's within a few blocks of their house. Closer, cheaper, more convenient are all common reasons one alternative seems more attractive than another. So, to help you figure out what's so special about your offering, try the exercise below.

The Power of Three

If you haven't noticed by now, three is a magic number for pitchers. For maximum impact, you need to be able to get your message down to its three most compelling points. Fewer than three and your pitch does not have enough weight or provide enough information for your prospect to make a decision. More than three and the message gets lost in verbiage. The following steps will help ensure you use the power of three to your best advantage.

Step 1: Ask yourself, What problem will my offering solve? Write all the answers you can think of.

Step 2: Go back over your answers and circle the three most important ones.

Step 3: Ask yourself, How will my offering make life easier or otherwise better for my prospect? Write all the answers you can think of, being as specific as possible.

Step 4: Go back over your answers and circle the three most important ones.

Step 5: Ask yourself, Why is my solution better than anyone else's? Write all the reasons that come to your mind.

Step 6: Look over the list and circle the three most compelling advantages.

Step 7: Look back at the three answers you've chosen for each question, and now pick the single most compelling point from each one. That's your three-point sticky note.

VARIATIONS ON THE THEME

We've just covered the basic ingredients of a pitch. Having tortured our sports analogies, I'm going to move to baking since I know about as much about baking as I do about baseball—that is, very little. So, the basic ingredients of a pitch are the equivalent of the flour, sugar, baking powder, and eggs that virtually every cake must have. But what makes one cake different from another, relatively more or less appealing, are the other flavors you put in, and the amounts in which you add them. Do you want a chocolate layer? Would your guests prefer cream cheese frosting or a fruit filling? How about spices and flavorings like cinnamon or vanilla? These beyond-the-basics decisions are what will make even those on a low-carb diet say, "Okay, maybe a micro slice."

So it is with pitching. Build your pitch around basic, universal ingredients, but use flavoring to give it style.

Here are a few standard recipes—that is, common pitch styles—and what you need to know about where and when to use them and how to make them work.

the "full frontal formal" pitch

This is the most straightforward pitching situation, where everyone in the room understands upfront that you are pitching and your goal is to gain their business or their support. Maybe you're making a presentation to a prospective client, maybe you're seeking funds from a group of venture capitalists, perhaps you're presenting recommendations to a group in your office or making a proposal to an established client. Whatever the specific circumstances, the agenda is to do a deal, and everyone in the room knows it. Since deals involve money and money is always blue, you need to go blue, too.

That means you must lead with your clearest and most direct explanation of the business offering and what the benefit is for your prospect. No pussyfooting—this is not the time to indulge a pink-hued need to verbalize (and verbalize and verbalize some more). You also need to credential yourself early in the pitch and be prepared to ask outright for their business rather than waiting in more traditionally feminine fashion for a subsequent meeting to close on the deal. In a Full Frontal pitch, you don't have time for a lot of foreplay.

In developing the written material for your presentation, think about visuals that can support your words—PowerPoint, graphics, models. Then craft the pitch, at least in part, around what their eyes will see (we'll talk a lot more about packaging in chapter 10). Emphasize data, which will appeal to a blue's natural love of numbers, and clearly articulate the financial returns, which is a blue's favorite way to keep score.

the "just us girls" pitch

At the opposite end of the pitching spectrum, the Just Us Girls pitch is a classic pink-on-pink exchange. If you're pink and you're pitching to other pinks—say, you're asking for support from a female colleague, or you're presenting to a woman-owned business or in a women-dominated environment—you need to put the emphasis on feeling good about each other and the prospect of doing business together. You need to establish trust and connection, and make your prospect feel comfortable about working with you.

Your language, therefore, needs more feminine markers—apologies, expressions of vulnerability, upward inflections at the ends of words, and inquiries about what would make the person on the receiving end of the pitch feel more comfortable. Sentences that begin "I'm sorry, but . . ." or questions like "Is that going to be okay with you?" work really well in a Just Us Girls pitch. So do words that soften the message, like "Maybe we might consider . . ." and "Can we think about . . . ?" as opposed to bolder declarations of suggested action that may sound overly aggressive to a pink, as if you were too interested in pushing your agenda and not interested enough in fulfilling her needs.

Here's how I recently used a Just Us Girls approach in a telephone meeting with a woman representing a major company for whom I was scheduled to do a presentation. They had wanted to videotape the presentation, which was to take place at the company's headquarters, so it could be shown to their other offices around the country, at their discretion. Since they have more than 100 offices nationwide, that would in essence mean they were getting 100 presentations for the price of one—a great deal for them, but a very bad deal for me. I invoked the Nancy Reagan defense and just said no.

That's when the sweet young woman from their office called to see if she could change my mind. She was really, really pink and said the company really, really, really wanted to videotape. Because I'm really pink too, I felt bad. But I didn't feel so bad that I was willing to give my work away. So I used a Just Us Girls pitch to see if I could move us to a solution that was comfortable for both of us. I said, in essence, "I am really sorry, I would love to help you, but I am a Material Girl and this is how I make my living. Can we think together about a different way to do this that would work for both of us?" I then suggested that we might add a training program for a few of their local offices on top of the presentation, which would increase my fee and make me feel better about allowing them to videotape the initial presentation.

What made this a Just Us Girls pitch? I used an apology opener—classic gender communication. I made her laugh, which made her more comfortable, and acknowledged both her pain point (her boss *really* wanted her to come away with a yes from me about videotaping, and they were on a tight budget for this project) and our mutual discomfort talking about money (because two pinks would rather pull their skin off than talk about money together), which made it easier to do. Then I suggested a mutually acceptable solution without being insistent or intransigent about the outcome.

That is the heart of a Just Us Girls pitch: making it clear that you want to work with each other to get results that satisfy both parties and leave you feeling good about each other and the working relationship.

the "it's not about me, it's about the team" pitch

For anyone uncomfortable with self-promotion, and that means most women, the team pitch is a great way to present your offering without getting caught up in the cultural stereotypes and self-limiting beliefs that so often undermine

Ronna Lichtenberg

us. When you put yourself in the mindset that you are pitching on behalf of a cause rather than pitching for your own advancement, you don't have to worry about appearing immodest or unfeminine or be concerned that you're not good enough or don't deserve a positive outcome. Or, at least, you can worry about all of those things a lot less. Because, after all, it isn't you you're trying to promote; it's someone or something else. And we can be very powerful advocates when we're pitching on behalf of others in whom we believe.

I, for one, certainly find it easier to work up a good head of steam when I'm pitching other people to prospects instead of trying to sell myself and my own work. Nothing gives me more joy than to rave about a colleague or friend who does a great job. The same principle applies to a team pitch: Most women I know can more clearly articulate what another person, company, institution, or cause has to offer, and with more confidence and passion than if she is describing herself and what she can bring to the table.

Writing a team pitch is often easier too because you get to rely on the first person plural: *We* can do this for you, *we* can do that for you, we can fix it, we can handle it, we can fulfill your every need (well, no we can't, but we can certainly try to fulfill the most important ones). You do not have to dwell on the insecurities you may have as a woman about not being good enough; you have others with you and that automatically makes you feel better—in your mind, they're better simply by virtue of not being you.

This is a pitch, then, that is best used to give yourself strength and courage to make your best presentation. It allows a partial shift in focus, from me to them, that many women find liberating, and I highly recommend it as such. You cannot choose to use it in every pitching situation—you need to be part of a company or other institution, or working with partners, to rely on it. But when you can, it is a powerful mental tool.

One caveat on this one: Do not use the team pitch as a way to indulge your own insecurities, to collapse into "I am nothing, the team is everything" in your head or in your delivery. Nor should you overuse the team language to the point where it comes across as fake humility. As former Israeli prime minister Golda Meir once said to a visiting diplomat, "Don't be so humble, you're not that great." To help you own your strengths without going to either the humility or "look at me" extreme, try the team spirit exercise above.

the "hey, big fella" pitch

There isn't a straight woman alive who hasn't used this pitch from time to time, particularly in personal relationships with men. Come on now, admit it. Maybe you leaned on a Hey, Big Fella when you were trying to convince your boyfriend to get a date for your best friend or when you were trying to get your husband to fix a leaky faucet. You probably used it on your daddy when you were a little girl trying to get a new toy or stay up past your bedtime, and you might occasionally still use it on Dad today. Anytime you are trying to get a guy to do your bidding and you've looked up at him admiringly, or with an edge of sexy sass, conscious that he's conscious of your attractiveness, you're using a Hey, Big Fella pitch, even if you're not doing it deliberately.

Ronna Lichtenberg

We use this pitch in the business world, too. If you are pitching to a man and you know that part of the reason he's willing to listen to you is because you're attractive, you're in the midst of a Hey, Big Fella pitch, whether you like it or not. In fact, there are often elements of the Big Fella present anytime you are pitching one on one to a man, or to a group of men, or to a male-dominated larger audience, particularly if you are young and pretty. Sometimes a guy thinks you're cute and it gives you a bit of an edge, and sometimes it doesn't. This is not inherently good or bad, it just is. So don't beat yourself, or them, up about it.

What's important is not to deny the existence of the Big Fella pitch, but to acknowledge it and make conscious decisions about when and how to use it—or not use it.

First and foremost, in any potential Big Fella situation, you must be really clear upfront about the business value you have to offer and how you intend to apply that value to the prospect's business needs. The younger, cuter, and less experienced you are, the stronger your business content must be. Otherwise you risk your creditability, and that's a mighty big risk, given how hard women have to work at establishing credibility in the first place.

Conversely, the older and more experienced you are, the better able you are to use the Hey, Big Fella effectively, partly because the sexual energy you give off is not as intense and partly because you're simply more experienced about how to apply it. By the time you've been around the block a few times, you know how to be playful, to make the recipient feel good without giving off a vibe that says, "Do me now, Big Daddy, please."

One of the most masterful Hey, Big Fella pitchers I've ever seen is Charlotte Beers, who was rightfully known for many years as the most powerful woman in advertising. I remember the first time I saw Charlotte, some fifteen years ago, at a conference for working women in a big New York City hotel. She was riding an escalator, and at the time, I didn't have a clue who Charlotte was; all I saw was this fabulous middle-aged woman, dressed to the hilt, with enough vivaciousness and sexual energy to fill the whole hotel. And I remember thinking, Who is *that*?

Throughout her career, Charlotte routinely flirted her brains out, with women as well as men. She dressed in an overtly sexy yet tasteful way, had a very feminine and provocative demeanor, and somehow it all worked for her: partly because she worked in an industry in which creative and personal flair is admired; partly because she'd already established her business acumen and authority, as the former head of both Ogilvy & Mather and J. Walter Thompson, so she didn't risk credibility; and partly because with Charlotte, the flirty playfulness was such an authentic part of who she is. Charlotte never used her sexuality in an affected way or to manipulate an outcome; she is just a genuine hottie, with an outsized zest for life, who will still be hot when she's 400 years old.

What's the lesson here? Don't be afraid to use the hint of sexuality that is an integral part of being a woman when you pitch as long as you have strong business chops to back up your offering. If you have the basic ingredients and you want to add a dash of flirtation, just because the sun is shining and you're feeling foxy, it's okay.

I have a friend, a hotshot in financial management, who is so worried that showing even a trace of playful sexuality in the workplace will undermine her credibility that she shuts down that side of herself completely. She is so closed down that she tends to makes the guys around her feel insecure, as if she hates them all. It's like she's delivering an anti-pitch and, in so doing, does her cause no good. I confess to being guilty of that myself in my early years at Prudential. Working in a very male environment, I came across guys all the time who, in retrospect, just wanted me to vaguely admire them, to look at them as if they were somebody. I refused—I wouldn't give them the satisfaction of letting them think I even saw them as human, let alone potentially attractive. And I did my own cause no good either.

On the other hand, a little bit of Big Fella goes a long way. Just as you shouldn't be afraid to use it a little, you don't want to abuse it, either.

Case in point: the women of the first season of *The Apprentice*. Early on in the contest, the eight female contestants—all smart, accomplished business-

Ronna Lichtenberg

women in their twenties and early thirties—blatantly used their sexuality to pitch and succeed at the assignments they were given. In one of the earliest episodes, the ladies needed to sell lemonade at a lemonade stand and, to boost sales, decided to sell kisses to go with it. Naturally, they won the challenge. Later on, Katrina, one of the lemonade kissers, was asked to pull a rickshaw by her male project manager, who believed that tourists would pay good money to be physically carted around New York City by a pretty woman while staring at her shapely bottom. Katrina was outraged. I say, you set the terms, girlfriend. You used your attractiveness very assertively in a sales situation before, so you don't have room to be uppity now.

Eventually, Katrina was fired by the Donald, and all viewers remember about her now is the way she leaned on her sexuality, not her business acumen.

The moral of the story: She who lives by the Big Fella dies by the Big Fella.

USE PERSONAL DISCLOSURES JUDICIOUSLY

While most women recognize the danger inherent in leaning too much on sexuality while pitching (even those of us who go ahead and do it anyway), we often don't see the risks in another traditionally female tendency: sharing personal stories to make a business point and strengthen a professional relationship. Sometimes it works very well indeed, but sometimes it falls flat, and it's vital to know what makes the difference.

When you are pitching to other women, particularly pink women, you'll find personal anecdotes are a powerful and compelling way to make a point. We're wired, after all, to value relationship, and there is no faster, more effective way to forge a connection with someone than to share a story about your own life. We prefer a human face on issues, and when you make that face your own, you communicate the importance of this particular issue to you and your deeper and more intimate understanding of what's needed and why.

My friend Diane Perlmutter, even though striped, knows how to throw a wicked Just Us Girls pitch. Diane is the chief executive officer of Gilda's Club, an international nonprofit organization that provides support to individuals and families living with cancer. Diane often starts meetings the same way, saying, "I'm here for the same reason many of you are: I lost someone close to me. My younger sister died of breast cancer." The message is simple yet powerful, and it always works because it's so consistent with the club's culture and true meaning.

The pinker the woman with whom you are interacting, the more personal the disclosure can be and the longer the time you can spend talking about it. The disclosure should be somehow relevant to the pitch—don't go on and on about your alcoholic first husband unless you're pitching to raise funds for a rehab center—and must be genuinely meaningful to you. Leave the personal out of your pitch with a pink, or do it superficially, and you risk losing her goodwill entirely.

I saw this happen on a fifth season episode of the HBO series *The Sopranos*. Adriana, who was engaged to one of the mob captains, was talking with an FBI agent who had strong-armed her into becoming an informant. The very pink Adriana was agonizing over selling out the people she loved, and the very blue female agent recognized that this moll was badly in need of a girlfriend moment. So the agent put down her pad and pen, shared three sentences about what a jerk her first husband was, then picked up the pad and pen again, signaling the end of said moment. But pink women need more than a moment, particularly when the stakes are high. Instead of feeling—dare I say it?—mollified, Adriana shut down after this little exchange, feeling angrier and even more confused than she had before. If the FBI agent had only understood the importance of a more meaningful disclosure in that moment, she might have gotten poor Adriana to spill enough beans to put Tony Soprano and his family away for life.

When you are pitching to a blue woman, you may still want to share a personal story, because most women value connection to some degree, but the revelation should be less intimate. Wait to see if the prospect invites a moment of

Ronna Lichtenberg

disclosure first. If she does and you are pink yourself, you may mentally shout hallelujah, sister, and be ready to dish. Don't go there. What's typically called for in this situation is a personal disclosure that's not all that personal.

Consider this scenario: A pink colleague of mine named Audrey regularly deals with a client named Anna, who is very blue. Audrey was taken aback recently when the brisk and to-the-business-point Anna, who had never gone in for personal chitchat before, stepped out of character to congratulate her on her recent engagement and ask how her wedding plans were going. The sudden transition from blue to pink momentarily rattled Audrey, who luckily recognized quickly that true disclosure was not called for here. This was not the time nor was Anna the person to whom she could complain about her overbearing future mother-in-law who was threatening to ruin the wedding with tasteless demands. Instead, Audrey said, "Yes, it's very exciting. I've just registered at Fortunoff and decided to go with Lenox for my china. Thanks for asking." End of disclosure. Anna was satisfied with what she'd gotten, and she and Audrey then shifted smoothly back to blue business mode.

If you are instead pitching to a blue man or group of men, stay away from personal disclosure entirely. Whereas women's wiring leads us to see personal stories as a way to build relationships, men's wiring leads them to regard such stories as frivolous and beside the point. You risk being seen as less professional and annoying them by wasting their time with irrelevant anecdotes. You cannot change their minds; this is a matter of biology and no amount of proselytizing will alter the outcome. Go there at your own peril.

The one exception: if you are blue too. Remember the unspoken sanctions against women who present with a masculine style that we talked about in chapter 3. Including a personal moment in your pitch will help you demonstrate vulnerability so you won't trigger them. Typically, just a moment is all that's required, a casual inquiry at the beginning or end of the presentation (never, ever in the middle or heart of a pitch, when their single-focused brains are entirely in business mode—their necks will snap from the pain of shifting gears). You might ask your prospect where he went on a recent vacation and confide you've always hankered to go to Tuscany, too. Or you might ask about the ages of his children; then share that you have a teenager as well and commiserate about how challenging this time is. Do not, however, share any of the actual challenges.

In other words, find a personal disclosure you can make that is proportionate to a personal disclosure he could conceivably make. Then make it quickly and move on.

STRIKE THE RIGHT TONE

The final step in crafting your pitch is to make sure you have infused your words with the right tone and the right energy. If you're trying to launch a brand new product or service, it has to sound exciting. If you're addressing ways to reverse the tide of serious business losses, you have to sound somber yet urgent. The right tone, in effect, cues your prospect as to how you want them to respond.

Mary Taylor believes that almost every pitch needs a bit of humor. Some people get so serious during a pitch that they become a virtual caricature of themselves, she notes. This doesn't mean you should be funny, as in ha-ha, Mary says, but rather that you should convey a certain warmth to your audience no matter what the topic at hand.

I believe, however, that there are a few situations in which humor is wrong, period. For example, you should rarely use humor in a Full Frontal Formal pitch and never use humor directed at other people, no matter what kind of pitch you're throwing. Meanwhile, self-deprecating humor may go over well in a Just Us Girls pitch, in which a demonstration of vulnerability can be helpful. But it can be utterly disastrous in a formal pitch, in which you need to convey authority and confidence throughout (the exception is if the power person does it and sets you up to do it, too).

Last but not least, no matter what kind of pitch you're throwing, be sure you have conveyed your personal passion for your offering—not effusive, over-the-top gushing (please, no), but your quiet, heartfelt conviction that you have

Ronna Lichtenberg

something to offer that will truly benefit the person, company, and cause and that you are the best one to provide this service. As Mary says, "When you truly believe something, it is easier to sell." My corollary: When you truly believe something, you make it easier for others to buy.

Making life easier for your prospect is, in the end, one of the most powerful pitches of all.

The Pre-Pitch Checklist

As you create and refine your pitch, make sure you have addressed the following questions:

- ❖ Have you really thought through what's in it for them versus what's in it for you?
- ❖ How and why does your pitch solve their problem or ease their pain point?
- ❖ Have you considered your prospect's other options?
- ❖ Have you addressed, directly or indirectly, why you're better? What type of pitch will you use?
- ❖ Can you write your offering in one sentence—identify the three most compelling points and boil them down so they can fit on a single Post-it note?
- ❖ Have you clearly demonstrated that you really "get" what they need?
- ❖ Have you considered what works about your offering from a pink perspective? From a blue?
- ❖ Have you thought about who can say yes? Who can say no? Why would this person say yes? Why would this person say yes to *you?*
- ❖ Have you conveyed in word and tone your passion for the project and your conviction that you are the best one for the job or are otherwise deserving of their support?
- ❖ Have you prepared data about the value of your pitch?
- ❖ Have you prepared credentials sufficiently for a blue target?

CHAPTER 9
pricing the pitch

Women are great at selling stuff, be it cars, containers, cookies, or companies. Over the past couple of decades, women have made enormous strides in the sales and marketing arena, including business-to-business transactions in which the "offering" carries price tags in the millions and the deal is negotiated in an intensely competitive environment.

Yet when it comes time to price ourselves and our ideas in the marketplace, we still freeze. The same rising female stars who are so skilled at getting others to pay top dollar for the products they pitch are considerably less skilled at nabbing top dollar for themselves, according to the most recent salary survey by *Sales and Marketing Management* magazine. Among sales and marketing managers with eleven to twenty-five years of experience in the field, for instance, men took home an average of $155,298, including commissions and bonuses, in 2003. Meanwhile, women with comparable experience earned $125,410—a nearly 24 percent difference.

Those results are in keeping with the continuing overall wage gap between men and women in the workplace. Although the divide has narrowed modestly over the past twenty years, women still earn, on average, only seventy-seven cents for every dollar earned by men. African-American women earn just sixty-six cents, and Hispanic women earn only fifty-four cents for each dollar that white men earn. Moreover, as women get older, the wage gap widens. And that disparity remains even after accounting for all the sociological and demographic factors that can influence salary, such as marital status, number and age of children, years and hours in the workforce, and job tenure. Controlling for these possible variables, a 2003 study by the U.S. General Accounting Office found that women still earn, on average, only 80 percent of what men are paid.

Some of the disparity is undoubtedly the result of old-fashioned lingering bias in the workplace against women. But at least some of the problem lies with women themselves: We are so uncomfortable with the idea of being viewed as an "offering" in the marketplace, that we will be judged and literally valued, that the mere mention of money in a business context is enough to trigger emotional alarm bells that make us unable to negotiate on our own behalf. We often don't raise the subject at all, and, if and when we do, we're too uncomfortable to ask for what we really want and deserve.

In other words, if marriage is the "M" word for men, money is the "M" word for women—a subject so painful that we shy away from it whenever possible.

All about Eve

There's another aspect of asking that feels "bad." In a *Wall Street Journal* article about what might be holding women back from corporate success, Terry Dal, a former vice chairman at Wells Fargo bank, said, "Good girls don't advertise; only prostitutes advertise. We feel dirty promoting ourselves."

There seems to be a connection between feeling inhibited about asking for what you want, especially if it's money, and the stereotype that it is somehow wrong for women to ask for what they want sexually. Clients who get better at asking for what they want in the bedroom have told me they find it easier to ask in the boardroom . . . and vice versa.

This chapter is about taking that pain away. It is about getting truly, gut-level comfortable with negotiating for money. It is about understanding, at your core, that what you have to offer has real value in the marketplace. And it is about learning techniques for setting your price, asking for that price, and getting that price in a way that is thoroughly in keeping with your own natural style.

Every pitch carries a price tag. You need to be the one to set it—and you can, without sacrificing who you are in the process.

WHY MONEY IS SO HARD

Of course, you don't need me to tell you that money is a tough topic for many women. You already know this from personal experience. Research supports the idea, too. A 2003 survey by the American Institute of Certified Public Accountants found that some 70 percent of women indicate that they need help managing their finances. And, in an earlier, separate survey by Dreyfus and the National Center for Women and Retirement Research, far more women than men reported that they avoided making financial decisions for fear of making a mistake.

In the first part of this book, we discussed some of the reasons why pitching for money is especially challenging for women. They bear repeating here.

Perhaps first and foremost, we have to grapple with the culturally ingrained admonitions against asking for what we want and putting our own needs first. An executive I'll call Phoebe is usually direct, even blunt at times, in her professional style and is used to talking about big-time financial issues every day by virtue of her job, but she uses words like *difficult, scary,* and *intimidating* to describe talking about money on her own behalf. "I don't want to come across as greedy or grabby or as if I feel entitled," says Phoebe. "I worry that someone will look at me, laugh, and say, 'What are you smoking—what makes you think *you* are worth that much money?'"

It is the WHO DOES SHE THINK *SHE* IS? factor writ large, in neon.

We're also afraid to ask for money because we worry that such a stressful conversation may somehow ruin our relationship with our boss, client, or the friend with whom we're doing business.

While money can be an intensely emotional subject for both sexes, men seem to find it a little easier to distance themselves, in part because their biology makes it more difficult for them to access and process as many emotions as women do in the first place. Men often seem to be better able to make a distinction between who they are as a person and how their offering is valued in the marketplace.

Then there are all those personal feelings of inadequacy that money seems to raise. We say to ourselves, "I can't ask for X amount because I'm not good enough, I don't deserve it." We worry that if we do ask we may be rejected. We worry too that if we price ourselves too aggressively, our buyers will be entitled to expect more of us and everyone expects too much already.

One highly successful businesswoman confessed to me that she quite deliberately charges less than her competitors for precisely this reason. "If I charge at the top of the market, they'll be entitled to my life—calls at any time of the day or night, wherever I am, crazy weekends filled with work," she told me. "Lower fees take some pressure off."

a tale of two currencies

The final reason that pitching for money is so complicated for women—and even more complex when two women are negotiating with each other—is that we are typically dealing in two currencies at once: cash currency and emotional currency, as we saw in chapter 3.

Cash currency is all about the dollars that a prospective buyer will pay you to perform a particular task. Emotional currency is about all the non-financial benefits you get from your interactions with this person or in the working environment—praise, warmth, caring, friendship, recognition, and flexibility, just to name a few possibilities.

In calculating what we consider fair compensation, women constantly toggle back and forth between the two currencies, making conscious and unconscious decisions about the trade-offs we're willing to accept. The more we get in emotional currency, the more willing we may be to accept less on the financial end. The reverse is true as well. I've seen plenty of women stay in a job they hate because the position paid a bundle. On occasion, I've even been one of them. (This, by the way, is the main reason it's typically so much easier to negotiate money with a blue. You only have to deal in one currency, so the transaction is cleaner.)

Putting a dollar sign on task is relatively easy. Calculating emotional currency is a whole lot tougher. There is no established marketplace for it, and everyone tends to overvalue their emotional contribution.

This can be particularly problematic for women in a hypermasculine, strongly systemizing environment, like accounting or engineering, where people are not normally hired or promoted through the ranks for relationship skills (that is, not until they get close to the top, when these skills become really critical). What often happens is that it's hard to let go of the desire not just to make everyone happy, but to have them demonstrate it in the same golden retriever tail-wagging way that you might if someone made you happy on a good day.

You can rant and rave about it, but you won't change it. At least not in the short term. A far more productive approach, I believe, is to use our natural ability to read another person's style and make adjustments accordingly. In terms of money, this means we need to translate the pink relationship work that we do in blue marketplace terms. We need to connect it to bottom line outcomes that bosses and clients understand and show how the emotional work that we do ties to the buyer's business goals.

raise the subject

In workshops, when I ask women to sell each other a product, everyone talks about price. But when I ask women to sell themselves as a CEO candidate for the company making that product, no one mentions money.

Good girls don't ask. This common stereotype haunts our thinking about money and is one of the key factors that holds us back from getting what we want and deserve financially.

But learn this and learn it well: *It is our job to ask for money.*

Ronna Lichtenberg

Jennifer Buchholz at GE Consumer Finance puts it this way: "If you don't ask, you have a zero percent chance of hearing 'yes.' If you do ask, you have a 50 percent chance of hearing 'yes.' So open up your mouth and ask for what you need."

You'll find it infinitely easier to start the conversation if you first think through ways to make that conversation more comfortable for your buyer. Shifting the mental focus from you to them, even temporarily, helps get around many of the bad feelings we have about pushing our own needs to the forefront or appearing too pushy or greedy.

This mental strategy is particularly helpful if you are pink and your prospect is pink, too. Two pinks doing money together increases the discomfort level exponentially as both sides grapple with the same wiring challenges and cultural impediments.

Acknowledging the discomfort up front and finding indirect ways to have the conversation are two strategies I've found helpful in this regard. Recently, for example, it was time for me to renegotiate my annual retainer with a major client, who is pink *and* a close friend, which makes conversations about money infinitely harder. I knew she would never approach me about money, so I approached her, but I did so in an e-mail, so she would not have to talk to me directly. I labeled the e-mail "Yucky Money Stuff" so she would understand that I understand the subject is difficult for us and might get a small laugh out of my heading to help dissipate the tension. We finalized all of the financial details by e-mail. To this day, we have never spoken a word to each other about money, either in person or by phone, which is how I know we're cool.

Finding an indirect way to ask for money is easier for most women anyway because it is in keeping with our natural style of communication. Just be sure that you aren't so indirect that the person on the receiving end of the request doesn't even realize you've asked.

In a typical scenario, for example, a woman looking for more money might go to her boss and say, "I feel like I'm really ready for more responsibility." Her translation: "I want a promotion and a big fat raise to go with it." But if the boss is a guy, that's probably not going to be his interpretation. Instead, he hears, "Feel free to give me a lot more work without paying me extra."

Taking a backdoor approach doesn't get you out of raising the subject of money explicitly. You just don't have to be in-your-face about it.

FIGURE OUT YOUR MARKET VALUE

In fact, understanding our relationship to the market, where and how and why our work may be valued, is the first crucial step in ensuring we are paid as well as we want and deserve.

I learned this lesson the hard way. When I was a big muckety-muck in the corporate world, I was paid more money than I had ever dreamed possible. In terms of my compensation, I was one happy gal. It wasn't until quite a few years later that I discovered my employer routinely paid other people in similar jobs more than they'd paid me. You probably won't be surprised to learn that those "other people" just happened to be men.

I know many women, on all rungs of the corporate ladder, who have had similar experiences. For example, Judy Haberkorn, who was president of consumer sales and service at Verizon, the giant telecommunication company, was earning what she felt was "fair, if not lavish, compensation" for her big job. But it wasn't until she started sitting on corporate boards, and more important, on compensation committees, that she "realized how much people were being paid for jobs with a lot less responsibility."

The first step in getting the money you deserve is to understand the market rate for your offering. Not what you think you need, not what they're willing to pay, but the going rate for similar goods and services offered in your area by someone with your skills and years of experience.

This involves some homework. Maybe you go to your industry association to find out the salary range in your area for the position you're interested in. Or

Ronna Lichtenberg

check out one of the myriad Web sites, such as salary.com or jobstar.org, which post compensation surveys for various industries, positions, and geographic areas. You can also talk to people in the know—friends and colleagues who have provided or paid for comparable services and are willing to give you the lowdown on what's customary and reasonable.

Then—and this is a biggie, my friends—*you seek expert advice.* Madeleine Condit, who is a senior client partner for Korn/Ferry, one of the biggest recruiting firms in the world, notes that men routinely consult lawyers, financial advisers, executive recruiters, and any other paid counselors they can think of to help them assess what constitutes a fair fee, salary, and general compensation package for any given job or project. "They put more resources around themselves," she says. Women, on the other hand, will talk to their girlfriends about how they feel about the job in question. Money may be part of the conversation, but that's not the same authoritative guidance you might get from a professional counselor.

Sure, expert advice will cost you. But you are worth it. At a minimum, Madeleine recommends, hire a lawyer to review any employment contract you are asked to sign. The key questions you need answered: What are you being offered, in legal terms, and how are you protected? Ideally, you should also consult some kind of financial pro, either an expert in the field who can help you assess what constitutes fair compensation in this circumstance or an adviser who can talk to you about how this job fits into your general financial picture—or, in the best of all worlds, both.

The pinker you are, the bigger the job, and the more trouble you typically have with money issues, the more imperative it is to rely on professional advice—and the more you should be willing to pay to make sure you get the best counsel possible.

separate me from me, inc.

Once you've established what the market range is for the particular pitching situation, you need to figure out where you fit in that range.

The first part of the process is mental: You need to stop thinking about how to price yourself in the marketplace and think instead about how to price *your offering* in the marketplace. In other words, you have to separate Me from Me, Inc.

The way I help myself make the shift is to think about the difference between Ronna Sue and Mrs. Lichtenberg. Ronna Sue is that wild-haired woman who sits home with her husband on Sunday nights watching *The Sopranos,* wearing a threadbare T-shirt, old sweats, and thick glasses with black rims. Mrs. Lichtenberg, on the other hand, is pulled together. She wears a suit, classy jewelry, tasteful makeup, contact lenses, and she does the best she can with her hair. Ronna Sue is Me; Mrs. Lichtenberg is Me, Inc., a part of the offering. The transformation is so complete that now on weekdays, when I walk out of our bedroom after getting dressed for work, my husband, Jimmy, will say to me, "Oh, hello, Mrs. Lichtenberg, so nice to see you again."

Everyone has to find their own way to slip into the Me, Inc. mindset before coming up with a price for their offering. But getting there is crucial. Confuse the personal with the professional on money, particularly if you already have an established relationship with the buyer, and you risk sliding down a slippery slope that may not only cost you the job at hand but the goodwill of the buyer as well.

Sheila Wellington, former president of Catalyst, the national nonprofit research and advisory organization supporting the advancement of women in business, recalls just such an outcome several years ago. At the time, she was still at Catalyst and was pricing services for a new project that the organization was undertaking. Sheila went with the lowest bidder, to the consternation of a long-time friend who was in the running. The friend called Sheila to the carpet for using another vendor and refused to speak to her. But Sheila's obligation in this situation, as head of Catalyst, was to get the best deal for her organization; if the friend had come in with a competitive bid, Sheila would have been delighted to give the nod to her. Notes Sheila, "I had to do what was right for my organization—acting otherwise would have been irresponsible."

Ronna Lichtenberg

adapt to the circumstances

Your research into going rates should not lead you to a single price for your pitch but rather to a range of prices—both a market range and a personal range, which should overlap but won't necessarily be identical. A variety of factors will determine this range and where your offering should fit within it.

Think of it like buying eggs. If I buy eggs at the deli on the corner, I pay a lot more because of convenience than if I travel farther and pick up a carton at the nearest supermarket. I'll pay even less if I make the trek to buy my eggs at a big suburban warehouse store, like BJ's or Costco. I'll pay the most for the big brown organic eggs at my favorite fancy foods store. But even so, there is an established range for eggs—I won't be charged fifty cents at one place and fifty dollars at another.

In order to determine the right rate for you within the established range for any given pitch, consider the following factors:

❧ **How much can they afford to pay?** I may be hired to give the same speech by a multinational corporation and a nonprofit organization. But, based on their ability to pay, I will charge the charity a lot less. In pricing, one size does not fit all.

❧ **What else am I getting out of the deal?** There may be nonfinancial benefits that are worth enough to you that you'll agree to a lower price. Maybe this is a charitable organization that is near and dear to your heart; maybe the job entails an easy commute; maybe you'll raise your visibility by taking on this project, which will ultimately lead to more and even better-paying work. Or maybe this gig will lead to others or extend your skills, or just be fun—there are lots of ways to receive value.

❧ **Are there mitigating circumstances?** I cut different deals, depending on a variety of factors that may make a particular job worth more or less to me. I charge more for a workshop that requires me to be out of town for three days than I would if I were giving the same workshop in New York

The Emotional Side of Stress

Janice Kiecolt-Glaser, Ph.D., did a fascinating experiment about emotions and healing with married couples at Ohio State University. She gave the couples minor skin wounds and then watched the rate at which the wounds healed. In good marriages, the women healed well. In "bad marriages," defined as a marriage in which conflict was expressed negatively, even violently, the women healed more slowly, exhibiting higher levels of stress hormones that suppressed their immune systems.

Men, interestingly enough, healed at pretty much the same rate regardless of what was going on with their wives. Good marriage or bad, their wounds healed.

Men and women release different hormones in response to specific types of events. Men who are stressed by intellectual challenges, like a school examination, secrete more adrenaline and cortisol than women do. But in men, the release of these stress hormones tends to evoke feelings of accomplishment and triumph. Women in the same situation produce lower levels of adrenaline and cortisol, but also report feelings of failure and anxiety.

A major study of response at the University of California, Los Angeles, shows that women, rather than responding in a fight-or-flight fashion when threatened, may respond with behaviors Laura Klein, Ph.D., calls "tend and befriend." In her stress research, Dr. Klein found that oxytocin, a hormone that women release during childbirth and lactation, may also be released when a woman is stressed. Oxytocin decreases anxiety and depression and promotes an affiliation or friend-seeking response in females.

If a woman is stressed, she will get a burst of the same stress hormones men do, but then she will get a shot of oxytocin. (Men may, too, but testosterone reduces the effect of oxytocin.) In a woman, estrogen enhances oxytocin's role and triggers the tend-and-befriend response. Conversely, testosterone appears to enhance the fight-or-flight response in men.

Ronna Lichtenberg

City, where I live. I will give a discount to a client with whom I do business on a regular basis but may charge more to one I've never met before and may never work with again.

❧ **What are current market conditions?** We'd like to think that once we set our price, our work is done and that will be our price forever. But economic tides ebb and flow, market conditions shift, industries thrive or falter, and you need to adapt your pricing to the changing times. I've heard women say, "I'll never work for X amount," but sometimes you need to re-think what you're willing to work for. If your industry has hit hard times, you may have to settle for less money than you're used to making. Or an important client is struggling and you have to accept a lower fee or lose the account.

Do not feel dissed when the market is not in your favor: Sometimes it isn't about you. Everything with a market price—stocks, shoes, shawls—has price fluctuations.

There will be other times when the market bounces back in your favor, when the kind of work you do is in high demand and you can once again command a premium price. Over the course of a career, if you manage the upsides to their fullest potential and position yourself in the above-market range, even in down markets, you will end up living your retirement dream and not the bag lady nightmare.

pause for an equipment check

The final step in determining your price is to consider what you think you'd be paid for the same job if you were a man.

It's a lesson that I keep learning again and again. For example, a longtime client, whom I'll call Alice, approached me about a new project. We'd been working together for some time on women's programs for her company, and I routinely discounted my usual rates because (a) the company pays me an an-nual retainer and my best and biggest customers get my best prices; (b) I felt passionate about the subject matter and the payment that I received in emotional currency made me willing to accept less in cash; and (c) I really like this woman and enjoy our working relationship. Now she wanted me to give my presentation before the whole company, men and women alike, during a big fancy offsite training session. I hadn't done this sort of event for them before, and I didn't have a clue about what their budget was or what the market price for this particular program might be. I just knew that people typically pay a lot more for a sales training program than they do for a speech, and my price needed to be higher as a result.

So I let Alice know that I'd need more money to convert my speech into a training program for their event. She said, fine, what do you want? Because I am close to her, I was able to ask for her help. Please, I asked her, find out what your company would pay for the same content and presentation if I were a guy. She laughed, and we threw around some possible numbers. She then talked to a few people in her office and came back with an amount that was double the fee I'd charged for the women-only speech.

When I coach women on salary negotiations and ask them to think about what number they'd throw out if they had different "equipment," the number is always substantially higher than the initial amount they name. Then I ask them to think about why they can't just ask for that amount. After a pause, they realize there is no good reason and they go for it. If that sounds too scary, try the same exercise, on page 217, for yourself.

DOING THE DISCOUNT

If you are like many women, you are probably so uncomfortable with the idea of yourself as an offering that you lower your own "price" before anyone else has a chance to do it for you. We communicate this discomfort through a collection of self-deprecating behaviors that serve to reduce the value of what we do or say, which ultimately results in reducing the price that buyers are willing to pay for our services. Experts call this behavior "discounting."

Ronna Lichtenberg

Price Like a Guy

Even if you think of yourself as a fully confident woman, when it comes to money, it's worth a quick check to see whether you're clear in your own mind not just about what's right, but what's possible. Before you price your offering, quickly run through the following.

Step 1: Write down the amount you intend to ask for.

Step 2: Then write down the amount of money you would ask for if you were someone else—pick a colleague or competitor.

Step 3: Now specifically think about the amount you'd request to do the same job, under the same circumstances, if you were a man.

Step 4: Compare that number to the amount you were originally going to ask for on your own behalf.

Step 5: List the reasons why you can't ask for the numbers you came up with in steps 1, 2, or 3.

Step 6: See if you can ignore them, and go for the "guy price."

Consider just a few examples of discounting language that many women use while pitching to introduce themselves and their offering:

- I know you have probably already thought of this, but . . .
- I haven't thought this out completely, but what about . . .
- You probably don't remember me, but . . .

Or consider these examples of the sentences we use to deflect possible or anticipated criticism before any has even been offered:

- Well, the idea needs a lot of work . . .
- I know So-and-So said practically the same thing . . .
- Oh, I've had this suit for *years* . . .

Or these common self-protective phrases:

- Well, I will try and see if I can do it . . .

- Well, I have never been very good at . . .

- I'm sure So-and-So could handle that just as well or better . . .

Sound familiar? In fact, we spend so much time and energy cutting down our-selves and our efforts that it's a wonder anyone pays us at all. But I'd be willing to bet that So-and-So, wherever they may be, is making a bundle.

why we discount

Women have solid reasons for indulging in discounting behavior, or so it seems. We want to avoid looking overconfident so we won't trigger those nasty who-does-she-think-she-is sentiments that pop up when women flout culturally ac-cepted norms of female modesty. Discounting also reduces our personal exposure and emotional investment in case people don't like our ideas. Our wiring leads us to take rejection harder and remember hurts longer so, in essence, we do it to ourselves before they can do it to us to lessen the potential for pain.

Then too, sometimes we discount strategically as a way to elicit support, compliments, and other emotional yummies from whomever we're dealing with. In other words, we make a negative comment about ourselves to elicit a positive rebuttal from the other side. If I moan about how fat I look in a par-ticular outfit, you're supposed to say something like, "No, you look fabu-lous—on you, wide horizontal stripes somehow have a slimming effect." Never mind that you don't necessarily believe the return comment—it's the thought that counts.

Of course, sometimes discounting is nothing more than an old habit. We've been underplaying our abilities and accomplishments routinely since we were kids. We're so used to doing it, we're not even aware of the neg-ative impact. For example, consider this e-mail, which a friend passed along:

I'm Sure I Blew That One

A study by Patrice Rosenthal, Ph.D., David Guest, and Ricardo Peccei, Ph.D., in the *Journal of Occupational and Organizational Psychology* found that women managers attribute their success significantly less strongly to ability and are readier than men are to believe that their failures result from lack of ability, as in "It wasn't really so great" about a victory and "I just wasn't good enough" regarding a failure. Think about your own life. Haven't you ever said, "I can't imagine why they would choose/select/crown me"?

Modesty is part of it. But modesty isn't the only reason women sell themselves short. At least part of it, and I'm starting to think maybe the biggest part of it, seems to be our old friend, the focus on relationship. Because women are concerned with protecting the other person's self-esteem and want to maintain some equality in the relationship, we tend to downplay our own achievements and potential. We don't want other people to hate us, so if we think we are one up, we will take ourselves down.

"Judy: below is my invoice for copyediting (please note my hourly rate will be going up to $40—a big jump, but it's been at $30/hour for more than six years. I hope you'll still want to use my services at the new rate)."

Does that message give you confidence? I didn't think so.

The negative impact of discounting can be considerable—at least as damaging to your money-making potential, in my opinion, as the workplace bias that we're apt to blame loudly for the lingering pay disparity between women and men. Because if you honestly believe the discount, other people will too—and are likely to pay you less as a result. You don't give top dollar to someone who readily admits she's not top-rate.

Even if you are just saying the discount for effect and don't really believe it, other people may believe it, with the same results. If neither side believes the discount, your remarks will come off as gratuitous, which lots of people will find just plain annoying. That's not exactly the kind of reaction that elicits the big bucks, either.

Can discounting ever be an effective tool? Yes. If you're dealing with a pink and you're doing it strategically as a way to connect and establish relationship, discounting can work in your favor. Expressions of vulnerability can be a mechanism for two pinks to bond. But engage in discounting behaviors sparingly, if at all, under other pitching circumstances. The price tag is usually just too high.

discounting versus giving a discount

On the other hand, you may have good reason on occasion to offer your prospect a discount, which is an entirely different proposition than discounting.

A discount is when you offer your prospect a price less than your normal market rate. You negotiate a lower price for a specific business reason—perhaps as a way to invest in a long-term relationship with a new client or because the buyer can't afford your usual rate and you're eager to work with them anyway. You might say, "My standard rate is $X for this type of work, but I'm willing to do this first project for less as a way for us to get started." Or, "I know you don't have the budget for my normal fee this time out, but I really believe in this project, so I'm willing to move forward for $Y."

The trick is to make the discount explicit, for solid business reasons, and confined to the specific project at hand. That's very different from cutting down your own value in your head. When you offer a discount, you can move to premium pricing later, if and when marketplace conditions change—the economy picks up, the client moves to a company with the ability to pay more, you've established the relationship and wowed them with your abilities. Essentially, you position the discount as a gift.

But you can rarely, if ever, move from discounting to premium pricing. Once you've convinced them through your actions that you are worth less, you are likely to seem worth less to them forever.

ESTABLISHING A PREMIUM BRAND

The goal is to substitute a "premium pricing" framework for the discounting habit.

How can we communicate that we believe we are a premium brand without invoking all those icky feelings women traditionally have about money issues, without appearing immodest or to be putting our own needs first, to engage in an equal energy exchange instead of one-upmanship? The setup is always the bank shot I talked about on page 89.

The financial equivalent is to focus on what you can achieve for your buyer with your offering. For women, premium pricing should always be about convincing them that you can help them with their needs better, faster, more easily than anyone else.

So premium pricing is . . . "I know you need this quickly; is tomorrow morning fast enough?" Or, "I know this project requires that kind of industry experience; since I worked at Whatsit Corporation, I have a deeper understanding of the issues than anyone else would." Or, and this works especially well if you're dealing with someone in a big company, "I know you need someone on your team who backs you up; I am really impressed with where you're going here and totally support what you're trying to do."

Do you really state your reasons this starkly? Of course not. It takes finesse and technique to sink a bank shot. This is the right concept, however, as is the notion that you must make the benefit you bring and the added value very, very clear. (For more tips about how to convey you are a premium brand, see the box on page 222.)

Premium Pricing

To add value to whatever you are promoting/selling/tooting, focus on these ABCs.

Appearance: People pay more for something that looks good.

❖ Dress/groom appropriately for the situation.

❖ Dress your idea appropriately (good grammar, typing, paper, handouts, copies, printing, etc.).

❖ Make the product, even a prototype, high quality.

Benefit: People value, and therefore pay more for, what fits their needs.

❖ Do your homework; learn all you can about the situation, people, and business you are approaching.

❖ Look for what in your experience is common to (not exactly the same as) the current situation.

❖ Focus on the other's needs, reactions, etc.

Clarity: People like you to be clear, concise, and specific about the value you add.

❖ Identify your strengths and be able to state them succinctly, with relevance.

❖ Don't volunteer your weaknesses, but know them and be prepared to share the least threatening if needed.

❖ Be selective in what you premium price.

the risks of premium pricing

You can't expect a premium every time. Be selective about what, when, and why you charge a premium.

First things first: You have to tell the truth. If you cannot deliver on the promise of why you deserve a premium, your reputation takes a big hit.

Then too, sometimes charging a premium will damage the relationship. Now this is a tricky one for most women because we're all about the relationship, and we're always worrying about potential stressors to the relationship and trying to avoid conflict. So how do you know when pushing for a premium really will damage the relationship and when it's just in your head?

Use your color prism. If you're dealing with a blue, you will not—*cannot*—damage the relationship by talking about money because blues don't play by those rules. As long as you stay with marketplace language and don't verbalize the mental calculations you may be doing about emotional currency, you can disagree with a blue about the financial outcome and even have some conflict around money without destroying the relationship. To ensure a happy ending, go out for a beer together (or another social equivalent) after the negotiations are over. If nothing else, it will make you feel better.

If you are blue and your prospect is pink, on the other hand, you can inadvertently do damage to the relationship because you may not be adequately taking that second currency into account. Meanwhile, if it's a pink-on-pink negotiation, you can both get so wrapped up in connection currency that you never quite make it to marketplace.

In both circumstances, the solution is to stop dealing in unspoken assumptions about money and let the other person in on how you're thinking about the financial end of the offering and why. You need to look at the conversation as a way of honoring the relationship, not undermining it—you respect the person and the project enough to engage in a real dialogue about price and to think through both currencies in a thoughtful and conscious way.

Watch out for this tendency to play both sides of the net and avoid taking on too much emotional responsibility for what the people on the other side of the table are thinking. We think, "Oh, she's looking unhappy, I'd better not ask for more money, or back off from my request." But what if she's looking strained just because she neglected to eat fiber for breakfast? Do not assume that you know what they want and what's best for them without letting them actually engage with you in working out the details.

count on negotiating

Research shows that women are far less likely than men to negotiate financial compensation. In a study of recent Carnegie Mellon graduates with master's degrees, Linda Babcock, Ph.D., an economics professor at the university, found that only 7 percent of the women had negotiated their salaries, compared with 57 percent of the men. Similarly, a 2003 study of business students by Lisa Barron, Ph.D., an assistant professor of organizational behavior in the Graduate School of Management at the University of California, Irvine, found that 85 percent of the men, but only 17 percent of the women, felt it was up to them to make sure their employer paid them what they were worth. The rest felt that their value would be determined by whatever the company paid them.

It should come as no surprise that we mostly accept the money that we are offered without pressing for more. What may be eye opening, however, is the financial damage we do to ourselves as a result. In the Carnegie Mellon study, for example, the graduates who negotiated their salaries were able to raise their compensation by about $4,000. This amount, coincidentally, just happened to be the average difference between the men's and women's starting salaries. The implication, according to a *New York Times* interview with Sara Laschever, who coauthored a book with Dr. Babcock: "Women might have closed or approached closing the gender gap if they had negotiated."

The question, then, is not whether you should negotiate, but how you can negotiate in a way that is both comfortable and smart.

convince yourself you're deserving

Start in your own head. To negotiate effectively, you have to believe you're worth the premium you seek. This is tough for many women, because of both our culturally supported tendencies toward modesty and our inclination to engage in an equal energy exchange. Men, on the other hand, typically seek to be one up. Ask a guy how much he wants to be paid and he'll answer, "As much as I can." Ask a woman and she'll acknowledge the market range, then

Ronna Lichtenberg

give you fifty reasons why she cannot be in the top of that range but should fall somewhere around the midpoint.

The research supports this too: In the UC Irvine study, for instance, some 70 percent of the men said they believed they were entitled to a higher salary than other applicants, while the same number of women indicated that they were entitled to the same compensation as other candidates for the job.

The first pitch you need to toss, then, is to yourself. You need to convince yourself that you deserve a premium. Here is where the bank shot we talked about earlier comes in handy. You not only have to sell your prospect on the benefit you're offering, you need to sell yourself on that notion as well, and the way to do that is to focus on how much you can help them. High-powered attorney Judy Fryer, who is a principal shareholder at one of New York's most prestigious law firms and bills at a rate commensurate with that position, uses this technique routinely. Judy puts it this way: "The key is to really believe you can add value to something, someone, some process. If I believe I can really help, I don't feel dirty, I don't feel like I'm misleading anyone, I don't feel as if anyone is doing me a favor. I feel perfectly okay."

This involves a certain amount of mental cheerleading on your own behalf, to do whatever you need to do in your head to imagine yourself as a person who can make and deserves the amount in question.

One of my favorite stories about this kind of self-motivation involves actor Jim Carrey. Urban legend has it that when the rubber-faced star was just starting out and working menial low-paying jobs to support himself while he sought roles, he wrote himself a check for $1 million. He carried that check around with him at all times, looking at it as the spirit moved him, to help frame his expectations of himself and get used to thinking of himself as an actor of great value. As it turned out, what must have seemed like a ridiculously grandiose dream at the time was in fact low-balling it. The actor now nabs a cool $20 million per movie.

Take a cue from Carrey: Allow yourself to imagine, really imagine, the financial possibilities. Then give yourself permission to believe you deserve them.

connect the dots

One technique that I've found helpful when negotiating compensation is to think of the process in visual terms.

Imagine a horizontal line, with the market low price on the left, the peak price on the right, and a vertical line in the center representing midrange. In any given money pitch, you need to figure out where to place the dot that represents the amount you think you should be paid and make an educated guess about where your prospective buyer will place their dot and why. Then think about ways to close the gap.

Here's how the process usually works: Women place their dot at or somewhat under midrange. They imagine the prospect will place their dot somewhat below that point. Then, before the negotiations even start, women try to move their dot closer to where they think the prospect's will be, to avoid appearing big-headed and reduce the possibility of conflict.

In Ronna's alternate and newly improved universe, the process ought instead to go like this: You place your dot. You then think about why you really deserve premium rather than average pricing and move your dot to a more appropriate location, farther up the market range line. Next, you imagine where your prospect will put their dot. You then think about ways to get your prospect to move their dot closer to yours.

Get that crucial distinction? The goal is to get them to move their dot first, not the other way around. In the end, you may indeed need or choose to move. But your first thought should be about moving them. That's the purpose of pitching.

FURTHER UPPING THE ANTE

Okay, so you've established yourself as a premium brand. What else can you do to ensure you get the best money deal possible?

get the timing right

The best time to ask for money—a raise, a higher fee, a bigger budget—is just after you've delivered for your buyer. When you just went out and slew Goliath, that's a money moment. Let them savor the success briefly, then say something like, "I loved doing that for you, I can't wait to do more. Let's talk about what would make me feel *really* good. . . . "

Sometimes you can't choose the timing; the timing chooses you. If the timing is bad but there was nothing you could do to alter the events—say, you're up for your annual raise just as your company loses its biggest client or has announced a new wave of layoffs—don't make yourself crazy with what-ifs. Just negotiate the best deal you can under the circumstances and mentally move on.

You can pitch an individual when the company is in a bad situation, but you should lower your expectations. This is not the time you are going to do your best deal ever, and more often than not, it's not even a time when you can make a deal.

Corporate communications expert Mary Taylor recalls a time several years ago when she was negotiating with a prospective new employer while halfway through a two-year severance package from a former employer. The terms of her buyout stipulated that she'd lose the second year of compensation if she took a full-time job with a new company. So Mary worked out a deal with the new employer to work as a part-time consultant rather than join the staff full-time for the first year. They offered her an office and secretary, worked out a mutually acceptable reduced day rate, and indicated they'd hire her at the going rate for people in her position when her last year of severance was up.

By the end of the following year, however, market conditions had changed dramatically. The industry was laying off people, not hiring them. While the company still wanted Mary on board, the compensation offer dropped by $60,000 a year. Notes Mary, "This wasn't a case of, 'you're not so valuable anymore,' it was a case of the market telling them they simply didn't have to pay so much anymore." Mary stayed, but only long enough for the market to move back in her favor.

go to your me, inc. board

Sometimes the easiest way to get more money is to have someone else act unofficially as your agent and pitch on your behalf. Or, as Mary replied when I asked her how she'd advise other women to press for a raise, "You need satisfied customers to go to bat for you."

My consulting business has been built on women referring me to other women, and providing enthusiastic endorsements at that. When I went out on my speaking tour for my last book, I sent e-mails to people I knew in each of the cities I planned to visit, asking them who they knew who could help me drum up business. It was a girlfriend brigade. They delivered and the tour was a success.

This is a strategy in which women have a huge advantage. Because while women may have trouble asking for money, men have even greater problems asking for help. I can say to a good friend or associate, "Do you know anybody who could use somebody?" without losing face. Men typically feel they cannot.

GETTING TO YES ON MONEY

I've said it already, but it bears repeating: The single most important step you can take to get the compensation you deserve is to convince yourself of the value of your offering, which will empower you emotionally to negotiate from a position of strength, and then to make that value clear and visible to the other party.

Recapping the rest: Know the marketplace range for compensation, understand where you fit in that range and why, and take economic conditions and special circumstances into account to arrive at a figure that seems reasonable. Think about the financial trade-offs you'd be willing to accept for greater emotional satisfaction, and vice versa. Pledge to give up discounting behaviors before they drag down your prices, and wrap yourself instead in premium packaging (more on precisely how to do that in the next chapter). Be realistic about the numbers and never, ever confuse the price of your pitch with your own self-worth.

If you'd like to read more about specific negotiating techniques, I highly

Ronna Lichtenberg

recommend the work of Deborah Kolb, Ph.D., professor of management at the Simmons School of Management, founder of its Center for Gender in Organizations, and senior fellow and former executive director of Harvard Law School's Program on Negotiation. (How's that for some impressive credentials?) Dr. Kolb's specialty is looking at negotiation through a gender lens. In her book *Everyday Negotiation,* cowritten with Judith Williams, Ph.D., Dr. Kolb lays out some valuable bargaining strategies for women, including ways to overcome the negativity, doubt, and acts of self-sabotage that threaten to defeat us before the people we're dealing with have even uttered a word.

When self-doubt takes over, Dr. Kolb advises that you step back, take stock, and assess the personal resources you can call on to shore up your position. She suggests you ask yourself four questions (the side commentary is mine):

1. *Why is the other person negotiating with you?*

   In other words, what do you have that they need? This is the kind of benefit thinking at which women excel and is at the core of determining the financial value of your offering.

2. *What happens when you have been successful in a negotiation?*

   Try applying the techniques that have worked for you when you were negotiating money in the past to the situation at hand.

3. *What do you know about the other party and the situation?*

   Use the research you've gathered to tailor your pitch to the prospect. As I've previously noted, people pay more for goods and services that meet their needs precisely. Finding out how much the buyer typically pays for what you're offering can also help you put together a realistic pricing structure.

4. *What about the current situation makes you feel vulnerable?*

   Dr. Kolb notes, "Once you understand what trips you up, you can figure out what you need to do to compensate."

accentuate the positive

But my favorite Deborah Kolb technique is one that she calls "always say yes." The strategy is to identify what would constitute a wholehearted yes on your prospect's part. Essentially, you leave it up to the other person to meet the conditions, negotiate, or withdraw their offer. The idea is that you can as easily lay out your negotiating demands with a yes as with a no, and yes is infinitely more effective.

Here's a sample: Yes, I'd be happy to take on this project, for this amount of money. Yes, I can accept that salary, as long as I can work from home two days a week. Yes, I can deliver on sales, with the right budget behind me. Yes, yes, yes.

The strategy is not unlike the way that child development experts suggest parents deal with a youngster's demands. It's morning and the child wants cake for breakfast. The resourceful mom replies, "Yes, you can have a small slice of cake after dinner tonight. Now how about some cereal?" Or he whines and begs for a toy while shopping for a friend's birthday present. Mom says, "Yes, you absolutely can get that computer game for your birthday, which is coming up soon. Let's put it on your list."

The beauty of yes is that it forces you to clearly articulate what both parties need to make the working relationship work. In effect, you are saying to your buyer, "Here's my understanding of what you need, and under these circumstances, here's what I can give you." Framing it as *yes* indicates a willingness to work together toward a mutually acceptable goal and respect for the other's position.

By the way, this is completely consistent with knowing where your no is. If you don't understand what your boundaries are, or what you won't do, then you don't understand where your yes is, either.

So now you know what you're going to offer, to whom, and for how much. The next stage, packaging, is about how to make sure your offering is as appealing as it can possibly be.

CHAPTER 10
packaging the pitch

One way to enhance our chances of getting a premium price is to premium package our offering—that is, to add value to our pitch by presenting ourselves and our ideas in the best possible light. It is a simple yet steadfast rule: People pay more, and say yes more readily, for something and someone that looks good.

You should not only dress well yourself, but dress your ideas well too. This may sound like a "duh"—of course, you try to put your best foot forward—but, in fact, most of us find this proposition more challenging in practice than it sounds in theory. When it actually comes time to put ourselves out there, those old cultural stereotypes that tell us to present ourselves modestly and underplay our abilities reach out to pull us back. Yet showing other people the most flattering view of yourself and your ideas is every bit as "legitimate" as leading with your flaws.

The key to premium packaging is not to go out and buy yourself a couple of expensive work outfits that you think make you look good. The key is to think about what will make you and your offering look good to *them*. And not just in terms of the physical way you dress and present your offering, but in terms of your demeanor, the methods you use to help them understand and process information, the way you honor and respect the way they prefer to do business. You adapt to their needs in the workplace rather than inadvertently pressing them to see the world your way. And in so doing, you make it infinitely easier for them to fulfill your needs, too.

I call this process "style sync." Practicing it is part of the essence of pitching like a girl and puts you a giant step closer to winning at work while being who you are.

UNDERSTANDING STYLE SYNC

The concept of style sync is simple: The more comfortable someone feels around you, the likelier it is for them to say yes to your pitch. The goal is to make it as easy as possible for your prospect to support you, and a great deal of that work involves eliminating impediments. *Everything you do that doesn't fit with their style means they have to do more work to see the benefit you can bring to them. The more work they have to do, the less likely they are to do it.*

The process is akin to traveling in a foreign country where you do your best to respect the local customs. You don't want to walk into the Vatican wearing short shorts and a bikini top, smacking a giant wad of bubble gum. You don't want to walk into a pitch looking and acting like the business equivalent.

When you style sync, you demonstrate in yet another way that you care about the relationship in a way that makes the other party happy to do business with you. Just think about your own shopping experiences. If you go to a store and the person waiting on you is nasty or vaguely insulting or pushes you to make a quick purchase when you're in the mood to linger and explore the possibilities, you think to yourself, "Not only do I not have to buy this from you, I don't have to buy anything from you," and you leave without making the purchase. You may also mentally vow never to come back.

Same thing with pitching.

Not bothering to adapt at least somewhat to your prospects' style means you are pushing your style on them, which is really a form of arrogance. Of course, we usually don't see it that way. Instead we tend to go into victim head. Why don't they want to talk about their feelings? Why can't they read what's going on with

Ronna Lichtenberg

me? We have a mental list of the way they should be and how they should behave, and what it boils down to is that we want them to be more like us.

Well, that's being just as chauvinistic about style as we think men are. And it certainly won't get you where you want to go. For one thing, the brain sex research tells us that men aren't wired to behave like us; they don't even know how to behave the way we want them to behave because they are biologically built to function in a very different way than we are. As Ruben Gur, Ph.D., at the University of Pennsylvania, points out, "Men and women may be speaking on the same topics, but the context from which they are coming can be drastically different."

So lose the resentment. The answer to why can't they be more like us is, they can't. Sure, men can adapt just as we can adapt. But they are more likely to adapt if we pitch them to adapt than they are if we try to mandate it.

what really stops us

Perhaps the most important reason that so many women have difficulty with the idea of adapting their style to the needs of others in the workplace is that we fear we will somehow lose ourselves in the process. We risk authenticity. We hold being true to ourselves as a core value, and because of that, we find it hard to experiment with style. We think that by doing so we will somehow betray our true and deepest self.

Men do not seem to have this problem. Maybe they're okay with the notion of experimenting with style because the business world is their world—they've been in it longer, they set the rules, they feel more comfortable. They are making adaptations within their natural habitat, not trying to adapt to what can still seem at times like an alien universe.

Research by Herminia Ibarra, Ph.D., formerly of the Harvard Business School and currently professor of organizational behavior at the global business school INSEAD, supports the notion that, in their initial dealings with clients, men focus their energies on adaptive behaviors that increase the likelihood that those clients will approve of them. When faced with new business situations or prospects, men tend to feign or exaggerate confidence (no surprise there) and imitate the style of senior people in the room to tide themselves over until they find a professional style of their own that feels right in the situation. Women, on the other hand, try to make image and style a non-issue and base their credibility on technical competence. Our strategy is to work harder and be even more meticulous in our efforts so that the work alone will speak for itself.

You cannot, however, just ignore the issue of professional image and style and hope to pitch effectively. This is particularly true in the initial stages of a business interaction, when your prospects have no hard evidence yet of how you will perform. It is human nature to make a preliminary judgment based on image and first impressions—we do it, why shouldn't our prospects? The challenge then is to figure out how to be effective (that is, how to adapt to their style) and authentic at the same time.

Dr. Ibarra puts it this way: "You can't just say, 'I have to be me,' and that's it. You need to think, 'I have to be me' in a broader way. Acknowledge that there are things you have to learn that are not going to feel authentic because you have never done them before. Then worry later about how you convey more of who you really are."

In other words, you do not have to lose your core self in order to style sync. You do not have to walk into your office, act like a man for nine hours, then go home and be a woman again. We're talking about small adjustments here, relatively superficial changes, not because your natural style is somehow lesser, but because you consciously choose to make small modifications on behalf of your Me, Inc. offering. There is a vast difference between saying, "I need to be someone else," and saying, "I need to do something else in this moment because that is better for me and for them in the long run."

Jennifer Buchholz, at GE Consumer Finance, adapts her style to the very different people she works with all day long and says she loves watching them light up when she essentially chooses to speak their language. It makes connection possible. "This is the kind of change that is about seventeen layers more superficial than changing the essential female energy that makes us who we are and should be honored at all times." Jenn notes, "It's not changing who

Ronna Lichtenberg

you are, it's [akin to] changing the pocketbook or shoes to go with the outfit. It's like changing the bag from black to brown, if you know they prefer brown. That's fine, because surely you can find a brown bag that you like."

MASTERING STYLE SYNC

So now that I've hopefully helped you overcome your resistance to style sync, you need to learn how to do it effectively. There are actually two parts to style sync. One is learning how the people you're interacting with dress and customarily do business. The other is learning about and adapting to how they like to process information and handle emotional content at work.

In any potential pitching situation, you check two dials for style sync: You consider whether they're empathizers or systemizers for a fix on the culture they work in; and you check their color, pink or blue, for their emotional style and a hint as to how they might think and like to process information.

You don't have to style sync every minute that you are pitching. Focus on adapting your style during the opening phase of your pitch, when you are introducing the offering and credentialing yourself. This gets your prospect in the right frame of mind—read, most receptive—to hear what you have to say. Style sync is also crucial during formal presentations and when you close, so that your last impression reflects how easy it will be to do business together.

adapting your communication style

Think first about the medium you'll use to communicate. Should you send your prospect an e-mail, call on the phone, or meet face-to-face? If you choose a meeting, should it be casual or formal, one-on-one, or a larger group gathering? Although sometimes these decisions are not within your control, often they are. When that's the case, you'll be infinitely more effective if you let style sync guide your choices.

As a general rule, if your prospects are pink, you'll do better by emphasizing the more personal methods of communicating. In person is better than by

A Style Sync Checklist

Learning how to sync up to another person's style can take a little while and feel awkward at first. Eventually you'll be able to calibrate and adjust for style differences in a nanosecond. But for now, you might want to start with the following as a checklist to use pre-pitch.

1. Ask yourself, "Is my prospect pink or blue?" Write down one or two style adaptations you can make while you pitch to accommodate your buyer's color.

2. Ask yourself, "Am I dealing with a systemizing or an empathizing culture?" Write down any style changes you can make to adapt to the culture of the company or organization your prospect represents.

3. Look back over the suggestions you've written to determine which of the two dials seems most important to check in the pitching situation at hand and whether there are any additional modifications you should make to synchronize style in that area.

phone, which is better than sending an e-mail. Pinks are almost always happy to be asked to breakfast, lunch, dinner, or coffee. Blues are probably not. Blues want to focus on one objective at a time; don't let a nice grilled salmon or plate of tasty pasta distract them from your business offering. Then too, blues, particularly blues in systemizing cultures, probably feel some time pressure. They want you to get to the point, make the point, and move on from the point in the shortest time possible. Sharing a meal makes that impossible.

Also look at the cultural norms within your prospect's organization for clues about how information is routinely processed. In some cultures, meetings are the accepted way of doing business, with agendas and formal presentations. Some want ideas in writing and other backup documentation, some don't. If you're unfamiliar with the rules of a particular culture or the way a particular prospect likes to get information, ask. Would you like me to give you something in writing? Should we schedule a formal presentation? How do you prefer to do business? Asking about their preferences signals that you are putting their needs first and foremost. If you demonstrate in these initial stages that you are paying close attention to their needs, you indicate that you will be similarly attentive during the course of your business dealings together.

Mary Carol Garrity, owner of the home decorating emporium Nell Hill's, routinely practices this kind of attentiveness to style preferences with her clientele. Nell Hill's is located in Atchison, Kansas, some distance away from big-city shopping centers, and Mary Carol knows her customers don't just drive by, spot the store, and stop in on a whim. Nell Hill's is a destination. People have to go out of their way to get there, so Mary Carol goes out of her way to give them a shopping experience to remember.

Nell Hill's customers fall into two basic categories, Mary Carol says: working women who are pressured for time and need help getting their house together, and women who do not hold a job outside of their home and are simply looking for a pleasurable shopping experience. The Nell Hill's staff make it their business—quite literally—to find out which category each shopper falls into and adapt their pitch to her needs. They'll visit with the customer awhile, asking some leading questions about her shopping needs and goals. For the working woman, they'll then set out to make the decorating experience simple, removing a possible source of stress in an already stressful life by streamlining the process and guiding her choices. For the homemaker, they'll strive to make her time at Nell's entertaining, with a leisurely and playful look at the possibilities.

This keen attention to style preferences, I'm convinced, has contributed mightily to the store's success: Ninety-five percent of the people who visit Nell Hill's travel more than fifty miles to get there. Sure, the merchandise is charming. But it is the personalized service, particularly the attention paid to the shopping-style preferences of its customers, that really sets the store apart.

premium package the presentation

We'll talk more about effective ways to style sync while you're delivering your pitch in the next chapter. For now, let's concentrate on the outermost layer: how to use what you know about stylistic differences to help guide the way you physically present your offering and dress up that package to its best effect.

Once again, you're going to want to check those dials. The first assessment is what kind of culture you're dealing with. Say you're making a formal presentation and you've determined that you're pitching to systemizers. You know you're dealing with people who think analytically, who are used to developing constructs to make sense of ideas and the world around them. This suggests you should include some visuals: charts, tables, graphs, and models, packed with relevant data, as appropriate. These also work well if you're pitching to blues (who are likely to be the main audience in a systemizing culture), with their penchant for numbers and symbols.

If you're instead presenting to a group of empathizers, your visuals should be more people oriented, with photos and illustrations that humanize the abstract points you're trying to make. Try that with a bunch of systemizers and you will have lost half the battle before you've really begun.

I vividly remember seeing a death by visuals incident a few years back when observing the newly appointed female head of consumer affairs for an insurance trade association give her first presentation to the board. The woman had recently been recruited from the television industry and was smart, on the ball, and very creative—a little too creative for the situation, as it turned out. To illustrate the points she wanted to make about consumer affairs, she had had clay figures made and photographed in poses depicting the human issues that insurance consumers face, almost like an early version of Claymation. But her audience was made up of CEOs of life insurance companies, most of whom had achieved their positions because they were the smartest actuaries in the West. Talk about a room full of systemizers. They didn't hate the woman's presentation, they were just totally and utterly bewildered by it; they didn't have a clue what she was talking about. They found her efforts mildly charming, but didn't take her recommendations seriously.

In fact, they never took her seriously, although they should have. And that's what you get when you go into a roomful of systemizing actuaries

Ronna Lichtenberg

with Claymation figures: You become a decoration instead of a decision-maker.

The very same presentation, mind you, would have been brilliant before an audience of pink empathizers, who would have immediately gotten and appreciated the main message: that insurance speaks to a deep emotional need to take care of the ones you love most.

In general, overly creative and clever visuals do not go over well with systemizers or blues, both of whom like their pitches straight up, no rocks, please. They want to be able to focus single-mindedly on the central concept or the goal because that's the way their brains most comfortably work. The rest is just a distraction.

Similarly, avoid excessive use of color or subtle shades that men may simply not be able to perceive. Women have an enhanced ability to discriminate among colors. The retina at the back of the eyeball has about 130 million photoreceptor, rod-shaped cells to deal with black and white and 7 million cone-shaped cells to handle color. Color cells are on the X chromosome. Since women have two X chromosomes and men only have one, women get a greater variety of cones. For example, we see magenta; men see red. For a straight guy, it is almost a matter of pride not to know what, say, celadon is. (A gay man might instead say, "Oh, Ronna, celadon is so last year.")

PERSONAL PACKAGING

Deciding which colors to use in your PowerPoint presentation may seem like a trivial matter. But it is a series of seemingly small choices like these that sends powerful signals to your prospects about who you are and how comfortable they'll feel about doing business with you.

Consider the message in the bold color that Alexandra Lebenthal chose to wear to a recent board meeting of a major trade association. Alex, as you may know from her TV spots, is president and CEO of Lebenthal, an AXA Financial business and full service brokerage firm that specializes in municipal bond sales. Going to the board meeting, Alex knew that she would be the only woman in a room full of high-powered men, and that most of those guys would be dressed conservatively in the high-powered man uniform of a well-cut navy blue suit, white shirt, brightly colored tie, and expensive shoes and watch. She could have gone for the female version of that uniform—say, a gray Armani suit and small, tasteful earrings—which would allow her to blend in. Or she could have gone for what she did: her favorite power suit in bright orange, with a long jacket and big, gold jewelry.

Needless to say, Alex stood out.

What exactly was Alex trying to say with this choice of outfit? The message was simple yet powerful: *Here I am, deal with it.* Her goal was to let them know she was confident, because it takes courage to wear a color that bold. She was saying, "I refuse to blend in just because I am a woman, I am not afraid of you." And she was saying it loudly. As the doorman in an Atlanta hotel put it one day when I stepped out in a high impact outfit of my own, "Girl, you are making a lot of noise." I decided to take it as a compliment.

How you dress for pitching is not all that different from how you wrap a present. If I receive a gift that is wrapped in brown paper with Japanese calligraphy, I get a different feeling about the giver than if the present is wrapped in glossy paper with a premade bow or has a loving, handmade look with ends that don't quite meet. You are, in effect, a present to someone else; how you are dressed is the wrapping that gives that person a clue about what's inside the package.

Consider now the very different impact of my own choice of clothing for an appearance several years ago on the television game show *To Tell the Truth.* The 1960s game show had been revived for syndication, and a panel of celebrity judges had to guess which of three contestants was a corporate warrior who had written a book about office politics named, you guessed it, Ronna Lichtenberg. The goal was to stump the panel, who would get to ask each of the contestants pointed questions to determine who was the real Ronna. My two cohorts, with whom I had instantly bonded, stood to win $7,500 if the panel couldn't figure out the truth. We really wanted to win.

So contestant No. 1, a housewife, showed up in a black suit, serious makeup, big hair, and came across as very tough. Contestant No. 2, a singer who worked temp jobs, also dressed in a dark suit with a demeanor so serious that she almost seemed humorless. And then there was me, in a light-blue pants suit with soft lines, weekend makeup, no earrings, and a style that was relaxed and funny.

Not a single one of the celebrities ended up picking me to be me. In fact, they were so shocked and horrified at my true identity—one panelist told me I looked like a grade-school principal—that I was embarrassed to have fooled them so well. But we did win all the money, which was great, and mostly made up for what was in retrospect just a small humiliation, really. (Don't even try to find the tape: I've destroyed them all.)

the messages our clothes send

Alex Lebenthal knows it. My fellow game-show contestants knew it, and, if you didn't know it before, you know it now, too: The clothes we choose to wear speak volumes about how we want to be perceived in the workplace, how we perceive ourselves, and ultimately, how successful our pitching efforts will be.

Here are a couple of rules that will help you make this basic truth work for you.

Dress for Your Client

Once again, this means taking style sync into account. If I am dressing for a speaking engagement, for instance, I will first consider the culture of the place. If it is a high systemizing culture, filled with blues, I know they will be more formal than my usual style and tuned in to expressions of authority. So I will dress formally, too, which means (among other things) being literally more buttoned up—I will button one more button on my blouse than I would if I were speaking to a group of, say, marketers, who are more likely to be empathizers, and pink empathizers at that. High contrast (dark suit/light shirt) goes over well with blues, too.

Dress for the Situation

In a Full Frontal pitch, for example, the way you use authority markers in dress and jewelry matters a lot. Sometimes it only takes one stylistic mistake, in which you show up in an outfit ill suited to the occasion, to do you in. I learned this rule the hard way during my sixth and, as it happened, last appearance on *Weekend Today* a few years ago.

Dressing for television is all about simple lines and clean cuts, which is the formula I'd followed for each of my previous appearances talking about work and work-life issues. The producers seemed very happy with me, and by the time Appearance No. 6 rolled around, I guess I was feeling my oats. I was convinced by a well-meaning designer friend to show up in a very expensive pale green tweed suit with pink and blue threads. The material was so heavy that I immediately looked twenty pounds heavier instead of the usual ten that the camera supposedly adds. But the worst part about the suit, in retrospect, was the hanging threads on the collar and cuffs, which would now be considered quite fashionable but then made the outfit look frayed.

When I walked out of the house that morning, my husband, Jimmy, said to me, "You know, your suit looks a lot like grass." That should have been my first clue that something was amiss with my outfit, but I was convinced that Jimmy just wasn't as fashion-savvy as my designer friend. After my segment ended, one of the producers said to me, "That's a very interesting suit." I knew in an instant I was done. One thing you don't want your prospect saying to you is how interesting you look. What was called for in this situation—an appearance on a TV news show, specifically talking about business on a TV news show—was a businesslike look, with the authority markers to show for it. I looked too trendy, too tubby, and too unlike the viewer's image of what a smart businesswoman should look like. The suit was a distraction from the message I was trying to deliver.

Style Watch

Part One: What Their Clothes Say

Step 1: With a notepad in hand, randomly pick out women on the street or in the lobby as they make their way to work in the morning, and jot down the details of their outfits: clothes (style, cut, and color), jewelry, handbag, briefcase, shoes, hairstyle—the works.

Step 2: Note your impression of the message these women are sending with their outfits. What does her package say?

Step 3: Share the details of each outfit with a friend or colleague, and ask them for their impression of the message each woman was sending.

Step 4: Compare notes. Pay particular attention to the details of outfits that send the kind of message you'd like to send, and why and how they accomplish that goal.

Part Two: What Your Clothes Say

Step 1: Make an appointment at a major department store with their resident personal shopper. (This is typically a free—yes, *free*—albeit underutilized, service.)

Step 2: Go dressed as you normally dress for work, and ask the shopper, "What does my outfit say to you?"

Step 3: Ask the shopper, "If I want to send [fill in the blank] message instead, what would be the most important detail for me to change?"

Step 4: Have the shopper show you outfits and/or accessories that fit the bill. If you agree, buy at least one of the items, as an investment in your professional future. If you don't agree, try another store.

Of course, I haven't been asked back to that show since, although maybe some pink producer will read this and decide to give me another shot.

find the right authority markers

The best way for women to communicate authority and power in dress is through the use of color, fit, and accessories.

The younger you are, the less experienced you are, and/or the prettier you are, the more you need to go for authority and status markers in the way you put yourself together. If you are pretty and pitching to men, you already derive a certain kind of power from your looks; you don't have to work that anymore. You do not want your outer package to distract their wired-for-sex, single-focused minds from the business package you're offering. If you are pitching to women, you don't want them to think you are leaning on your looks; they'll know it and resent it. The message you really want to communicate is this: I want to be taken seriously.

On the other hand, if you are a blue woman and your natural style communicates hyperauthority—short hair, no makeup, severe pantsuits, dark colors, sensible shoes—think about softening the look. If you out-blue the blues with too many authority markers at once, you end up looking like a woman business soldier and risk frightening your prospects by bucking too many feminine social and cultural stereotypes at once.

A woman can act exactly the same way a man does and get punished for it. Actually, there is some chance that a woman with "masculine" behaviors experiences even more backlash in workplaces that are less macho and more consensual. Laurie Rudman, Ph.D., at Rutgers, found that women who seemed to present with male behaviors (and who we would call blue) were *particularly* likely to be discriminated against when the management position was feminized, that is, included relationship abilities. In other words, blue women were considered great when the job was about task; when it was about people, they faced the possibility of backlash.

But you don't have to change much, just a detail or two. Maybe you put on slightly higher heels and some lip gloss or a nice pair of earrings. If you feel uncomfortable with classic femininity markers, think about accomplishing the same goal with your communication style, particularly if you're dealing with pink or striped prospects. Look to establish some connection—add a small personal comment in your e-mail, ask how their weekend went, what's up with the kids, just something to put them at their ease.

Here are a few other pointers I've picked up along the way.

Ronna Lichtenberg

Jewelry: The Pretty Way to Say Money

You do not need to spend a fortune on jewelry, but you should invest in at least one pair of signature earrings that broadcasts to anyone watching that you are a person of status. I wear the same diamond studs almost every workday because they are appropriate for just about any professional situation and say to the world, "I am Mrs. Lichtenberg—a professional woman of some accomplishment and a force to be reckoned with." On the weekends, when I turn back into Ronna Sue, I favor a pair of gigantic wire hoops I picked up at a flea market for $1.50. They say, "Let's hang out—I'm ready to have some fun." Just changing the earrings changes the message.

The right necklace can accomplish much the same goal. So can an expensive, tasteful watch. Rings are another matter. You cannot win with rings—you can only lose, either by wearing too many, or wearing one that is so big it is garish, or wearing one on some body part other than your finger.

Short Hair Versus More Hair

Hair is the battleground upon which many of the wars between perceived femininity and perceived authority are fought. Is your hair short? Lacquered into place? Unless it's spiked and worn with a tongue stud, it probably looks more authoritative. Long, tumbling, highlighted blonde curls? More feminine, less authoritative.

You probably know which way your hair "reads" and are basically okay with that. Just consider, if it "reads" strongly in one direction or another, balancing that message with the rest of how you present yourself. A high contrast tailored suit balances the curls; pretty earrings and a little more eye makeup balances the short hair.

Hair color makes a big statement if it's one you've adopted and not your biological baby. The more distant the relationship between your natural roots and adoptive color, the more reaction you'll get. Whatever color you choose, avoid excessive roots unless you're in an '80s Madonna wannabe mode, and never wannabe taken seriously.

Being personally hair challenged, I only have two more pieces of advice about hair.

In a high systemizing culture, make sure your hair looks under control. Get a leash for that puppy, be it head bands, clips, or superglue. Whatever you do, no gently drifting tendrils, Rapunzel, which means no alligator clips to *mostly* put up your long hair unless you have a few more combs stuck in there, too.

Everyone knows better than to change hair styles all the time, unless you're in the fashion and beauty business. But do change styles when you're ready for a promotion, new opportunity, new kind of gig. Under those circumstances, having people think "there's something different about her" is a good thing.

Color Me Important

Few people can pull off an orange power suit the way Alex Lebenthal can. The more color you use, the more risk you are taking by calling attention to yourself. When you say, "look at me, look at me" in the loud voice of color, you must have the business chops to deliver. Go for a brightly colored accent piece, such as a shell or scarf, to express the same message.

Some people like to add color with tattoos. I'd recommend that if you've never seen a woman in your business who's senior to you sporting a tattoo, put yours where it will be a pleasant surprise for your sweetie, or dress to conceal.

Accessories Mean Business

Aim up for your look. Your shoes and handbag should reflect where you want to be rather than where you are now.

You do not have to break the bank to achieve the desired look. Scout out sales, shop on eBay. If you're on a tight budget, stay away from super trendy bags, which depreciate quickly—you do not want people (read: other women) recognizing whatever you're carrying as last season's hot bag (they will read: outdated, out of touch, or, worst of all, fashion victim). Instead, invest in a good quality, classically styled handbag, which can last forever (or at least a couple of decades).

Ronna Lichtenberg

You've probably guessed that I think shoes make or break a power look, but don't forget handbags can too. My be-all lavender bag has provided endless opportunities for bonding with other women who share my accessories habit because it sends a lot of messages at once: it's authoritative, feminine, and fun.

If you think my handbag is the only one that sends a message, consider all the hoo-hah over the two Hermès handbags Martha Stewart carried to court. In that case, her "clients" were the jurors, and clients never like it when you look like you make more money than they do.

In a hair and nails mood, I could go on about this at great length, but I'm not going to do it because this stuff dates quickly. What's important for you to know is that accessories of all kinds send powerful messages, and you want your accessories to say what you really want them to say instead of using them to act out when you shouldn't be.

take risks, but not too far, too fast

Ideally, you want to go for as much "look at me" as you can handle, and a little bit more. Dare to go outside of your comfort zone, but not so far that you can't think about anything else, like your pitch. You want to keep pushing to the next level until you settle into a fashion style that is right for who you are and what you want.

Think of it as a dialogue. You are making a statement to the marketplace and the marketplace responds. If you get the reaction you want, which is "You've really got it together," your prospects will take you more seriously. If you get a bad response, which is "Boy, you really look hot" or "What are you *doing* with your hair?" keep tweaking until you hit on a style that works.

Make changes gradually. If there are too many swings in the way you package yourself or the shifts are too sudden, you make people nervous and suggest that you don't really know who you are or what you have to offer. If you are unsure of what you've got, they will be too and will not be inclined to buy whatever it is you are selling.

In other words, don't be like early Hillary Clinton hair: changing too often, too dramatically.

Alex Lebenthal suggests starting by adding emphasis with one detail, such as your jewelry. If you typically wear a single strand of pearls, a good first step might be to switch to a triple strand of bigger pearls. Bigger jewelry, Alex says, is like wearing a bit of armor and typically has bigger impact. Or you might add a patterned blouse to your navy suit. Or trade up to a more expensive, stylish brand of shoe.

Ideally, you want to get to a place where your outfit expresses something about your personality and individuality. "Women who dress to blend into the background, or who dress like a female version of a man, end up looking less authoritative," Alex says. "My thought is that you should instead embrace who you are and what is different about you. Then you will be noticed and listened to."

work past your fears

I know that making these changes is easier said than done. Really, I do. Because the more you put yourself out there, the greater the risk you run of being judged. We fear being judged in large part because we have already judged ourselves and found ourselves lacking. We worry about not being young enough, thin enough, tall enough, well groomed enough, big busted enough, well coiffed enough, or well enough dressed. No wonder it takes us so long to get dressed and out of the house.

How do you work past your worries about being judged? First, bear in mind that attractiveness is a relative concept. Beauty really is in the eye of the beholder, and the judgment of the beholders is molded by the culture in which they exist.

I'm the image of death warmed over in Sunday morning yoga class but can look fine in my television appearances, after the makeup artists have had their considerable way with me. When I'm at a family reunion, I'm tall; in most other situations, I'm short. When I get on a plane in New York City to go home

Ronna Lichtenberg

to Missouri, I'm fat; when I get off the plane in Kansas City, I'm thin. Same body, only the cultural perceptions are different.

If you are going to be pitching in a culture in which you believe people will discount you because of how you appear physically, you must work even harder to premium price your appearance, to say to them, "I am Somebody." Focus on accentuating your very best features—your hair, your nails, your skin tone—to draw attention where you want it. And carry yourself like a queen. Great posture telegraphs inner strength.

What you don't do is buy into the discount.

Accept that with each initial encounter with a new prospect there will be a moment of assessment, but it will only be a moment. Okay, ten minutes, tops. Mentally and physically preparing for that moment lessens the chance that you will be distracted or hurt by what happens *in* the moment and frees you for the possibility of true connection.

creating a signature style

Ideally, after you get tired of trying to camouflage the physical parts of yourself that you regard as bad or ugly, or that you fear others will regard that way, you will come to accept them and even love them as a core part of who you are. You may accept them by making a physical change that allows you to be truer to your deepest self or by embracing them just the way they are. Either way, the act of acceptance brings with it a power that translates directly into the marketplace.

This is what happened to my friend Carole, an entrepreneur of a certain age who for years had kept the gray at bay by coloring her curly, shoulder length hair a lovely dark ash brown. Carole is not one to fuss about hair, and getting her curls colored and cut just so on a regular basis felt to her like a really big deal. One day, Carole just grew tired of warring with her hair and decided to go gray. To do this, she was advised to let her hair grow out as long as she could stand the two-tone look and then cut it really short so that all the remaining brown was snipped away. She went through a lot of soul searching, worrying that she was too old to carry off a super-cropped do and still look good. But she forged ahead, growing it out and then cutting it off so the hair was no more than an inch long anywhere on her head.

The change, going from a big head of dark brown curls to a skullcap of steely gray, was dramatic—and definitely traumatic for Carole. But it looked fabulous, and not just because it turned out to be a very flattering cut and color, but because the look was a manifestation of who Carole is. She had earned the right to that hair. As killing a lion does for an African male on the plains in a tribal society, the rite of passage to gray gave Carole a tremendous amount of confidence.

Soon after, Carole approached a long-time client that she'd been under-pricing substantially, pointed out the going market rate, and suggested they raise her fees by $500 a day. They agreed, just like that. She felt strong, like "I am woman, hear me roar"; it showed, and the client picked up on it. The new-found strength, I am convinced, was directly related to her new hair.

Not long after this incident, Carole pitched a new program to a new client and says she knew the deal was hers when she walked into the meeting and saw that both her client and the person the client had to sell to internally had hair just like hers. There was an immediate bond among women who had reached a certain stage in their lives; they were mature and proud to say, "This is who I am now."

For Carole, the simple act of going gray liberated a wave of energy that put her in a much more productive place.

So now Carole has her hair, the way that Jennifer Lopez has her bottom, and Lauren Hutton has the space between her teeth, and Tina Fey and Ashleigh Banfield have their glasses. Signature.

THE HEART AND ART OF THE FLIRT

No discussion of personal style would be complete without talking about the most personal styling of all: flirting.

Ronna Lichtenberg

When I was promoting my first book, *Work Would Be Great If It Weren't for the People,* I was often asked whether I think it's okay to date someone at work. My stock answer: Even if I were your mommy and told you it *wasn't* okay, you're going to do it anyway—if you're asking the question in the first place, you've got a reason (that is, you've already got someone in your sights) and nothing I say is going to stop you. Under those circumstances, the key question is not whether it's okay to date a coworker but how you manage to date that coworker without damaging your career.

The same holds true with flirting. If you're prone to flirting, you're going to flirt whether I tell you it's okay or not. The real question is how best to manage that flirting so it doesn't undermine your pitching and may even, in certain specific situations with particular kinds of prospects, mildly enhance it.

First, we need to establish the kind of flirting we're talking about. Because there's flirting and then there's flirting.

Serious flirting, or flirting with intent, is what you do when you're working with someone in whom you're interested in a non-work kind of way. You want something from him (or her) that is more important to you than your business goal; this is a case of Me winning out over Me, Inc. My highly unscientific research suggests that this kind of behavior is rare.

Ronna, on Flirting

Flirting is like hot fudge sauce. It can be very tasty, but . . .

- ❖ It's not good on everything.
- ❖ There are people who don't like it.
- ❖ It's hard to clean up when you make a mess.
- ❖ You don't want to use too much of it.
- ❖ Remember that it isn't supposed to be the main event.
- ❖ If you use it on a daily basis, you'll regret it.

Most flirting is casual, with no anticipation of physical follow-through. Used appropriately, this type of flirting can be another way of being charming, of making the people you're dealing with feel good about themselves. Used inappropriately, it can undercut your credibility, lead others to view you as unprofessional, and make anything and anyone you're trying to pitch that much harder to sell.

Let me be blunt here: Serious flirting during a pitch is a big no-no. If you are attracted to your prospect and would like to have sex with him or her, save the impulse to signal your interest until the pitch is over.

Remember, you cannot successfully pitch for two goals at once. To be effective, you have to focus on one desired outcome and put all your efforts into achieving it. If you're pitching to a straight man, particularly a blue straight man, the brain sex research tells us he can't focus on more than one objective at a time. Flirting will serve to distract him from the professional message you're trying to deliver. If he sees you as a place to profitably spread his seed, there's not much else he'll be able to concentrate on.

The waters are murkier when it comes to the other kind of flirting. Once again, intent is key. You should not flirt in a way that suggests you might be open to having sex if you are not. Nor should you flirt as a way to create an advantage. That merely implies that you don't have any other advantages, or at least not ones strong enough to get the job done. In benefit thinking, the intention is to understand them better so you can take care of their problems, not to understand them better so you can use their vulnerability to get what you want, which is what flirting is about sometimes.

Make sure your intentions are as clear and clean as possible. People can and routinely do misread the intentions of flirting—not only the object of your flirt but others who observe it. Remember what we learned about brain sex: male bias is to think you're attracted to him even when you're not (they can't help it—they have a larger hypothalamus, the sex center of the brain, where hormones, especially testosterone, stimulate the desire for sex).

Above all, remember that sex is a power tool; you shouldn't use it as a weapon. If you're an attractive woman and you misuse your sexual energy, it's

Ronna Lichtenberg

no different than a guy using his physical strength to overpower or intimidate those who are weaker. Unfair. Bad. Wrong.

a flirting checklist

How best then to think about flirting? Consider it a seasoning, something to sprinkle on your offering, so it won't overpower the taste. A little goes a long way. The following questions will help you determine how to use this particular spice.

How attractive are you?

The more attractive you are, and the bluer your prospects are, the bluer you have to be too. Remember, guys in general can only focus well on one thing at a time, and because of the way they're wired to move through the sexual buffet, flirting is a major distraction. Given a choice between concentrating on a message about business and what they construe as an invitation to get down and dirty, sex trumps work every time. If you're very attractive, you already have the benefits that come from being attractive. That's enough.

How attractive are you to this audience?

Everything is relative. I may not look like a hot tamale anymore to a roomful of twenty- and thirty-somethings. But wearing a flattering outfit on a good hair day, I can still look pretty sparky to a not-yet-geriatric crowd. Use your powers of empathy and extra-sensory abilities to see yourself in the eye of the beholder; even if you think you're chopped liver, they may think you're chopped salsa. Proceed accordingly.

How well do you know your prospects?

If the professional relationship is new, focus on establishing credibility, being authoritative, and showing confidence. As we saw in chapter 3, these qualities aren't assumed if you're a woman; you have to prove them. If your prospects are thinking about you as one of many potential mothers for their children, they're not dwelling on your credibility. Conversely, if you've been working with someone for a while and have developed something of a sibling relationship, or everybody's married and you all know and are comfortable with each other's spouses, a little flirting is fine.

How old are you?

Men are wired to respond to a woman's fertility. The younger you are, the more fertile you're presumed to be and the more distracting the sexual energy that's generated during an interaction can be, even when you don't mean to be flirtatious.

After menopause, it's easier to flirt because no one takes it seriously anymore. In fact, sometimes a bit of flirting helps get their attention, signaling that you are still a vibrant person. In general, as soon as you're old enough for a business associate to say to you, "You remind me so much of my mom," you can flirt without doing damage (after you smack him).

What's the culture you're dealing with and your role within it?

If you're dealing with a systemizing culture, where the work is analytical and technical, there will likely be fewer women around and flirting will be much more noticeable. Proceed with extreme caution. Particularly in a systemizing culture, the lower your rung on the business ladder, the less you should flirt and the more you need to focus on establishing authority.

Are you looking for power?

The more direct power you hope to wield, the less feminine and flirtatious you can be. Flirting is for influence, not power.

Are you looking to start a conversation?

A bit of flirtation can work well when you're opening with a pink because it's a good way to indicate interest and establish connection. With a blue, there's a bigger chance it's a no-no.

Ronna Lichtenberg

Are you looking to reach agreement?

When you're closing, you're talking about money, and then it's serious. Money is always serious and money is always blue. Never flirt when you're talking about money—especially somebody else's money.

Do you want to set the stage for future transactions?

You've pitched, you've done the deal, and the interaction is just about over. If you've delivered successfully and hope to do business together, a little flirting at this point can be helpful, as a reminder that you not only get the job done and done well, but you're also personally pleasant to work with.

Here's an example in which I was on the receiving end of exactly this kind of flirt. I had just finished writing a particularly challenging section of this book and took myself out to a shoe store for a little retail therapy. I was helped by an older salesman named Salvatore and ended up buying two pairs of the same shoes in different colors, which I had some anxiety about and hadn't ever done before. As I was paying, Salvatore looked at me with absolute sincerity and said, "You have exquisite taste. You picked out the best shoes in the line."

Not one item of my clothing was clean, and I was so grubby from work that I needed someone to scrub me down with a Brillo pad. Yet the almost flirtatious way Salvatore spoke to me, as if to say, "You are something, girlfriend," made me feel terrific. I thought to myself, "I am definitely coming back to this store to buy shoes from you, Salvatore, because your shoes look great and you make me feel great."

That's what the best kind of pitching does: makes someone feel good about themselves, and in so doing, makes them a little more eager to do business with you.

CHAPTER 11
delivering the pitch

The Big Moment is finally upon you. You've crafted, you've priced, and you've packaged your offering with a big red bow. Now your name is called to take the mound. You are warmed up and ready to deliver your pitch.

In this phase of the game, you are going to bring all you've learned to bear on a singular goal: to share the benefits of your offering with a prospect so that they will want to play ball with you. To accomplish this, your style of delivery needs to be in sync with the buyers. Good timing helps. So does serendipity.

You can't control the serendipity part (although you can help foster the circumstances under which serendipity is more likely to stroll your way). But you can certainly use the advantages and skills that come naturally to you as a woman to turn the odds of winning greatly in your favor.

Let's play ball.

PICK YOUR MOMENT

Sometimes you are able to pick the moment to deliver your pitch and sometimes the moment picks you.

If the timing is within your control and it is a formal pitch, try to schedule the meeting during your best part of the day, when you typically have your best energy cooking. If at all possible, look for a match between your ideal time frame and your prospects' stated time preferences. You want them to have their best energy cooking, too.

Whether the timing is within your control or not, do some warm-up work before the meeting to get into the right frame of mind to pitch. Revisit the techniques we talked about. Don't go in hungry or tired; at the risk of sounding like your mother, make sure that you get a good night's rest beforehand; try, if possible, to work out sometime within the forty-eight hours prior to your pitch to get the knots out of your body.

Do some emotional prep work, too. If there is someone you know who drains you, try not talk to them right before you pitch. On the other hand, deliberately engage with those who make you feel good and generally brighten your day. Take a bubble bath the night before, listen to your favorite music. When you know the pitch is coming, do what you can to prepare on every level. The point here is to be as nice to yourself as possible.

the surprise pitch

Sometimes the opportunity to pitch comes as a complete surprise. You get an unsolicited job offer. Or your boss offers you an unanticipated promotion or the possibility of a new assignment or project. You have a chance meeting with a prospective new client or employer or financial backer. These chances are likely to pop up more often when you have done your homework about visioning. When you have a deeper clarity about what you really want, you are better able to recognize opportunity when it's out for a stroll in your neighborhood.

Not every surprise is pleasant, though. Maybe your boss hands you a demotion instead of that promotion. Or your best client threatens to cancel a lucrative project. Sometimes you can see the darkness coming, but some thunderstorms just pop up out of the blue—clear skies one moment, steel-gray clouds and the occasional lightning bolt the next.

Or maybe the energy of the interaction is simply and completely different than what you expected. Maybe the person you're pitching to had a fight with her mother that day and walks into the room in an ugly mood. Or your boss told you that he had twenty minutes to hear your idea but something came up that he hasn't told you about and he is mentally hoping to get you out of his office in less than seven minutes. Or maybe you feel like you just don't have it today, for whatever reason—you didn't sleep well or you had dairy for breakfast. Whatever.

Throughout the day, in any given moment, you are going to have to evaluate situations and potential opportunities and decide if this is a moment when you should be pitching. If it is, you then have to figure out the best pitch for the moment and situation, or whether you need to change the pitch you've already prepared. Good or bad, the key to handling the surprise pitch is first to recognize it, then focus on figuring out what to go for in the moment. Ask yourself, "What is my goal here? What benefit can I gain, here and now, that will also benefit them?"

One of the things that's pleased me most in the course of writing this book is that women who've read early versions of it are finding more and more opportunities to pitch. As Eileen said, "My client called with what could have been a big problem, but I just took a step back—and pitched."

To someone with a hammer, the whole world looks like a nail. To someone with skills as a pitcher, almost any interaction is one that might be improved with just a little pitching, instead of a lot of bitching.

PRACTICE WHAT YOU PITCH

Practice won't make your pitch perfect—no pitch is completely 100 percent perfect. But rehearsing before you go in, at least the right kind of rehearsing, will get your pitch a darned sight closer to perfect than it would be otherwise.

Saying your pitch out loud is crucial. Say it in front of the mirror, say it to your pet, say it to a friend or peer whose opinion you respect. (Don't say it to your kids, though. Kids are too wiggly.) But you must say it out loud. People spend a great deal of time writing speeches, presentations, or other kinds of

The Panic Room

If you are prone to anxiety before a pitch—and who isn't?—the following exercise can help you to create a safe place within your own head where you can go if and when you start to panic.

Step 1: Take a minute by yourself, away from distractions. Bring up an image of a place where you feel secure and at peace. It may be a beautiful beach. It may be your home. Your body should feel warm and relaxed while you're "seeing" it.

Step 2: Practice visualizing your refuge as clearly and vividly as possible so that when you need a safe place to gather energy, you'll be ready.

Step 3: Before an important pitch, take a few minutes alone. Call up your image, sticking with it until you feel your tension begin to ease and a sense of calm prevail.

pitches that are meant to be spoken but say the words out loud for the first time when they are in the situation. They find out too late that what appeals to the eye and what appeals to the ear are often very different. The speaker sounds halting and insecure because the words may be too formal or the phrasing is awkward when verbalized.

The real point of writing down your pitch, after all, is to be able to say it. You want to be able to ignore the printed page and talk, really talk, with your prospect.

One technique that I've found effective is to tape yourself delivering the practice version of your pitch, take a break, then listen to the tape a short time later to hear what that stranger with a voice oddly like yours sounds like. Your ear will pick up what you need to modify—sentences that run on, awkward wording, phrases that sound stiff. As a bonus, listening to the tape will help you remember the pitch better, so you'll need to refer less often to your notes. The way that memory works, hearing your own voice say something makes it far easier to remember than reading over the same material a hundred times.

If you choose to do a dry run in front of another person, make sure that someone is either a close friend or a peer or mentor you admire and is willing to give you the time and a frank assessment, recommends Mary Taylor, vice president of communications at AXA. "You want someone who knows you respect their judgment, so they will give you an honest opinion. They need to tell you what makes this pitch not a good pitch. You don't want someone who will say, 'that's great' to everything."

BE AWARE OF THE DOUBLE PITCH

Pitching is never just about the prospect and the pitcher. Chances are the person you are selling to will have to sell your ideas to someone else for ultimate approval. Your prospect is in effect your representative, your agent in that second interaction.

Even if your prospect *is* the final decision-maker, you still have to assume they will talk to someone else about your offering or forward your e-mails. This is particularly true if your prospect is pink. Women like to talk (duh) and like to talk to each other about other people (double duh), so you should just assume when you are talking to a woman about your offering, you are also talking to others.

In essence, you are double pitching even when you think you aren't.

So before the meeting begins, do some thinking about whom your prospect needs to sell to internally, or who will be offering opinions about your offering, and what information they need to give those people to nail the sale. Your goal is to make it easier for the buyer to pitch your idea to someone else.

If the involvement of others is formal and obvious, you can simply ask your prospect to whom she will show your offering and what those others need to see. This conversation also provides the perfect opportunity to move away from "I" and start talking about "we." What do *we* need to do to make this work? You want them to understand that you are on the same side. It is us against the pain. We hate that pain and, together, we can beat it.

This is a prime objective in any pitch: to move to "we" as soon as you can.

OPENING THE GAME

Okay, you're in, you're on, you're ready to go. Before the official part of your meeting begins, warm up your audience with a few opening techniques that will help put them in the mood to do business with you.

Start with something as seemingly innocuous as your response to their polite inquiry about whether you need anything before you begin. If someone offers you water or a cup of coffee, for instance, always say yes. If they don't ask, make the request yourself, without apology. "Could I have some cold water, please?" If you start the session by saying, "Oh no, that's okay, I don't need anything," you are indulging in a form of discounting: "Oh no, that's okay, I'm happy to sit here all alone in the dark." Get used to asking for what you need and get them used to the idea of extending themselves for you and treating you nicely, which they'll need to do if you are going to do a deal together. Besides, if you are nervous, your throat is probably dry. Water will help.

Then try to find something they like that you genuinely care about. Probe someone's interests so you can find something you really have in common: Even some blues respect the social niceties. Doris Meister, a top-ranking private banking executive, always finds something to say related to her buyer's community. "I always love coming out to southern California. Have you lived here long?" Or, "I had a wonderful time last night at your Performing Arts Center. The acoustics are fantastic and the production was world class."

Connecting yourself to them and their world in a positive way predisposes them to listen to what you have to say, Doris believes. It also helps you assess their business style, so you can modify your approach to their needs and preferences.

To mix my sports metaphors for a moment, you hit a social ball across the net to see where it lands and how they respond. If they hit the ball back with some energy behind the return, you are probably dealing with pink or striped players and you can proceed accordingly. If they just let the ball land, or catch it without lobbing it back to you, you probably need to go blue and quickly end the social chitchat and shift the meeting to the business at hand. (When you're playing with someone new, I think it is worth a "diagnostic" such as this to find out style, so it's worth the risk that they might be blue. You can minimize the risk by making the question not too pink, and being able to back away fast. If you play it totally safe and don't try anything, you aren't going to find out their style until later.) What you want to watch for, notes Doris, is not just what they say, but how they say it. "Look at their facial expressions, their body language, whether they're making eye contact," she says. "What you're aiming for is engagement, to connect with them and have them connect back to you."

In opening the official part of the meeting, Doris also always says something like, "Thank you for arranging to meet with us; we appreciate your willingness to find out more about us." Or, "We're really excited about this opportunity to meet with you." The idea is to convey enthusiasm for the project right from the start.

identify the power person

If the meeting involves more than two people, these opening gambits also give you a chance to identify the real decision-maker in the room. Introductions with titles will provide the first important clue about each person's role in the process. Then concentrate less on how they react to you and more on how they react to each other, advises Janet Clarke, entrepreneur and seasoned public board member. Janet, who has attended more than her fair share of meetings in her career, notes, "People naturally focus their attention on the power person in the room."

The power person is usually not the first person to speak, says Janet, and in fact typically says very little. But when the lower-on-the-totem-pole types talk, they keep glancing at the power person to gauge their reactions. And when the power person does make a comment, everyone else in the room stops, looks, and listens.

If you see the power person defer and let the less-powerful people do most of the talking, play the game, says Janet. But always stay tuned in to the reac-

Ronna Lichtenberg

tion of that power person, who even in silence sets the tone and mandates the approach for the meeting.

TAKE BRAIN SEX INTO ACCOUNT

The gender and color of the decision-maker will help you determine how to proceed with your pitch. In the absence of definitive clues about color, always go blue, particularly in formal presentations and mixed-gender groups.

Now, here comes the big payoff for all the work you have done to learn about the business implications of the different ways in which men and women are wired.

if your prospect is blue

If you are delivering your pitch to men in general, and blues in particular, here are some of the key points to keep in mind.

Cover one topic at a time.

One great advantage of women's multifocal brains is that we bring a richer perspective to our prospect's pain point during a pitch. The disadvantage, if we're pitching to men, is that we're often inclined to share all of those perspectives at once, which makes their single-focus brains spin.

To avoid information overload or labels of indecisiveness, focus on one topic at a time. Make yourself notes on the others; you can catch the important ones later.

Stick with logic.

Discussions based on reason are easier to comprehend for men, who, you'll recall, have a harder time accessing and processing emotions than women. If you stick with logic, you are living in that single-focus, step-thinking part of the brain where they are happiest. This is particularly true if you're dealing with a systemizing man, whose brain is organized around analytical concepts.

Personally, I think of logic as just one way to get to an answer and not always the best way. Intuition has often served me better than logic. So I think it's fine for you to get to an answer intuitively; just explain it logically, at least until they've worked with you long enough to trust and value your intuition.

Use numbers more than words.

We like language—stories, explanations, details, grace notes. They like data. Use the former sparingly and the latter liberally and you'll do okay. Which leads me directly to the next point . . .

Rein in your verbal tendencies.

You don't need me to tell you that men think we talk too much. Men do not want to hear everything you know or think about the issue in question. The same biological tendencies that make talking a great shared activity for women make it a shared pain in the eardrums for men.

Do not give three paragraphs worth of explanation when a couple of sentences will do. If there is silence, do not rush in to fill it. Learn to shut up.

The real crux of the problem is our natural reaction to their reactions while we're pitching. Or rather their lack of reaction. Men will often not give the signs of affirmations that are instinctive for women—no nodding, no uh-huhs, no nothing. That makes us nervous because we are busy processing emotionally and applying our self-limiting beliefs and concluding that they must hate our ideas or us or both. So we resolve our discomfort by talking more.

Catch yourself if you find yourself feeling anxious about a lack of affirmation from your prospect. Put this note to yourself in the margins of your presentation: S.I.G., which stands for Silence Is Good.

Participate in an activity together.

Remember, just as talking is a great shared activity for women, so activity is a great shared activity for men. Often, women opt out of the golfing excursions, Outward Bound trips, brandy-sipping, cigar-puffing post-conference sessions

Ronna Lichtenberg

Some Men *Can't* Express Emotions

Not only is it easier for women to access emotions, because of the multifocal connectedness we have going on, it is also easier for us to talk about it. In fact, there is a lot of research being done now on gender differences in a condition called alexithymia, which is marked by the inability or difficulty in describing or being aware of one's emotions or moods. There may be a biological basis for this condition. Sebastian Kraemer, M.D., notes that alexithymia is associated with inter-hemisphere transfer across the brain.

Why does this matter? Women tend to have a larger corpus callosum, which connects the brain's hemispheres. Simon LeVay, Ph.D., author of *The Sexual Brain*, found that the corpus callosum also occupies a larger fraction of the entire brain volume in women than in men, which suggests a greater number of nerve fibers connecting the two hemispheres of the brain. As we process emotion and reason in both hemispheres of the brain, there is also a bigger pipeline between those hemispheres so that more information is flowing back and forth.

Harvard psychologist William S. Pollack, Ph.D., suggests that most men display what amounts to a full-blown case of alexithymia, the result, he argues, of a gender-specific rearing and socialization process. Research shows that by age two, boys are less verbally expressive than girls, and by age four, they're less expressive facially.

Now think about it. Men have the capacity to separate their emotions from other mental tasks. They may even have difficulty accessing those emotions. And it isn't as easy for them to talk about it because we are the better talkers. That's why getting men to talk about something we want to talk about because we feel emotional about it is so difficult.

and other assorted male-bonding rituals that guys favor. Rather than take yourself out of the action entirely—and therefore miss out on opportunities to foster business relationships and do deals—consider finding a way to join in on your own terms.

Non-golfer Diane Ruebling, a former vice president at MONY Life Insurance Company, recalls being invited to participate in a golf tournament for their biggest clients. At first, Diane considered refusing, but then hit on an ingenious solution. She drove the beverage cart around the course, supplying pop, candy, and chips to anyone who wanted a snack, all while wearing a tiara and posting a sign that said "Omnipotent Putter." Guests could ask her to putt for them, and if she missed they could try it again. "I could have opted out, but decided to adapt instead because it was important for me to be there and be a part of the group. And I ended up having a blast with everyone."

Mind you, a tiara is only for the very brave. But you can certainly have yourself a good time tooling around on whatever golf cart equivalent is handy.

Translate the benefits of your offering into a "win."

Men and women tend to keep score in different ways. In business situations, men are conditioned to look for an advantage, while women traditionally seek an equal exchange of energy. Men tend to define advantage as I win; you lose. A successful sale to a man is overcoming your objections and getting you to do something you might not otherwise do. We have a different idea about power and aren't necessarily looking for the same kind of win.

At work, this different way of keeping score often leads men to keep a mental tally that they update throughout their day. They calculate "I won" or "I lost" on every transaction. I won in this meeting. I lost in this conversation. I won in that e-mail. It's always vertical. I'm up, therefore you're down. We, meanwhile, are busy looking for ways to keep our transactions even.

Once you understand the way that men keep score, you can boost your effectiveness as a pitcher by translating the benefits of your offering into competitive terms that speak to their desire to win.

Ronna Lichtenberg

Limit your use of personal stories.

Men do not share our predilection for humanizing the business points under discussion. Where we see anecdotes as a way to gain valuable perspective on an issue, men typically see them as entirely beside the point. Your pitch to men generally will be more effective if you use people stories sparingly in your presentation, and make sure to tie the stories you do use directly to a possible business outcome. Make the connection clear to him so he doesn't have to work at it.

The best stories to use are about people who are successful, particularly people who somehow resemble people your prospect aspires to be like. Biology makes him want to go up the food chain. Remember the research by Herminia Ibarra, Ph.D., that tells us that guys want to be like the guys who are senior to them? Illustrations that use the exploits of the powerful to make a point are likely to be the most powerful for your prospect.

Limit expressions of emotion.

Women have an easier time accessing, processing, and talking about emotions than men do. If you are a pink woman pitching to a blue or in a blue-tinged environment, you are at risk of talking too much. If you are a blue woman pitching to a man in a mildly systemizing environment, you need to make a conscious decision about just how much emotion to show—too much makes you seem vulnerable, and men typically interpret vulnerability as lacking power and authority. Too little and the old bully broad syndrome will come back to haunt you because of stereotypes about femininity. Generally, a little goes a long way. Then you can shift back into business mode.

Be clear about time.

This is one that pink women often get wrong because our sense of time can be so different than a blue man's.

When You Pitch to a Blue

1. Cover one topic at a time.

2. Stay with logic.

3. Use numbers more than words.

4. When listening, keep your face still and avoid offering too many verbal affirmations.

5. If it's important that you have a longer talk with him, see if you can do it during an activity. If golf isn't your bag, at least give him a stress ball to squeeze, or meet somewhere he can pace around the room if need be.

6. Explain the advantage of your offering in competitive terms (e.g., "With this kind of investment, chances are you will beat the S & P by 20 percent").

7. Limit the use of personal stories to illustrate points. If you do use them, make the connection for him in advance and after you've done it. Otherwise, use stories that refer to others who are successful.

8. Use visual illustrations, preferably charts and graphs, not pictures of people.

9. Defer to his rank if he is your superior.

10. Avoid excessive use of color or subtle shades he might not be able to see.

First off, realize that during your pitch, he is focused on the task, not the interaction. He is running the clock to get this job done efficiently and move on to the next task. We're ready to schmooze our way to the deal. If he walks into a meeting thinking that the pitch will take ten minutes and you use up eight minutes on a story, you are toast. So be sure to check how much time your prospect has for the meeting ahead of time and proceed accordingly.

Second, we tend to view time in human terms, always considering the consequences of what we do now on future relationships. Your prospect often does

Ronna Lichtenberg

not want to hear about potential relationship impacts. Keep your thoughts to yourself on the secondary and tertiary consequences (unless those consequences are so dire that you must share them immediately) and focus the discussion on the here and now.

Last but not least, our well-deserved reputation for patience sometimes spills over into an equally accurate rep for taking too long to get to the point, or failing to get to the point entirely. (Please don't get mad at me for that—you know it's true, girlfriend.) We are so geared to relationship that we get lost in the setup—I feel good, you feel good, I feel good, you feel good—and wait too long before we close. Don't get so lost in building connection that you fail to state what you want directly and set the terms for what you hope will happen next.

When You Pitch to a Pink

1. Make spatial and abstract concepts real. Use examples to get them off the page and into life.

2. Tie the benefit to people beyond her, people she cares about.

3. If she toggles between emotion and ideas, recognize it as a sign that she wants to connect with you.

4. Don't be surprised if she brings up an old emotional pain that is influencing her current decision. You don't need to fix it; just make it clear you've heard it.

5. Expect that she is going to want to talk about you and your offering to someone else she trusts and that their opinion will matter a lot.

6. Show her you are listening by giving her facial cues and verbal affirmations.

7. Make points by using personal stories, or stories about individuals.

8. Let her talk.

9. Use more than one color, as well as pictures of faces.

10. If there is a way you can appeal to more than one sense at the same time, do so.

if your prospect is pink

In many ways, pitching to another woman, particularly a pink woman, is the mirror image of pitching to a man. She considers many variables at once, he doesn't. She likes words, he doesn't. She likes personal stories, he doesn't. And so it goes.

But life is never quite that simple. If the woman is blue, you will need to incorporate some blue techniques into your delivery—some numbers, statements of advantage, and bottom line impact, for example. The culture she's operating in matters, too. If she's a natural pink working in a high systemizing culture, for example, she's probably adapted to the needs of the organization with a few big blue stripes. You'll need to go blue enough to match those.

Here are a few other pointers to bear in mind while pitching to a woman, particularly if she's pink.

Make abstract ideas human.

Women think in human terms rather than conceptual ones as men do. When you're pitching to a pink woman, always translate theory into practice and explain how your offering will play out in real life.

Say, for example, you are a broker trying to convince a client to open a 529 college savings plan for a child. If your client is a blue man, you might start off by explaining the tax advantages and support your points with a handy dandy chart illustrating the superior returns generated by these accounts over time compared with an ordinary taxable investment account. If your client is a woman, however, you'll do better to open with a question about her child. You might say, "Have you thought yet about sending little Susie to college, and where she might go? Gee, that school is kind of expensive; let's talk about how we might make that happen." Then you'd talk generalities about some practical steps she could take to save for college before getting down to product specifics.

One broker I know even drives home the point with visuals: The walls of her office are decorated with banners from all the different colleges attended

Ronna Lichtenberg

by the children and grandchildren of her clients. The message couldn't be clearer—at least, not to a pink.

Tie the benefit to the people she cares about.

The college-banner broker's selling strategy also works because she shows her clients how her offering will help the people they love most. A woman exists in a web of relationships, and she is always going to be thinking about herself and your offering in the context of those other people. If she works for a big company, she's worried about her team, her employees, her customers, and the shareholders. If she's an entrepreneur, she's concerned about her customers, her suppliers, and her backers. No matter where she works, she's thinking about her boss and her colleagues and, while she's at it, her family, too.

If you honor those relationships by thinking through the impact of your offering on them, in addition to the benefit for your prospect, you let her know you understand her priorities and really know how to attend to her needs.

Address old pain points.

Women carry hurts much longer than men do. So don't be surprised if your prospect brings up an old emotional pain that is influencing her current decision. Maybe you remind her of a consultant she worked with in the past who overcharged her. Or the junior employee who flaked out on a big project or the boss who passed her by for a promotion. Or maybe, just maybe, you look like the sister of her seventeenth boyfriend who cheated on her with her best friend.

You probably can't know what old pain is going in. But you can listen for it and, when you hear it, speak to it. You can say, "I heard what you said about the consultant you worked with last year. Let's talk about that so we can make sure we don't repeat it."

Now that's a perfect pitch.

In general, you don't want to get so caught up in delivering your pitch that you don't pay attention to the signals that are coming back at you. Because no one pitches in a vacuum. You are pitcher to a catcher who is giving you cues about what kind of pitch she wants, as in, "Don't be sending me a fastball, Sparky, I don't want it." If your toss is all about you, and therefore one-sided, you might as well go practice with a batting machine and give up pitching entirely. (More on signals in a moment.)

if your prospect is striped

You will run across a lot of people with striped styles in the course of the day, and you may wonder how to pitch to them. Cases where you are most likely to find stripes: pink women who've added blue stripes in order to make progress in a systemizing culture; blue women who've added pink stripes because they've been criticized for being too cold and/or domineering; blue men who've made it to the top of their particular food chain and added pink stripes as part of an effort to lead the troops in a friendlier way; naturally pink men working with a lot of blue men, who've added stripes in order to fit in better.

In most of these cases, people have added stripes in order to adapt to a certain kind of workplace culture—in other words, their stripes are more cultivated than natural (there are some natural stripes, too, but care and feeding of the born striped is the same as for an adopted stripe). Given that your prospect probably has stripes in order to adapt to certain kind of situations, your response should be "situational" as well: Treat them like a blue in public, including group e-mails, and look for opportunities to be pink when you are face-to-face or somehow alone.

With given individuals, you can get really precise about what will trigger behavior that is more pink or blue: at home it may be balancing the checkbook (does anyone do that anymore?), or at work it may be that at 3:00 on Friday afternoon there's a style shift.

And whatever you do, don't feel betrayed when someone you thought was pink "blues up" in public. That's just someone with a striped style, and after it happens once, you can safely predict that it will happen again.

A caveat: A striped guy is more likely to respond to an expression of emo-

Ronna Lichtenberg

tion or vulnerability from a striped or pink woman because it is socially acceptable for a woman to express those things. So you can selectively use such expressions as you lead into a pitch to help create a feeling of comfort that may make them more inclined to do business with you.

Praise works for everyone.
Men and women both want and need praise, possibly for slightly different reasons. Researchers at the University of North Carolina, writing in the *Journal of Experimental Social Psychology,* found that men felt the greatest regard for an individual who flattered them unstintingly, even if the comments were untrue. For men, praise tied to status enhancement is great.

For women, praise is an affirmation and provides connection glue.

Remember to find good things to say about your prospect while you're pitching. My preference is that you make the effort to find something you actually believe while you're at it.

a word of warning to the blues

If you are a blue woman, your desire when pitching to another woman will be to get right down to business. You may be mildly annoyed, even downright pissed off, when she does not want to go there immediately with you but meanders down another path.

The most important and most challenging style shift that blue women have to do with pink women is to carefully keep checking in with her during the delivery phase to make sure the connections are holding. If you are blue, you are likely to get lost in task. You'll have your head in the binder. You want to focus on the numbers and the models. You want to get in all the reasons why what you want is a good thing.

But you need to hold back. Because you are a woman too, you will be able to tell what's going on with a pink, and what will be going on is that she is feeling uncomfortable, disconnected, out of her element. Because you are blue, you don't want to have to bother with that, but you have to. It is really easy for a blue woman to make an enemy out of a pink woman, without even trying, by ignoring her need for connection.

Instead, set your style monitor on full track. Give her lots of feedback. And participate in bonding activities, to the extent that you can. A little seemingly idle chitchat—about family, common interests, the void left in the lives of working women everywhere by the ending of *Sex and the City*—goes a long way toward sealing a deal.

bringing in a partner

By this point in our journey together, you know enough about corporate cultures and colors to know what will be an easy environment for you and what will be hard, who will be a comfortable target and who will be tough. The further away the pitching environment is from your natural style—say, if you're a strong empathizer going into a room full of systemizers or a bubble-gum pink woman pitching to a deep navy blue—the more you should think about bringing a partner into the room with you.

In my corporate life, I always pitched with guys because I worked mostly with guys who were all blue, but I didn't have a clue about how to sync up styles, so I just did my best blue imitation. In my own business, for the first few years I always pitched with women, who tended to have similar styles to mine, because it felt more comfortable, so I still didn't have to flex much.

In recent years, I've done a lot of pitching with Steve Safier, Ph.D., from HayGroup, who is a mostly blue guy from a systemizing culture. Our collaboration has taught me a lot about style syncing with a colleague, and about how valuable this can be.

We were introduced by a mutual client, who thought we would be a good team. The potential advantage to clients was immediately clear to me— HayGroup is highly respected for its intellectual capital. Steve is a psychologist who specialized in anxiety disorders when he had a private practice; as a consultant, he's had decades of experience in organization change and individual coaching. He has extensive technical HR expertise that I don't have,

Ronna Lichtenberg

coming from the business side. But I wasn't sure that pitching together would work because our styles and backgrounds are so different.

But I've found that having a mostly blue pitching colleague gives me more room to do my pink thing, knowing that the blue stuff will get covered because it's natural to him to make sure it does.

What I've also learned from working with Steve is that being explicit about a pink/blue relationship can be extremely valuable in pitching when you respect each other's contributions and can talk through differences; when you're both committed to delivering maximum value; and when you establish the pattern of working through the hard stuff with each other instead of trying to avoid it. You know that you have a great dynamic when you're willing to take a temporary back seat when your prospect has a clear style preference that matches your colleague's, because you know that your collaborator will recognize both your intent and your contribution.

Steve has had to listen, for example, to so many conversations about shoes that he has volunteered to explain to the IRS that I should get an accessories deduction. And I have learned that the models he draws for other blue systemizers are often exactly what they need to understand the offering.

If you can choose to have a teammate who's committed to working with you on style, especially for a big pitch, go for it.

Of course, sometimes you don't have a choice. You cannot choose, for example, to take a colleague with you to a job interview. What you can do in that case is get a lot of coaching beforehand from someone who is the color of your buyer or a more natural fit with that environment. Then when you go into the meeting, you keep the voice of that coach in your head, and essentially partner yourself.

SELLING YOUR IDEA INTERNALLY

The context in which you're pitching also plays an important role in how you make your case. One important distinction is whether the meeting is public or private. If I'm pitching to another woman on the phone or in person and it's just the two of us, I can be a lot pinker than if I am pitching to her in a meeting of forty other women, and I have to be even less pink if we're in a room full of guys or in a mixed gender meeting in a systemizing culture. *Pitching in a small group means paying the closest attention to the style preferences of the person across*

Top Ten Mistakes in Selling Your Ideas Internally

1. Selling the idea too broadly. The more you can define the audience, and who would benefit from knowing the idea, the better.

2. Relying too heavily on a superior's megaphone. People get tired of having higher-ups' names used for what feel to them like routine purposes.

3. Forgetting to lead with a strong, specific statement of the benefit. Too often, we communicate by starting with why we care instead of why they should.

4. Using the wrong medium for the message. This is particularly true for an idea that is somehow linked to bad news. Bad news needs to be delivered as personally as possible.

5. Lacking credibility. Either you haven't established sufficient expertise or you have squandered your credibility by sending too many e-mail messages marked "urgent priority."

6. Sending in the wrong messenger. Often there is someone who would be more effective delivering the message than you are, if you could be strong enough to pass the ball.

7. Deciding you don't need to practice. You do. And if it is really important, you should probably videotape yourself doing it.

8. Expecting too much. If your idea requires fast turnaround from a completely overwhelmed team, or it's really too late in the process to incorporate it, no one will pay attention.

9. Aiming for the big hit. In other words, putting all your energy into one big bang message instead of a lot of little ones dripped in.

10. Neglecting to build a fan base. That is, failing to recruit a constituency with a shared interest in getting the message out.

Ronna Lichtenberg

from you; pitching in a large group means paying closest attention to the style pref-erences of the culture in which you find yourself.

You're also likely to present differently if you're pitching within your own organization than you would to an outsider. In one way, internal pitches are easier: Presumably, you already have some credibility in your own company and will have to expend less energy to establish your authority and gain trust. You may also be able to inject more of your "real" self into the offering. Then too, you should find it somewhat easier to gain the ear of your prospect and garner support from other interested parties.

But that same familiarity can also lead you to neglect some of the basic lessons of effective pitching. You think, "I don't have to bother with all that brain sex stuff, these guys already know me. Systemizers, schmistemizers, I'll just tell them what I think."

That is a serious mistake, my friends, because you should always be con-sidering this stuff when you pitch. Maybe you don't have to give it the full power treatment when your own company is the prospect; maybe you can take a few more style risks. But you should always, *always,* be using brain sex and style sync techniques to give your pitch more muscle.

For a look at other common mistakes that pitchers make when selling their ideas internally, take a look at my version of a David Letterman Top Ten list on the previous page.

TIPS FROM TV

During the course of my career, I've appeared on television a number of times, first as a representative of Prudential Securities and later, after my first two books were published, as a commentator on business issues. Several of the techniques I learned from the media training that I received prior to those ap-pearances and the TV professionals I've observed over the years have proved enormously helpful to me during the delivery phase of a pitch.

Here are a few tips I think are worth passing along.

Tip No. 1: Get in your "must airs"

The first time I went on television, I immediately hit the Big Time: an appearance on *60 Minutes* with Mike Wallace. Unfortunately, the circumstances were less than ideal. Prudential was in more than $200 million worth of hot water over how they'd sold a complex product.

Fortunately, Prudential's public relations experts schooled me in what to do in potentially hostile interviews. The key, they told me, was that you must get in the answers you want to give, no matter what the question actually is. These answers are your "must airs," or the central talking points you must make sure to communicate. The interviewer asks, "What do you think about X?" Your answer needs to be, "That is a very interesting question, which ties directly to what I wanted to say about Y."

Every pitcher should have her must airs—an agenda that you make sure you get across. Yes, you want to be responsive to your buyer and his agenda as well, but you have to be in control of your own game. If you let your prospects drive the agenda entirely, you are only returning the ball to them—you aren't really pitching, which involves tossing the ball to a target with clear intention, or keeping up your end of the game.

Tip No. 2: Sit up really straight

The way you carry yourself, particularly the way you sit, matters a lot to your prospects' assessment of you. On serious television news shows, you'll notice that most of the women sit, stand, and move in much the same way. They cross their legs at an angle; they never, ever slouch (you immediately lose all presence); and any hand gestures they make are purposeful. So they sit mostly with their knees together and off to one side, spine straight, shoulders back. Their posture says, "I'm calm, sure of myself, and in charge of this situation," which is exactly what you want your prospects to think of you. By the way, it also makes your thighs look slimmer.

278
Ronna Lichtenberg

Tip No. 3: Fake confidence

Of course, real confidence is better than the fake kind. But if you're not yet mentally in a place where you truly feel that what you've got to offer is the best offer your buyers can get, I'm a big believer in faking it. You don't really believe that all those anchor people and interviewers know what they're talking about on every subject they report, do you? I don't think so.

The way to physically fake confidence is to keep your shoulders down and back, your chest lifted, and your head up. And smile. Research shows that if you force yourself to smile, the very act of curving your lips will release hormones that will automatically make you feel better. (For a cinematic view of this technique, rent *The King and I* and watch Anna and her son whistle a happy tune before meeting the king of Siam.)

DELIVERY IS A DIALOGUE

Delivering your pitch is not a one-sided event. You don't go in and do all the talking while they do all the judging. You are making assessments as well.

In effect, you want to carry a mental tape recorder into the room with you, taking note of relevant details that will later help you assess whether you really want this deal and under what circumstances. In addition to the questions you ask to better understand what they need from you, you also want to get a better sense of what they can give you and what they can't. Will this be a situation in which you can get an energy exchange that works? How far apart are your learning, emotional, and cultural styles? If the gap is wide, how much will it cost you emotionally and psychically to deliver? Will they be paying you enough money to make the inherent difficulties worth your while? Because the bigger the disparity between your styles, the more energy you will have to expend to deliver and the more you need to get paid to make the experience worthwhile.

Understanding that you are not a supplicant helps balance the energy exchange and allows you to pitch with greater authority.

picking up their signals

One of the great advantages women bring to any pitching situation is our ability to pick up nonverbal cues about how our pitch is being received. The brain sex research confirms that we have heightened sensory abilities that enable us to hear better, see better, and be better at interpreting facial expressions than men. This in turn gives us more information about what our prospects think about our offering and allows us to quickly modify our approach as needed.

But this is a disadvantage, too. Biology helps us pick up the signals but, combined with cultural forces, can prompt us to misinterpret or be overwhelmed by them, too. Our wiring leads us to process the reactions we observe analytically and emotionally at the same time. Meanwhile, the stereotypes with which we've been raised and the self-limiting beliefs we carry with us often translate these cues into negative conclusions about how the buyer feels about us. What complicates it is that voice inside your head that you believe is intuition might, in these circumstances, really be paranoia trying to pass itself off as something else.

So at the same time as you're delivering the pitch, you have a running commentary going in your head. Are they listening? Do they like it? He's not talking, he must really hate this idea. He's tapping his pencil, he's not really listening, what a jerk.

Test Your Hearing at Home

If you're not convinced of our superior senses, wait until there is a faucet quietly dripping in the bathroom (this is a test that is easier to administer if you are in bed with a man, but you can manage it even if you aren't). See who notices it first.

Ronna Lichtenberg

This is a really dangerous point for women. First, you can get swamped by all the emotional data you're receiving and become distracted from the task at hand. If you get lost in pondering what this means about how he feels about you, you've lost the pitch because you are so tangled in your own mental underwear you can't break free.

The second danger is that you may be wrong about what all those cues mean.

Take the tapping, for instance. You think he's tapping because he hates what he's hearing. But maybe he's tapping because his wiring makes it physically harder for him to just sit still and listen. Maybe he's expressing the male sense of time—he's got another meeting coming up shortly and just needs you to speed things up.

You cannot let the signals you receive give license to the voices of darkness in your head to take over. Do not let yourself go from "Oh, he's sounding a little impatient" to "I knew I shouldn't have tried this. I'm dirt. I'm nothing."

Instead—and you can do this in a split second because we process this stuff so quickly—say to yourself, "Okay, he's tapping. That doesn't necessarily mean what I'm doing is bad, but it may mean he's in a hurry and he needs me to pick up the pace." Then you try picking up the pace and see if that works. Or you say to him, "I realize I didn't ask you at the beginning of the meeting how much time we have for this. How are you doing on time?"

That is the great beauty of our ability to pick up and process all these signals: We get an opportunity to tailor our pitch more precisely to our prospect in midstream. We know how they are responding, without them telling us directly. And that information is vital to our ultimate success.

the signals you give off

Just as you are picking up cues from the people to whom you are pitching, you are giving off signals too, consciously and unconsciously. The single most important point for you to remember is that if you are pitching to a man, he is not wired to receive all of your signals. I often hear women making comments along the lines of, "Of course, he should know that I was upset. He must have seen it." Well, no. The only way you know for sure that a man knows how you are feeling or what you are thinking is if you tell him so directly.

Men often just do not get it. Literally. Nonverbal cues don't count to them. Neither does indirect speech. (For example, a female manager might ask a male subordinate, "Do you think I can have that report by Thursday?" and if he says yes, she thinks that she has just made a request and that she will have it by Thursday. When it isn't done on Thursday, she gets ticked. But he might not have even known that it was a request, let alone a priority, and thinks, "If she wanted it, why didn't she just tell me?") This is a profound realization, a change-your-life kind of insight. Because once you understand this basic truth, you can stop banging your head against a male concrete wall, expending unproductive emotional energy trying to get a guy to do something that he isn't biologically equipped to do.

In fact, the fewer signals you give off the better. Giving a man too much feedback may distract him and make you look less powerful in his eyes. When you give him nonverbal signals, you are calling upon him to interpret them, which he finds hard. And your purpose in pitching is to make life easier for him. Plus, he's not very good at it, and when guys are pushed to do things they can't do well, they tend to get very grouchy.

A female prospect, on the other hand, will usually be eager for your feedback. Bear in mind that when you are pitching, you are not the only one who is anxious. Your prospect is nervous, too. If she buys something from you, she is putting herself at risk—maybe she's worried about spending her company's resources and the questions she may get from her boss about it. Or she's caught up in 318 other things she has to take care of in her inbox. Or she's just not sure she's making the right decision. The more you can help her be present and calm, the better off she is going to be and the more inclined to say yes.

So, because she is a woman too, she is looking to you for signs that will help her assess the relationship. She is scanning your face, she sees you out of the corner of her eye. She knows if you are uncomfortable, which will make her uncomfortable. It's a bit like riding a horse. If you tighten up, so will she. Instead you want to do the equivalent of "Whoa, Betsy, everything is just fine."

Like you, she is taking the temperature of the relationship on a moment-by-moment basis. You want to broadcast back: It's warm; it's warm; it's still warm; yes, it's warm even now.

Hint: If a female prospect wants to tell you how she feels about your offering, you are in good shape.

SETTING UP FOR THE CLOSE

The delivery phase of your pitch is also the beginning of closing. Toward that end, you need to set up crucial aspects of the offering that are necessary for closing: what needs to be done, pricing, and the next steps. In effect, you need to say to your prospect, here is my understanding of what we are talking about doing, this is roughly how much it will cost you, and here is what we have to do to move forward. You have to make it clear that you are asking for something, that it's going to cost them, and that you expect the proceedings to move along.

Instead, we often wait and wait and wait some more for our prospects to take the lead, know what we want, and set the terms for a deal.

This is not unlike a woman who really wants to get married but never makes it crystal clear to her boyfriend that this is her goal. In fact, a whole genre of self-help books has developed and prospered based solely on this phenomenon. The woman lives with her commitment-phobic boyfriend for seven years without ever clearly articulating that she wants to get hitched and make babies. Then she is devastated when he runs off with young Miss Cookie-Face who has made it clear from the beginning the size of ring that is acceptable, and the size family.

Being clear about what you want sets the stage for getting it, in life and in the close.

CHAPTER 12
closing

All the work you've done so far is in preparation for the moment when you ask the person you're pitching for something, and you are hoping that her answer will be yes. You've done everything in your power to get ready, and now—you're waiting to hear if you get a yes. That moment can be, to use a technical term, a real booger.

Here's why. In the moment you've asked for something and your prospect is thinking about an answer, the relationship winds shift a little. You feel it, and you think you need to do something to "fix" the relationship and make everything be okay—after all, taking care of other people is our job, right? It's easy to see it from the prospect's perspective: She's been feeling connected to you, and then, suddenly, she realizes you have just asked her to give up something she likes and values—like "her" money (even a budget can feel like personal property). Doubts and self-protective thoughts bubble up in her head about the value of your offering.

Because of all of our brain sex gifts, we can almost see those doubts like little cartoon bubbles over our prospect's head, and, in the bad times, we think it's all about us and start to freak. Maybe the prospect is thinking "I don't really need this," or "I thought she was trying to help me but she just wanted something from me," or "I can't afford it." You read all of her signals and her thoughts, and the empathy that has been such a powerful tool in building a relationship becomes a barrier to your moving ahead. That's because as women we are at risk of taking our empathetic observations and making them be about us in a bad way. Empathy can turn out to be a giant trigger for all of those demon negative beliefs.

So we go right from noticing that she is thinking maybe she doesn't want/need our offering, at least not at our price, to thinking she's right and the universe would be better off without us sucking up all that oxygen. Or we decide that she's the enemy and we hate her because she is thinking bad things about us that only we are allowed to think. Or we feel bad because we get so flooded with her needs that we abandon our own and find surprise comments coming out of our mouths like "Oh, that's okay. I'll take care of it," or "I can do it for less money," or "I'm happy to wait another seventeen years for a promotion," or "I don't really need that department to clear things with me first." Often, our instinct is to act to preserve the relationship, at any cost, particularly if the cost is "only" to us.

I have said that I am glad that I am a woman, and I am. But I will admit there have been times when I envied men who couldn't read all those mild distress signals from a prospect, and who weren't sensitive to all the relationship nuances, because it makes it much easier to just forge ahead with a traditional close, which is some version of "are we going to do it, or what?"

Because guys are not wired to talk about how they feel about closing, there's no way for me to really know what's going on. What it looks like from the outside, and what the brain sex research suggests, is that it is easier for men to focus on the task of closing because they are not as distracted by the fluctuations in emotional currency that happen during a close. (On the other hand, they do have all the winning and losing stuff to deal with and, in some ways, a higher perceived social cost of losing, including losing face, than we do. Which means men get to torture themselves about closing, as well, just for different reasons.)

Not surprisingly, the emotional fluctuations of a close are a particular challenge for pinks. One young broker I'll call Macy described her difficulties in closing as follows: "Typically, the conversation is going fine and then it feels like there is some kind of a breakdown. The body language that I read from the other person suddenly isn't as welcoming and . . . it starts to feel like I'm trying to persuade them. Then it seems like there's a stopping point where everything comes to a halt. I don't know if I lose them, or if I'm not as confident as I need to be? I must be losing control over . . . something. So I work on a team with my husband, and at that point he comes in and reestablishes control." For Macy, the shift from relationship building to talking specifics about an offer is gear-grindingly difficult, because in her mind, closing is about establishing control, which is how guys do it. Short. Direct. Solution oriented.

If you are comfortable closing like a guy, you are able to comfortably think of closing as winning over someone else. You may even be able to take a little secret joy in putting something over on them—or at least be able to enjoy the act of closing as a way to establish dominance and reap riches. Nothing wrong with that, and nothing wrong with a little victory dance over that, if that is what works for you.

But for many women, a definition of closing that is based on directly imposing one's will feels alien, maybe even alienating. At an extreme, it can feel so "not who we are" that we never even try to pitch, because that way we don't have to close. Or, as I've seen many times, women can feel so awkward about closing that we somehow just don't do it.

For example, Phil, an insurance executive, was telling me about a young saleswoman on his team who wasn't getting great results. He confided in me that he thought her issue was that she was so cute, no one was willing to tell her that they weren't really interested in buying from her. My guess was that she just didn't know how to close.

I asked Phil to describe to me the difference between the way he closes and his understanding of the way she closes. He said that in his first meeting with prospects, he starts to move his buyer toward a close by saying something like, "I've listened to your dreams and goals, and I want to help you make all of that come true, but it's expensive. Do you care enough about this that the expense is worth it to you?" They agree or they don't, but Phil has made his "closing"

Ronna Lichtenberg

intention clear. In contrast, the young woman has told Phil that after the first meeting, and the second, and the third, she knows everything there is to know about the family, the nickname for Grandma, and where they hope Junior will go to school, but not whether they would prefer premiums to be level or lower in the first years. She gets the relationship, but doesn't know how to get from connection to closing.

You cannot get results—in business or in any group effort—unless you can close. *You need to be able to close a deal, any kind of deal, in order to succeed.* You need to be able to say, "I would really like you to consider me for this job," or "This is why I think you should promote me," or "Once we have your approval, we can get started on this new program right away." As Doris Meister, a top-ranking private banking executive, puts it, "In most businesses, the people who are viewed as the winners are the closers."

For me, closing used to be a lot like turbulence on an airplane. After one particularly colorful flight, where the flight attendants' faces and the hurricane-season Atlanta sky both turned an evil greenish yellow, I started to think that maybe my future employment should be limited to places I could walk to. But even as I kissed the ground in gratitude immediately upon landing, I knew that I couldn't live the work life I wanted without flying. Coming to terms with turbulence was essential to living my life on my terms. Same thing with closing. You may not ever love it, and I'm not going to tell you that you have to love it—I figure that telling you in chapter 3 that you might want to learn to feel fond of fear is obnoxious enough.

But, as with turbulence, you need to deal with closing to get where you want to go. You may also find that pretty soon it doesn't bug you so much, and that anticipating it is not so sweaty palm making. And, unlike how you feel about turbulence, you may even find that you get to kind of like not just what it does for you, but how it makes you feel, when you learn a woman-friendly style of closing.

The goal is to find a way of closing that works for you so that you can see it for what it is: an opportunity to start a new phase of a relationship that you have reason to believe will be valuable to both of you.

TAKE IT TO THE BRIDGE

Ideally, what has happened during the pitch is that you have established that you are working as a partner with your prospect. You've demonstrated that you know and care about what she needs and that you are the one who can help her get past whatever her pain point is, even if it's one she didn't even know she had before she talked to you.

One great technique for achieving a woman-friendly close is to use questions as a bridge from delivery to the close. In a bridge, you use questions to demonstrate that you value the relationship as a way to get to an agreement about how you are going to *continue* to work together (because that's what you've been doing during the pitch) toward some mutually agreeable goal. You are bridging from a discussion about what might be to what could be, with their support.

When you create a bridge with questions, you recap the conversation, get the prospect to agree to the things the two of you have accomplished in the conversation, and the close kind of happens by itself—and doesn't seem so abrupt.

Leaders in general, and sales leaders specifically, are often intuitively gifted at creating a bridge to close. A great example of that kind of talent is Mary Barneby, a divisional sales manager for a major global financial services firm, responsible for almost three thousand salespeople in her territory. Mary coaches her team on what she calls a question summary phase, which is a bridging technique.

Here's how she describes a question summary interchange. "You say, 'So we've talked about your goals,' and you repeat them to the client and say, 'Is this correct?' And the client says, yes, or let me expand on that one, or whatever, and you listen and clarify, if that's what you need to do. Then you go on and say, 'We've talked about [whatever your program/offering/idea is], and does that seem to make sense to you? Do you have any questions?' And the prospect says, they have a question here or there, which you answer. But it's a basic step-by-step, restating the goals, restating the offer, restating all the agreements that you already have."

This approach uniquely plays to a woman's strengths in a couple of ways. First, you don't ever have to "ask for the order" in a way that feels like a bank holdup . . . gimme the money, now. It lessens the potential for a money discussion to have a relationship-jarring impact. It also is an approach that works best when you're patient, which many women are. The relationship orientation that women have to time that we discussed in chapter 11 means that we will spend the time it takes to get from one question to the next.

As impressed as I am with Mary Barneby both because of her career achievements and for her history of service to women (as chair of New York's Financial Women's Association), what impresses me even more is that she has learned to use the bridging technique to come to agreement with her teenager. As we all know, pitching a teenager, let alone your own teenager, has got to be the toughest pitch of all.

For example, Mary described how she could use the bridging technique if Charlie, her teenage son, asked for a cell phone.

The first step is to ask questions as a way to both move things forward and clarify where there's agreement. So in the hypothetical cell phone saga, Mary explains, "I'd say to him, so this is what you want to do, you want to buy a new cell phone because—and I'll have the reasons why he wants to do it." This is exactly the same as with any prospect; you start with a statement of your understanding of their goal, and why it's their goal.

Mary's next question to Charlie would be, "What are our options out there?" They'd go back and forth on that, and the answer would be something like, we can get one that is on sale, we can get a new service where you get a cell phone for free, whatever. With a prospect, you already know the options, because you've done the homework, so you can say, "I know you have other options, like x, y, and z," just as a way to make sure that you've both considered alternatives and that there aren't any surprises out there that could tank your pitch.

This is the point where price often comes up. In Mary's case with her son, the question would be, "How are you going to pay for this?" which generates another set of options. You can have this kind of discussion with your client, too, since you've already had some kind of conversation about money, as we discussed in chapter 9. Your question might be something like, "I know it might be tough for you to make a commitment for second quarter, but you said third quarter looked good," or "I know the range we talked about is a stretch, but you thought it might be possible," or "I know that money isn't as big an issue for you right now as head count." The point is to offer a statement that they've agreed to before that they can agree to again or, failing that, to expand upon how they are thinking about money.

In Mary's cell phone example, after the money stuff is addressed, she quickly restates the conversation and makes a preliminary recommendation. "This is what you want, these are the options, and here's the option that makes the most sense for you." And because they've walked through the process together and looked at the logic of one solution versus another, he's in a position to say, "Yeah, I think that one makes sense," or "Let's do that one." (Of course, since Mary is Mom, the partnership goes a little further than it would with another kind of prospect, as in, "I'll lend you the money and you can pay me back.")

But the way Mary steps through the cell phone conversation with her son is the same way you can step through the conversation with your prospect. The emphasis on agreement at each stage is the same. And the orientation to partnership, to an equal energy exchange, is the same.

REPRISE ON RECEIVING

When I was talking with Mary Carol Garrity about her stunning success with Nell Hill's, a store that is pretty much literally in the middle of nowhere, I asked her what crossed her mind when she first saw a customer. She said, "You know, I want them to have a good time in here, and I don't care if they spend five dollars or five thousand dollars because I want them to walk out of here with something good. It's a reflection of our merchandise. I want them to walk away with something, and to walk away talking about the experience."

Ronna Lichtenberg

When you are closing, you have to be very clear that it is okay to want them to do what you want them to do. It may feel bad to ask for something, particularly when it feels like you are asking for yourself, but it isn't bad. All the homework you've done about the benefit to them works for you in this way: You can be passionate about asking for their support because you know that you are offering them something of value, even if it is "just" your continued efforts and energy on their behalf.

THE COLOR OF CLOSING

Just as we've discussed how introductions and credentialing reflect "color" preferences, closing will, too. The same technique of "taking it to the bridge" works with pinks, blues, and stripes, but the questions you ask, the pacing of the questions, and the responses you get will vary.

With a blue, you can often step through the bridging questions pretty quickly. In a formal situation, you and your blue will be working through some kind of written recommendations and you will have a summary page followed by next steps, which represents the close. The blue will expect this. In workshops I've done with sales teams, even the pinks say that a closing discussion happens much faster, one way or another, with a blue.

The Kinds of Questions You Can Ask a Blue

- ❖ Is there anything else you need to know to make a decision?
- ❖ Should we go ahead with X or Y?
- ❖ Is now a good time to talk about terms? (meaning, how money will be handled)
- ❖ Is there anyone else we need to talk to about this?
- ❖ What is our next action step?

The Kinds of Questions You Can Ask a Pink

❖ Does what I'm describing make sense to you? Is it helpful?

❖ How will this affect people you care about?

❖ I know that talking about money can feel more awkward when you like somebody. Do we need to talk more about how we are going to handle money stuff?

❖ Would it help if I drafted a note that summarizes our agreement?

❖ Is there someone else's support we need, and can I help you enlist it?

❖ Are you able to make a decision about this now?

I was eavesdropping on a classic blue conversation in an airport—I couldn't help it, the two thirtyish businessmen were talking pretty loudly about a colleague who bugged them. One said to the other, "I keep wanting to say, 'You are just like my mother. Would you get to the point?'"

A blue man always wants you to get to the point, as directly and logically as possible, and the point of a pitch is the close. He will respect you for pitching; he will respect you even more for trying to close. And since respecting, not liking, is often as good as it gets with a blue man, it is an ideal way to strengthen a working relationship with him.

With a pink, the bridging questions may take some time, and it may take more sessions to get to a close. Pinks, if they like you, may have trouble telling you what they need, or telling you no, so closing requires more interpretation. A great deal of patience may be required, because every question you ask, and every bit of information you give, could trigger more questions on her part.

It is also easy to mistake the pink's enthusiasm for a yes: "She likes me and she's engaging with me, so clearly she wants us to work together in this way I've proposed." Maybe, and maybe not. Remember, even a yes from a pink can just mean, "Yes, I'm listening."

Ronna Lichtenberg

Also, remember that someone who is giving you money may feel less obligated to give you emotional yummies. That's part of what complicates the relationship dynamic around closing a sale. If I've asked Ms. Prospect for something, I'm supposed to be giving her emotional treats instead of vice versa. It may feel like she is pulling back a bit when we get to that part of the pitch. It will, in all likelihood, feel like she doesn't seem as approving and connected as she did in the moments before you asked for money, or more resources, or whatever it is you're asking for.

Stripes, as I said earlier, are situational. Many stripes tend to go blue on closing, though, because if anything brings out the blue in a person . . . it's cold, hard, green cash.

What makes someone with a striped style tricky is that it is harder to anticipate their needs until you get to know their preferences in a given situation. If you're unsure, then just go back to bridging with questions, as in, "It seems like now would be a good time to talk about money/terms/the agreement." Either they will say yes, which is "take it to the blue," or they will say yes and then digress. The digression means that they want a pink moment, and you should follow their lead and give them a little more time before you try to build a bridge back to the close again.

for pinks or blues, silence is golden

One thing that is the same, no matter what the color, is that it is critical that at some point during the close you stop talking. Stop. Talking.

This is another of those brain sex/cultural expectations double whammies. Here we are. We are wired to talk. We are wired to talk about our feelings. We are wired to talk about their feelings, and we are reinforced for taking care of them. We know that they are feeling/thinking something about our offering, possibly including some mild anxiety. Every shred of our being wants to talk, and to fill up that aching silent space with something. Let it be.

Mary Barneby compares this silence challenge to doing business in Japan. She said when you are doing business in Japan, "you have to be able to deal with long periods of silence, and as an American, don't jump in. Maybe you've said, 'Okay we'll do the deal and it'll be ten dollars per unit.' And if the Japanese person is very quiet, as an American, your impulse will be to jump in and say, 'Okay, nine.' They'll think you're crazy! That's not what they're expecting from you. And I think as women, we have a tendency to jump into those silences. You have to let your client think about it."

To many women, silence feels like a relationship disconnect. It feels that way for good reason—for us, silence *is* often a sign of a relationship disconnect. It is not good relationship news when we give someone the silent treatment. But when closing, silence is just part of the process. It is as normal as a child's runny nose at day care.

Wait as long as you can possibly wait before speaking into a closing silence. Copy the guys and do multiplication tables in your head, or see if you can figure out how many pairs of shoes you actually own. Go elsewhere in your head, to give both of you a little room.

Know that a blue, especially a blue man, is likely to interpret your silence as power. Donna Lopiano, Ph.D., head of the Women's Sports Foundation, told me a great story about how she inadvertently learned this lesson. "Every year, the meeting I dreaded most was with my president at the University of Texas about budgets. I never realized the power of silence until we were in the middle of this budget conversation. We were just battling it out and I announced my bottom line, and he looked at me and said, 'Are you going to tell Ann?' (meaning, are you going all the way up the food chain to share our disagreement with the big boss, Ann Richards, the governor of Texas?). The question just knocked me for a loop. He thought I would, but I would never think of doing that. The reason I was silent was that I was really set back, but he interpreted my silence as my thinking, 'Yeah, but I'm not saying it.' There was this silence that seemed like forever. He is looking at me. I am looking at him, but I am thinking, 'Where is he getting that?' And finally, he looked at my boss, sitting to his right, and said, 'Give it to her.' That was the product of silence because he thought I was more powerful."

Ronna Lichtenberg

When you absolutely can not take the silence another second, you can come back with a question or two, if you are sure you can manage it without sounding desperate. If you think there is any chance the question will come out with even the vaguest hint of "are you ever going to call me again?" you just have to wait a little longer. While you're waiting this time, mentally go over all the good things about Me, Inc. See how many of the beliefs you can remember. Remind yourself of your three pitching points. Dwell on why this offer is so good.

If you are closing with a blue, you can then ask, "I see you're thinking about this. Is there anything that might be helpful for me to answer to get you closer to a decision?" If you are closing with a pink, you can say, "It feels like this might be something we should be talking about. I really want to understand this from your perspective. I'd love to get your feedback."

the death close

The "death close" is when you help somebody else close on something that is not in your interest. Take Rose, for example. Rose was a part-time association employee negotiating for benefits. Her boss's boss, Martha, called Rose to discuss it when Rose's boss was out of town.

It became clear to Rose that Martha was hoping to avoid having to pay benefits, but Martha was being indirect. Out of frustration, Rose said, "Then, what you are telling me is that you won't provide benefits, is that correct?" So all Martha had to do was say yes. Rose let Martha off the hook; she closed for Martha by putting the words in her mouth. And all she got from it was what she didn't want.

It seems weird, but this happens a lot, particularly with pink pitchers. What happens in the death close is that you get angry, but because you are a woman, you don't feel comfortable expressing that anger, so you turn it toward yourself. You may even hope that by doing that, the other person will feel guilty and ashamed and back off. Usually they don't. Usually they are like Martha and happy to use the weapon you just handed to them—on you.

When you are tempted to close for someone else, think, "Is this an outcome

I want?" If it isn't, avoid a close at all costs. What you need instead of a close is time to reposition the discussion to your liking. Tell the person, "This issue is really important to me. I need time to think. Can we schedule another time to do this?"

IF THE ANSWER IS YES

Hurray! It is rare that you can get a yes, even more rare that you can get a yes the first time you ask, and rarest of all that you can get exactly what you want.

But before you rush out to celebrate by taking a bath in a tub of champagne, remember a couple of things. First, movie star legend is that you have to make sure the champagne has gone flat before you climb into a tub of it, because otherwise you could sustain alcohol burns in important places. Second, now, more than ever, you need to make sure that the focus of your offering remains on them, and not on you.

Your prospect needs praise now, and reinforcement for making a good decision. You say that you are happy to have the chance to work together. If you have closed with a blue, you remind them of the competitive advantage they will achieve as a result of this. Your praise connects to how whatever it is you're doing together is going to create a win for your blue and your blue's "tribe." Then you move on quickly to do whatever you need to do to make sure that you deliver more than they thought they were going to get so that you are well-positioned for the next pitch.

With a pink, you take a little time to make sure the relationship is in a good place. You can even explicitly separate the business and the personal components at this point and say, "Maybe we should take our business hats off for a while and just plan on a triple crème caramel latte next week." If you've just reached agreement about the offering and your pink starts talking about something that feels personal, stay there. Don't try to take it back to the task at hand prematurely, even if you are blue and think if you can't start actually doing something you are going to implode. Your pink may have been stressed

Ronna Lichtenberg

by closing, and she may need a little time to process her emotions before moving forward. Don't rush her.

No matter what your prospect's color, do not express doubts about your offering. The temptation may be there to do it because it could feel as if you have "won" and your prospect is in a one-down situation. As we learned in the section on cultural stereotypes, you may really want to express vulnerability, as in "I really hope that I don't disappoint you." Expressing your vulnerability at this point is selfish, because it is asking the prospect to take care of *your* emotional needs and she is doing enough by supporting your offering. The best thing you can do for your prospect is make her feel comfortable by doing everything you can to appear confident that you are going to deliver on your offering at least to the level promised, and hopefully more.

Even if you don't get as big a yes as you would like, remember that you have gone into the pitch expecting to receive. The yes you get may be a surprise ("No, I don't think we can promote you, but we should be talking about getting you line experience to set you up for something bigger later"), or it may be smaller, but remember throughout the closing process that you are ready to receive a yes.

IF THE ANSWER IS MAYBE

Much of the time, maybe is the best you can do with a first pitch. The best maybe is the one that comes with enough feedback to help you get to a yes. When maybe is the answer, you move on to concentrating on learning even more about your prospect's pain point, resources, and decision-making capacity.

Your job is to figure out what this particular maybe means.

Take, for example, a common maybe, the "maybe later." When I was a little girl, my father would respond to my most outrageous requests with "maybe later." That was how he said, "The answer is no, but I don't want to have to deal with your response to the no, so I'm just going to see if this one will fade out on its own." There are a lot of people in the world who use the "maybe later" technique to say no. In an attempt to be nice, they take your card, give you a smile, tell you that they liked what you had to say, and then go back to what they were doing before just as if the encounter with you had never happened. For those people, "maybe later" means no.

Other times, "maybe later" is real and means that the prospect anticipates having a need for your offering, or the resources to "pay" for your offering, at some time in the future.

The way to figure out if it's real or as phony as a fake Fendi bag is to say, "Would it make sense for me to get back to you in X time period?" If your prospect says, "No, X plus six weeks would be better," or counters with something that will eventually appear on the calendar, the pitch is still alive. If they say, "No, thanks so much, I'll just plan on calling you when something comes up," your pitch is probably on a respirator.

In either case, your job is to follow up in a way that keeps the idea of working with you alive, because sometimes this kind of maybe turns into a great yes.

Another kind of maybe is the "maybe, but." The "maybe, but" means that your prospect has some concern that you don't fully understand, because if you fully understood it, you could help her work through it.

"Maybe, but" means "There are disturbances in the political winds," or "Yesterday I was pretty confident about my budget but today I'm not so sure," or "I just found out that the big boss's future daughter-in-law is applying for the job I was thinking of having you fill."

With a "maybe, but" you shift into very high active listening gear. You ask a lot of open-ended questions, as in, "Tell me what you see as the potential issues," and do a lot of paraphrasing of their responses, as in, "So, you're saying that if X happens, there is some chance they are going to want to hang you at high noon," and wait to see if you can get additional detail.

Sometimes a "maybe, but" is pretty simple and is just "I want to do it, but I want it to cost me less." If that's the case, it will come out pretty quickly, and you can decide if you are willing to negotiate and how much.

Ronna Lichtenberg

With other maybes, it is just a matter of waiting it out, because most of the time "maybe, but" relates to what other people may or may not do. This is another one where patience is a virtue.

If you've been waltzing with a maybe for what seems to be half your lifetime and aren't getting anywhere, another way to test the waters, and get to a yes, is to ask for something else that doesn't cost as much. If you're on the outside selling into an organization, you can ask for a referral: "I'm really looking forward to working with you on this, and I've told you how much I like to work with clients like you. Is there anyone else you know who could benefit from my offering?" If you're inside and asking for a promotion, you can say, "You know I really want to move to a line job/head up this new area/start supervising others. I know that now may not be the right time for that, so I was wondering if we should talk about putting me on that task force/getting financial support for an advanced degree/sending me to a special educational program."

All maybes offer a great opportunity to get better at eliciting feedback. At a minimum, you can make your prospect your partner by getting them to tell you what about your offering really works for them and what doesn't. Dr. Lopiano advises treating feedback, including criticism, as a kind of coaching. "Whenever you get a criticism, you don't discard it; you take a really objective look at it. The first decision you have to make is whether or not you should reassess what you're doing as a result. If I think it is valid, I will retreat, revise, and move forward. But if I don't think it is valid, I will just move forward. In either case, it's not personal. It's like when a coach criticizes you, he's not saying 'You're bad'; he's saying, 'I don't think this idea or performance is good.'"

Once in a while you'll get a maybe that is the "I've fallen and I can't get up" maybe. For whatever reason, your prospect can't decide to move forward and you end up in the call-back carousel, going around and around and around.

It's hard to step off that carousel because you can see the gold ring almost within reach. But at some point, you must make a move. Mary Seebeck, a legendary insurance saleswoman and author of *American Dream Women*, told me a great story of how she learned to make her move.

A local dentist was a prospect, and Mary had gone through a detailed fact-finding process with him. Mary made recommendations. She followed up regularly. He kept telling her to call back later.

Finally one day Mary had her assistant call the dentist and say, "Mary is cleaning out files because we need more space and wanted you to know that we're going to throw away all her notes about you." "No!" he said, and proceeded to move forward on her recommendations.

The only way to make way for the new, for any opportunity, is to let go of what isn't happening. Just don't threaten to let go of a maybe—if you're going to let it go, actually let it go. Otherwise you run the risk of making it an empty threat that leaves you looking powerless, which is exactly the result you don't want from a pitch.

IF *YOUR* ANSWER IS NO

There are some prospects who fall into the "life is too short category," although more of them fall into that category in a good economy than in a bad.

There are good reasons why you may have pitched someone and then decided that you don't want to move forward. The best reason is that what they want you to do doesn't help you build toward your vision. You've built one kind of offering; they want something slightly different. Or, more commonly, you used to do something and now want to do something new, and they want you for what you used to do. One of the most frustrating things about a job search is that employers often want you to have already done the job they want you to do, which eliminates some of the risk for them and increases risk of slow-death-by-lack-of-challenge for you.

One of the most courageous stories I've seen about a great no was in a *New York Times* story about a company called New Technology Management, founded by Lurita Doan. In 2000, her company was offered a $22 million con-

Ronna Lichtenberg

tract to supply hardware to the government. At that time, the company had $14 million in revenue. Faced with the opportunity to more than double her revenue, Lurita turned it down.

She also reports that she never regretted it, and I can see why: Four years later, her company is a recognized leader in border surveillance technology. She credits the company's growth to staying true to her vision, which is why she said no to what seemed to her like the wrong offer. "We've never been about selling hardware. We're a very service-oriented organization. If we went down that path, churning and burning technology, we would lose our edge."

Here's the trick with saying no to their offer. Make sure you wait to hear the offer before you decline it. If they haven't made you an offer, the answer isn't no. Once they make you an offer, you might be able to do something else with it, as in, "Thank you so much. That is a lovely offer. What would make it work for me is . . . " If you really don't want it at that point, you just ask for something that you really think they won't do—like give you more money than you can imagine. And if it turns out they have better imaginations than you do, well, maybe the answer is yes after all.

Which brings us to the other reason to say no, which is if you are sure in advance that you just can't charge enough to even out what it is going to cost you in emotional currency to satisfy this prospect.

I often see this situation with working moms, particularly new moms, who are recalculating the "cost" of their job. Things that used to be personally expensive in terms of the energy it takes to sustain the effort, like being on the road, or long hours, or clients who teeter on the edge of outrageously demanding, can become prohibitively expensive when there are young children at home.

You need to figure out if you are in a situation that more money can fix. Ask yourself, would this be worth it for twice as much money as we're talking about? If the answer is no, that it would take more than twice as much, it is not an offering you can support and you need to graciously extricate yourself from the situation.

If the answer is yes, then there may be a way to negotiate through it, for example, by aggressively cutting down the amount of time you spend on it or the scope of responsibility.

IF *THEIR* ANSWER IS NO

Take a deep breath. It's not the answer you wanted to hear, and that first moment of rejection can be as shocking as diving into the ocean off the Maine coast in July.

Then go to your strengths. Now is the time to put your ability to pick up nonverbal cues to good use.

If they clearly feel some regret about telling you no and seem to find some appeal in your offering, treat it as a "maybe later." That kind of no means, "I really like you and would like to do business with you, but this doesn't make sense for me right now." Don't pressure them, because the line between feeling sorry for you and sorry for themselves for having to put up with you can be pretty thin. Distinguish yourself by graciousness. Tell them that you would like the chance to come back to them in the future, with other ideas, and then do so, being extremely careful to follow the rules of follow-up (which I'll get to a little later in this chapter).

There is also the "What the hell, I've got nothing to lose" pitch as a response to a no. A reporter I met was working for an organization that was in pretty serious financial difficulty. Her beat was expensive; it got nuked. The boss asked her to propose another beat, which she did, but they didn't like that one, either. My take was that whatever alternative she pitched wouldn't have worked because they just wanted to cut head count, and her head was an easy one to cut. When her boss turned that pitch down, it was instantly clear there was no job for her. She shut down, and understandably felt bruised.

What she missed was a great opportunity to pitch. Her boss had been a big supporter of hers before and couldn't have felt good about firing her. There was a lot she could have asked for, from the simple ("I would love your active sup-

Ronna Lichtenberg

port and counsel in looking for something new") to the more complex ("After I digest this, could I come back to you to talk about possible options?").

A friend once told me that for men, no is just the beginning of a conversation, and for women it is the end. Trust me on this one. Every time you hear no from a guy, just go back in another way one more time. Guys see conflict as a way to engage. His no could just be an invitation to negotiate—tire kicking because he wants to buy the car. It's worth coming back with another version of the offer just to see if his no is actually an indication of serious interest.

Finally, keep a good attitude, because cheer in the face of a no can eventually bring a happy ending, even if it doesn't work immediately.

Three years ago, I was scheduled to have lunch with someone with whom I'd been negotiating a contract that was a big deal for my company. Things were on track. In fact, at 10:30 that morning, things were great. My prospect was psyched. I was psyched. She was saying things about getting the show on the road. When I met her at 12:30 P.M., she didn't look psyched. She looked wrecked. Her introductory comment? "Before we start lunch, I think I should tell you that I just quit my job." My first concern was it wasn't a very good thing that my prospect, a single mom, was out of work. My next thought wasn't a thought. It was a compelling visual image of my lovely potential contract being flushed down the toilet. My mood threatened to follow it, and it took considerable effort to pull myself together and bring my focus back to my prospect's loss instead of mine.

But I managed, and for the next hour or so I let her talk it out and tried to help her think about what to do next. The big project was clearly a non-starter, but as she talked about plans for her job transition, I thought I could help her. It was one of those weird observer moments every author of self-help books must have. I thought, "Would I tell someone to risk a pitch under these circumstances?" I decided that I would advise at most a very soft one, which I went on to offer. It was so small and so soft, it was more of a roll than a toss. It was the "oh, by the way" pitch. I followed up for the next few months to offer support during her job search. Last year she called, with an invitation to do a terrific project together based on my "oh, by the way" two years before. You can't count on no growing up into yes, but sometimes, when you least expect it, it does.

if the answer is hell, no

The first Prudential chairman I ever worked for, the late and much-beloved Bob Beck, was one of the world's great salesmen. Bob was a master at getting his mind in a good place and always said that he loved it when someone told him no because he had figured out how many nos it took to get to a yes and could receive every no gratefully because he knew it was moving him toward his goal.

I used to not be able to fathom this level of optimism, but now I kind of get it. Even a "hell, no" can be productive. All it means is that this pitch didn't work, this time. It's like Edison experimenting with light bulb filaments. It didn't work the first time. Or the next six thousand times he tried different filaments. Eventually, he found one that worked because he learned something from every one that didn't.

There is a certain inner feistiness that you need to summon up from somewhere to deal with a "hell, no." If you let the "hell, no" stop you, you lose. "They" win, because they were able to convince you that you couldn't find a Me, Inc. offering that would move you toward your vision. But if you figure out what didn't work, if you learn from the no, you win. It's as simple as that.

IF YOU GET FEEDBACK, YOU'VE SUCCEEDED

Whether someone said yes, no, maybe, or "please take it away, I hate it," it is vitally important to get feedback about your pitch. My experience is that it is best for all concerned not to ask for feedback immediately after pitching: You're too revved up and the person you've asked hasn't had time to put things in perspective.

The best way to ask for feedback is always a variation on the same theme:

Ronna Lichtenberg

"Please tell me what I need to know about you, and your needs, so I can do the best possible job for you." Here are some others: A comfy request for feedback would be, "You seem to be okay with this. Is there anything about it that isn't working for you?" If your prospect is pink, you can ask for feedback by saying something like, "I really want you to love this, so please tell me the parts that aren't quite working for you." If your prospect is blue, you can ask for feedback by saying something like, "Obviously I don't know you well enough to get this exactly right. Could you tell me what's working for you and if there is anything we need to tune up?" Remember, a blue can hear a request for help as vulnerability or a "one-down," so make sure your tone is strong.

The clearer you are in your own head that you are asking for feedback about your *offering,* not about if they really love/need/trust you, the easier you will make it for them to actually provide it to you. If this is someone whom you've pitched before and you sense that they are worried about you being fragile—maybe because the last time they told you what they thought you had a hissy fit/got quiet for two weeks/were overheard sobbing in the ladies' room—you say, "Look, I know you might be worried about my reaction. But I've learned that you are doing me a big favor by giving me real feedback, and I promise that I will be happy to hear what you have to say."

True, feedback, even feedback you solicit, can hurt. Sometimes the answer to the question Do I look fat in this? is yes. No matter how kindly it is said, it ain't great news.

But if you don't know what is working for you, and what is working against you, there is nothing you can do about it. Feedback is a source of power.

Judy Haberkorn, who was president of consumer sales and service at Verizon, told me a story about how she handled feedback that has become my personal standard for how it should be done. One day, her then-boss was giving Judy a performance review, and it was all positives. You know the corporate system—many boxes to be checked, and he had checked off all the right ones.

Judy was properly grateful. But then she looked at him and told him she wanted him to tell her all the stuff that wasn't so good. He demurred. So she

Give Yourself Feedback

You don't have to do this self-evaluation exercise after every pitch, but once or twice a year it is good to step back and get a sense of how you are doing with the whole pitching process. Fill one out for two or three specific pitches, so you can see any patterns. Remember that you're doing this just as a learning exercise, not as punishment. Do it because you are working on your game, and the only way to do that is to break down how well you are doing with various techniques.

On a scale from 1 (strongly disagree) to 10 (strongly agree):

1. I was credible.

   1   2   3   4   5   6   7   8   9   10

   My credibility would be increased if I . . .

2. They thought my offering addressed their needs.

   1   2   3   4   5   6   7   8   9   10

   The best fit was . . . and the part that didn't quite fit was . . .

3. I flexed effectively on style.

   1   2   3   4   5   6   7   8   9   10

   My prospect was a . . . and I adapted to their style by . . .

4. Me, Inc. distinguished itself from competitors.

   1   2   3   4   5   6   7   8   9   10

   Competitors have an edge with . . .

   The Me, Inc. offering is more appealing because . . .

5. I responded to their feedback and reactions.

   1   2   3   4   5   6   7   8   9   10

   The big nonverbal cues I got were . . .

   The best way I could have responded to those cues was . . .

6. The offering was fairly priced.

   1   2   3   4   5   6   7   8   9   10

Ronna Lichtenberg

My prospect (did or did not) need time to think about price. I handled that by. . . .
I'm confident that I asked for enough because. . . . I feel like my prospect "owes"
me something emotionally, and I am going to deal with my reaction by . . .

7. I maintained positive healthy energy.
   1   2   3   4   5   6   7   8   9   10
   My energy was good because I did . . . for myself.

looked him straight in the eye and said, "Tell me what they say about me when I'm not in the room."

To the degree that you can know what "they" say about you when you're not in the room, you can change what happens in the room.

That's why it is your job to:

❖ Ask for feedback. Say that you really want to know what worked, and what could have worked better.

❖ Make it easy for them to give you one or two specifics. You can't do much with global praise or criticism. So ask for feedback on something, like, "Did you think the competitive advantage was clear?" or "Were there too many slides?"

❖ Listen to the answer. If you're going to interrupt and get all defensive, it's better that you don't even ask. Your job is to actually listen, and to get real examples if you can.

❖ Say thank you. Even if you think they are full of garbanzos, they have taken a risk by sharing their perspective with you. You should acknowledge that, both when they tell you and then again at the end of the conversation.

❖ Don't get too into it. If they say the equivalent of "yes, you do look terrible in that," it is not an invitation for you to launch into, "I know, I know. I should have never bought something that made me look like I need a liver transplant." Acknowledge it and move on. It's just like a compliment, by the way. They say, "You look great in that!" and you say, "Thanks!" not "Oh do you think so? I think I look like a shar-pei in a tutu."

☞ Be good about giving feedback first. It's a gift to them if you do it the right way. And if you coach them on your style, it can make for an incredibly productive working relationship. You don't have to attach style labels if you don't want to. You can just say something like, "I can always give you a better answer if I have time to think," or "I need more explicit positives first from you if you can handle it—it will help me hear the harder stuff better." Make sure it's an "I" statement if you think there's any chance they will hear a "you" as criticism.

FOLLOWING UP

The world is full of people who get follow-up wrong. You know this because people follow up with you the wrong way all the time: They call you at bad times; they send too many messages; they leave urgent messages when you feel no urgency; and they try to make you feel guilty, which can make you feel guilty at first but which sooner or later makes you mad.

Bad follow-up can turn a great pitch sour. Follow up the wrong way and your previously appetizing pitch can become as unwelcome as a taped telemarketing call just when the baby finally stopped crying and was falling asleep.

As a woman, you have a tremendous potential advantage in following up. The advantage is that you are oriented to relationship and you know how to convey that, and strengthen it. Here are some specifics that will help you keep playing to that strength.

remember Dr. Pavlov

Ivan Pavlov, you will recall, trained dogs to associate a ringing bell with food being served; soon, they would salivate at the sound of the bell, without any food present. (I've re-created that very experiment: When the buzzer to our apartment sounds, the cats run to the door because they know Chinese food is coming.)

Ronna Lichtenberg

Here's the Pavlovian question for you: When your prospect sees your name, what is the first thing that comes to mind? If it's, "Oh, Lord, what does she want now?" that is not a good sign. You want them to think that there is a chance that hearing from you means something good for them.

That's why, particularly in a longer-term relationship, like with your boss or with any other internal client, you have to be in touch with them just to be helpful to them. Sometimes the only agenda you should have is their agenda. Congratulate them on something good that happened to them. Make sure that they heard some news. If nothing else, at least be fun, and invite them to things that they might enjoy.

By the way, this is a time when you can look manipulative if your real intent is not to focus on them, but to focus on you. Everyone eventually spots a Trojan horse. When you go immediately from "Oh, congratulations to you" to "And how are we doing on my raise?" your prospect is not going to feel you ever had any real concern for them.

If they bring up your agenda, use your scanning ability to see if they really mean it or are just testing you. Feel free to say, "I'm happy to talk about me/my offering later but right now I am perfectly content to focus on you," if you think they are just being polite and are rushed or otherwise preoccupied.

Taking attention turns is fine, and expected. When it's your turn, you can say, "Hey, just following up to see how we're doing and if there's anything you need from me to move forward."

if you bear gifts, be cool about it

The Forbes family, at least the ones who publish *Forbes* magazine, have really mastered the art of the follow-up. When I had responsibilities for advertising at Prudential Securities, they would have elegant functions sponsored by the magazine. Once there, their focus was on my having a good time.

The next day, or the next week, I would get a call from someone on the magazine who said basically, "Now that we've gotten to know each other better, may I tell you why your team should be buying more pages in my magazine?" It worked because I felt obligated, they made it a point to provide a very strong offering, and I didn't feel strong-armed. Gifts that work are the ones that are a little unexpected and have something to do with the receiver.

Remember that praise is a gift, too. Your prospect feels powerful to you, so it is hard to remember that he needs praise, too, but he does. If he's a guy, we know that he is wired to be constantly monitoring for status, so try to hook your praise to advantage and positioning. Even though research shows that guys like praise even when we don't mean it, try to find something that you really do mean. With blue guys, remember always to tie the praise to task: something he did, not something he is.

Women like praise, too, because it is simultaneously great relationship glue and helps us quiet down those negative internal beliefs. With a pink woman, you are free to praise something unrelated to task, including how she looks. (By the way, this advice doesn't hold if you are a guy reading this book, especially in a high-systemizing culture, which is likely to be all paranoid about anything related to gender. Under those circumstances, limit yourself to something like, "Wow, the grass in this photo of your family looks great. What do you do for lawn care?")

choose the benign interpretation

When you reach out to follow up with someone, there is a good chance you will get a response, or non-response, that is open to interpretation. You get to choose if you see it as benign—that is, okay—or bad.

For example, "He said to call on Wednesday morning, and I did, and now it is Friday afternoon and I haven't heard from him." The bad mental interpretation you may immediately go to is, "This means that he is not interested/hates me/has pursued another opportunity and that all is lost." It is possible that you are right.

However, a more likely, and a more useful, interpretation is the benign one, which is, "It's Friday afternoon and he must be really swamped. He's not going to get back to me today, or on Monday, which is always a bad day. If I don't hear back by Wednesday, then it makes sense to ring back and check."

Your pitch is never as important to your prospect as it is to you. When you're looking for a job and someone says they will call you back and you are living on savings and not sure what's going to happen, it feels like that return phone call is the most important thing in your life. But it doesn't feel the same way to your potential employer.

To them, it's another item on the To Do list. Important, but not life-altering. If you keep that in mind as you interpret reactions, you are less likely to go to something too negative, and to overreact.

it is not their job to provide closure

The day will come when you have tried to follow up with someone fifteen times and haven't heard anything back. You think that this is their way of saying no, but you aren't sure. You are feeling really frustrated, and what you want them to do is end the frustration so you can go on and lead your life.

It's like those bad romantic moments in movies, when the disappointed would-be lover says to the object of their desire, "Just tell me. All I need for you is to tell me that it's over." You know perfectly well that this is not something you want to do in your love life, unless you are searching for inspiration for your next tragic poem, song, or painting.

You don't want it in pitching, either. If you can't think of a reason to talk to them that is about them, and if you have already followed up, and definitely if you are feeling like a stalker, you have to let it go, at least for a while.

Here's a classic stalking story. An ad agency sent its capabilities material to a client conducting an agency search. The agency exec called the client a couple of times to see if the materials were "in" and the client, busy sorting out responses, didn't return the agency exec's calls.

So the agency exec tried again and got the client's voice mail message that said, "If this is urgent, you can call my cell." The exec, thinking the status of their candidacy was urgent, went ahead and called the client on the cell.

The client's response? A testy "This does not count as urgent." Outcome: The agency was eliminated from consideration on the spot.

Pressing them to close under these circumstances will never get you the answer you want, so you have to do what you do when disappointed in love—move your attention elsewhere and hope you'll hear from them.

treat their team with respect

A quick way to turn off exactly the kind of person you want to do business with is to diss her team. The more senior the person, the more she counts on the people around her to screen for her: It is their job to decide if Ms. Big will think it is valuable to be in contact with you.

It is just as important to know the style preferences of the assistant and to track his cues as it is to know the boss's. It goes without saying that you know and remember his name, and that you make some effort to know and connect to him as a person.

If you think that you are Ms. Thing and the person answering the phone is Ms. Nothing, you will communicate that. She will remember that. Your follow-up messages will get delivered . . . maybe. Later. You run the risk that there will be just a touch of spin when she says, "Diva called. Again."

Remember that anyone who works with, and especially anyone who reports to, your prospect is also a prospect and should be treated as such. By the way, never complain to the boss—even indirectly—with a voice mail or e-mail that says something like, "I left a couple of messages for you—maybe so-and-so didn't give them to you." This is a huge mistake; there's a good chance the person you're complaining about will hear the message before the boss does.

You can, however, blame lack of response on inanimate objects including Mars being in retrograde or a low-grade virus. One trick my friend Pam uses is to say something like this: "Sent you a note last week. With this crazy weather another client of mine told me she was having e-mail problems. In the event that cyberspace ate my message to you—or horrors! cyberspace ate your return message back to me—thought I should forward my note again." She adds that, "I hate to say it but this technique works more often than not." This one, though, has to be handled in a cheeky manner or it will fail.

mind your manners

When you are in a competitive situation, and you wouldn't be pitching if you weren't, you can lose points for bad manners. Bad manners include any demonstration of thoughtlessness. On her list of follow-up no-nos, Joanne Davis includes these faux pas: calling late on Friday when there's a good chance someone's trying to get out for a holiday weekend, calling your prospect on her first day back from vacation, calling on Monday morning, calling from a cell phone (who knows what the call will sound like on the other end?), and assuming that they have your contact information at hand when maybe they do and maybe they don't.

As Joanne told me, "My key pet peeve of bad manners is when callers don't leave their phone numbers. Yes, I may have it, but I may be on the road without my complete contact file. The five seconds they take to leave their number twice, slowly, saves me from having to open my Palm address book or file to find a number. Plus I may be checking voice mails walking through an airport and don't have a pen and pad handy while I'm in the middle of taking my laptop out for security and explaining to the security guy that my underwire bra is what's triggering the metal detector."

Be cheery when you call or e-mail, and hold down the harangues. Remember to mind your manners too when someone's pitching you. You gals are somehow connected in business: Next time the glove could be on another mitt.

PUT REJECTION IN ITS PLACE

If you got an answer you didn't like, you need to make yourself feel better before you can move on. It's okay if you feel like you've taken an emotional hit, and it's okay if it takes you more than twenty seconds to snap out of it; it is what happens to many women, and it is how we are wired to respond. The guys in your life are wired to tell you that it's no big deal and to brush yourself off and get immediately back into the game. Men need to find a recommendation that will fix it for you, and it doesn't hurt to thank them for this advice. It also doesn't hurt to ignore it.

The way to feel better is to take care of yourself. Go back to your list of things and people that give you energy from chapter 7. You need them now. You may feel like now is a great time to punish yourself, or to deprive yourself of things that give you pleasure because you haven't "earned" them. You have earned them. You have earned the right to take care of yourself by being brave enough to be in the game, which all by itself deserves a reward.

My best advice is to plan on a small treat for yourself after you pitch so that you are ready to reward yourself no matter what. That will make it easier to go right from rejection to recovery. It doesn't have to be big. Maybe a manicure. Or asking your sister to baby-sit so you can have twenty minutes in the mall. Or sitting down at the Starbucks and reading something adult for fifteen minutes instead of standing up and slurping while you do three other things.

Another technique that can help is having your own Comeback Kit to fall back on. If you are pitching, you are going to be rejected. Knowing that, it's good to have prepared in advance something that reminds you that you, and your offering, are in fact pretty wonderful.

Women who like to put scrapbooks together, and women who are so organized that there is a place for every photograph in their house (there is in mine, too, it's just that the place is likely to be stuck to the bottom of a seldom-used drawer), sometimes put together a portfolio or photo box of the things that remind them of what in their life makes them feel valuable.

Things you might include:

- Awards
- Check stubs
- Photographs of people you love

Ronna Lichtenberg

- An image of a special place

- A poem or saying that inspires you

- Letters of acceptance

- Engagement, wedding, or birth announcements

- A fortune cookie slip predicting great things

Part of what works about putting together a Comeback Kit is just "normalizing" rejection, as my shrink friends would say. If you know you're going to get rejected sometimes and you've prepared for it, it's a little easier to handle. Putting the good stuff in one place not only makes it easier to find on days that you could use a lift, but it honors what you've done—"Yes, I did do this, and it was good."

A few years ago I was Scholar-in-Residence at Youngstown State University, as part of a special entrepreneurial program. One morning, I was treated to a breakfast with local women business leaders, who, both individually and as a group, were delightful and impressive.

One of them owned a gym and had established a system of offering regular instruction in breast self-exams to help keep her clients healthy. She said that her Comeback Kit had only two letters in it, from clients who found their breast cancers early as a result of the training offered at her gym. Both had been treated successfully. On bad days, it's an instant way to remind herself that what she did had value and that what she offered went beyond toned triceps.

choose to move on

Nobody likes to be rejected. Guys don't wake up in the morning and say, "Boy, I hope I get turned down on that big pitch today." A gift that guys are more likely to have, though, is the gift of attributing it to something other than their own failings. Everything can feel more personal to us, including rejection. That's why we need to make a conscious choice about how we're going to handle rejection instead of defaulting to our wiring.

Mary Barneby was gracious enough to talk to me about something that didn't work out in her business life, and I think her story offers a terrific model of what to do when it doesn't work.

Before joining her current firm, Mary had a start-up business that she ended up having to close down. The company's concept was great; it was the only company in the world with this particular offering. People had put millions into it. But after 9/11, the venture capital market dried up and there was no way to make the company successful.

Mary struggled with the decision for months. She tried everything, including using her own money to meet payroll and to save the company.

"And then," she said, "when I realized that I could not personally do that, I sat myself down, and said, 'Look . . . I have to go on. I have to take my career and go elsewhere where I can be really successful; this is not an environment where I can make this happen.'" She went ahead and called a bankruptcy attorney and the company took Chapter 11.

After she did everything she had to do to liquidate the company, "I just moved on. I knew that there was nothing to go back to there. That I had to go forward . . . I didn't live in it. I didn't dwell on it."

Talking to Mary reminded me that if you live long enough, and you're lucky, you are going to try things that don't work out. If you've never failed in your work life, you are either very young, incredibly lucky, or have avoided taking the risks you should be taking to fulfill your potential. If your offering didn't work—it didn't work. The only possible response is . . . Next! All the other responses go in a little black box to be put away.

Early in my writing career, I took a nonfiction writing class taught by Jacob, a poet. Jacob told us that his rule was that when he sent out a poetry submission and got a rejection letter in response, he had to send out three more poems right away. As in my Bob Beck example earlier, Jacob trained himself to associate rejection with activity.

What's lovely about this is that it doesn't make rejection global and of cosmic importance. It doesn't make you a loser for life. It just means you take what you can with you and keep moving forward.

WHAT WENT WRONG?

After you've done whatever you need to do to feel better, it's time to take a look at your offering to see what would make that work better. You may not ever know exactly why the answer was no, but here are some possibilities.

repackage the offer

Now is the time to figure out how to make your offer attractive to someone else. Did it feel like the offering itself was good and the three sticky points were compelling? Which one was the strongest? Did you lead with that? Which one was the weakest? Should you lose that?

reprice your offering

The only way to know the marketplace value of your offering for sure is to find someone who will pay that specific amount for it. Up until that point, it's all theoretical.

Let's say I think my house is worth $250,000. If I put it on the market and the high bid is $147,000, that tells me that right this minute the house is not worth what I hoped it would be. My choices are to drop the price, leave it on the market and trust that someone else will come along, or take it off the market and wait it out.

Same thing with your offering. If you are in your market range, your prospect's first reaction is likely to be that it's too high. The nature of the human beast is to want to pay less than market. Why else do we all take such joy in saying, "I got it for 20 percent off!"? So whenever you pitch, if you are asking for enough, there is going to be price resistance when you try to close. Price resistance is a good sign: It means your potential buyer is serious.

But there is price resistance and there is "No way, sweet pea." If you've had more than three pitches in a row that break down over price, it is time to think about how you are pricing, and how to make your pricing more appealing.

bad timing

Sometimes the stars just don't align in your favor. When the economy dipped, particularly because I was doing so much work in the financial services sector, it got to be kind of a sick joke around the office. I'd pitch and get a maybe. Then we'd get a phone call that the company I was pitching was about to be taken over, or about to take over someone else, or getting ready to fire a big chunk of its team in order to be more attractive as an acquisition target, starting with the person who had just said maybe to me.

In this situation, the best thing you can do is focus on the relationship, if it is someone you like and want to work with in the future. If there is any way you can be helpful to them, now is the time to reach out. Otherwise, respect their needs by leaving them alone until whatever is happening that is bigger than both of you stops looming so large.

bad chemistry

Maybe you remind your prospect of his mother and he has residual ill will about the way she handled his toilet training. Who knows? As adorable as you are, sometimes your prospect is going to have a bad attitude.

Or sometimes, particularly if it is an internal pitch, you may come under attack for reasons you just didn't have any reason to expect. The person you consider your prospect has a competitor who attends a meeting unexpectedly, or someone you didn't think was your prospect feels that she was and now she feels dissed and is having a low blood sugar moment. Or, if you're an outsider, a group suddenly forms a quick game of "gotcha" just because they get abused all the time themselves and what a great opportunity it is to abuse someone else for a change.

Who knows? But there you are, having come into a meeting with good attitude, a great pitch, and a good tone, and suddenly you are flailing in a sea of other people's anger.

The best thing to do—in fact, the only thing to do—is to avoid engaging in the craziness. What you are going to do in the meeting is impress them with how calm you are, and the degree to which you concentrate on taking things back to facts, and on understanding what to do about whatever the purported problem is. Concentrate on physically relaxing. Inhale. Exhale. Lower your shoulders. Uncross your arms. And your legs. Communicate body language that indicates confidence and comfort. Hold your head as high as Nicole Kidman does at a movie premiere.

If you think you are totally losing it, ask for a quick break. They can probably use it as much as you can. Go to the bathroom and steady yourself. Get a drink of water. It sounds silly, I know, but if you can, take off your shoes and just stand for a moment and try to reconnect into your feet. You want to feel grounded, which is helped by being able to feel the ground.

Listen for opportunities to partner with your critics. Praise them for good points—that will make you look powerful. And then see if you can bridge with questions back to a pitch, although maybe not exactly the one you started out to give.

If nothing else, by the time the smoke clears they'll be saying, "Boy, she really handled herself like a pro, didn't she?" Which is a terrific way to get into position for the next game.

A personal agenda ambush is a variation on bad chemistry. No matter how much homework you do about your prospect's agenda, there is going to be something you miss. You aren't necessarily going to know if they just got told by the boss that they only have six months to shape up, or if they think they are in hot competition for some great new opportunity, or if they hate one of their colleagues so much they would give up a victory if it would somehow hurt that person badly. People are complex critters.

It is often possible to reposition to serve someone else's personal agenda, but be careful here. If their agenda really is out of sync with the organization's, and it often is because it isn't about creating value, your winning pitch could have a very short life expectancy.

when pitches disappear

The one thing I actually understand, and love, about string theory is that it hypothesizes that there may be not just the three dimensions we accept as everyday reality, but eleven dimensions.

I believe this to be true, because the existence of eleven dimensions is the best explanation I've ever heard of where single socks go when they go missing. My friend Jean, a banker with an extremely orderly and rational mind, told me that she once had a sock disappear from a pair of socks, which is not all that unusual. What is unusual is that the sock suddenly reappeared out of nowhere, four years later. I think maybe her sock went to the eleventh dimension. Sometimes pitches go there, too.

On the other hand, sometimes opportunities to pitch pop up from the eleventh dimension, just like socks—when you least expect them.

FILL 'ER UP WITH HIGH-OCTANE

You did it. You pitched. You closed. You got an answer. You followed up. Perhaps you dealt with rejection.

There is only one thing left for you to do. You must do something to reward yourself for being out there, for being in the game. You must do this especially if you don't want to and if you think you don't deserve it. Why? I'm the Mommy and I say so.

If that is not a convincing enough argument, consider this: Pitching takes energy—physically, mentally, and spiritually. If you've done all the work I've asked you to do, even if at first you feel flooded with adrenaline, the reality is that you're probably a little depleted after the pitch.

Now is a great time for a reward. One mom with three kids under the age of seven told me her reward was just to hold a glass of wine as she walked

Ronna Lichtenberg

through the house—she didn't even have to drink it. Another woman said that her reward was that old favorite: a bubble bath behind locked doors. Do whatever it is that brings you back. Go dig in the garden. Or in the closet, if that's what brings you energy. Check out the sales. If nothing else, at least put something on the calendar you know you'll enjoy.

Then, say thank you, however you say thank you, in whatever way works for you—through your own kind of prayer, in church on Sunday, or in the mosque, or in the synagogue, or with an amen to early morning inspirational television programming. If you're an agnostic, say thank you at the beginning of a meditation. If you're an atheist, say thank you to Charles Darwin for the theory of evolution, or to Ayn Rand for her celebration of capitalism, or to your mom for paying for the dentist who gave you that great smile.

Be grateful for the gifts you have, even if in the moment those gifts didn't get you to the answer you wanted. While you're at it, be grateful for the chance to pitch. Living in a society where anyone gets to participate in the marketplace, and particularly in a society where women get to participate fully in the marketplace, is a wonderful thing.

Being grateful helps you fill yourself back up so that when you get ready to pitch again, you will have even more to draw upon.

You'll need it, because my final bit of advice (you knew this was coming, didn't you?) is to keep going. You will notice that there are opportunities to pitch all the time. You know how to do it now. You know how to enjoy it. You know that it is the way you can create the success you want. It's good to take a breather, but now . . . You! . . . back in the game.

conclusion

By now, you know I am totally opposed to over-promising in a pitch, so let me just say that if you do the work it takes to really pitch like a girl, you will do better at work, make more money (if that is what matters to you), lose weight (if that is your desire), and have a better sex life (unless you are a nun).

I'm kidding. And I'm not. The lessons you've chosen as the right ones for you from this book are lessons that should help you achieve any goal you are ready to set for yourself.

The challenge that you and I have been partnering on in this book is the challenge of finding what you really want in your work life and doing what you can to help make it happen. In the course of this book we've looked at some of the things that might be making that hard for you—including brain sex differences and cultural messages—and some of the unique advantages you have as a woman, and as the unique woman you are.

"Putting yourself out there is the sign of a champion," says Donna Lopiano, the head of the Women's Sports Foundation.

Within you lies a champion. My vision is that the tools, techniques, and tips we've talked about in this book are what your inner champion needs to win at work, her way.

And now, as my yoga teacher would say, Enough talk. Go. Do.

APPENDIX 1

a word to the guys

I don't think work life is easier for you than it is for women. You have wiring and cultural expectations that are in conflict, just as we do. (I've watched while good guys try really hard not to stare when a gorgeous coworker in a miniskirt bends over to pick up something off the floor.) Most of you want to be good guys; you want to be caring, and you want to compete and achieve in a way that seems natural—authentic—to you.

Not only do you have these disconnects between what you want and what you are supposed to want, but it feels to you like women get a lot of special treatment. You feel you don't have the "luxury" of thinking about what you really want because you are expected to work to feed your family, and that is that. And on top of it, women are often confusing. Working through gender differences is hard work even with a woman you love, let alone with a coworker you may not personally care about.

Why should you bother to spend the time and effort it will take to learn how to work differently with women? Because working well with women offers a guy tremendous competitive advantage. If you are the guy at work that women trust, you will be in information flows that the jerk isn't. If women care about you, they will go beyond the extra mile to do what you need them to do to succeed. You will hear new ideas and perspectives you may not have considered. You'll be smarter; your decisions will be better informed.

Where do you start? If a woman gave you this book, it means that you are being invited to do things differently. The good news is that she thinks you are worth investing in; if she thought you were a jerk, she wouldn't give it to you. The bad news is that she is probably giving it to you because she thinks you don't "get it."

In that case, the first thing you do is say thank you. The second is seize the opportunity to make her your "translator." Tell her that you do want to understand and ask her to give you specifics that would make you a better business partner.

If she gave you the book, she will want to know that you read it. You don't have to read the whole thing. Just read the parts on brain sex differences and on pink and blue styles. What she will want to hear is that you believe that the differences you observe are potentially valuable. What bugs women most is when it looks like a man just assumes that the male-brained way of doing business is the best way.

Other action steps? Pick a couple of women and ask them for feedback on style differences. Tell them what works for you so that you can negotiate. It's okay to say, "Look, when I'm really busy, I just don't want to talk about my weekend, or hear about yours." You can also say, "Wait, you're talking about too many things at once." You can even get close enough to say, as a close guy friend of mind did, "Look, I don't like to talk about that girly crap." (By the way, he was good-natured enough to do it anyway, because he knew it was important to me. But telling me that I was asking for a lot kept that part of the conversation down to the bare minimum I needed.)

Look carefully at how your organization sets objectives and measures performance. In my consulting practice, this is the area where I consistently see male-brain bias creeping in. What you believe you are measuring, and what you believe to be the fairness of your measurements, may not be in sync with reality. If you are seeing "cliffs" in your company, where women and people of color reach a certain level and then leave, it is almost certainly the case that there are problems in this regard. You may also have a culture problem if your top male management thinks that "executive presence" is the biggest issue your future women leaders have, since that is often an unconscious code for "they don't look or act like us."

Understanding exactly how relationships drive your company's numbers will help you see whether you value relationship skills sufficiently. Most companies value technical talent but take relationship talent for granted.

Support women's networks and programs. Not all women, but a lot of us, find support and stress relief in being able to talk to each other. I know that it's hard not to think, ". . . gee, why do *they* get to get together when if us guys tried to do it all hell would break loose?" Here's why: if you let us get emotional support from each other, most of us will feel and do better in subtle ways, which is good for the organization, and therefore good for your paycheck.

Encourage women to pitch. Go out of your way to provide training and positive reinforcement to women who are trying to sell ideas and move forward. One CEO, faced with complaints from guys on his team about their women colleagues, realized what was going on was a style issue. Not only did he support the women receiving presentation training that addressed the kinds of differences I've covered in this book, but he set an example by getting the training for himself, the ultimate leadership statement.

Finally, although this book wasn't written to you, it was written for you, too—it was written so that men and women can find a way to create more value together. What men have brought, and bring, to the world of business is obviously valuable: sustained focus, spatial ability, systemized markets and organizations, physical and mental stamina, strong competitive drive. Even the capacity to put emotions aside has been, and often still is, an asset. As a dear guy friend said to me, "Hey, we've been doing this for centuries and we've done a damn good job."

Yes, you have. But I think you can do even better. Want to know how? Listen carefully the next time a woman pitches to you. She'll tell you.

APPENDIX 2

the empathy quotient (EQ)

Read each statement very carefully and rate how strongly you agree or disagree with it.

	strongly agree	slightly agree	slightly disagree	strongly disagree
1. I can easily tell if someone else wants to enter a conversation.	☐	☐	☐	☐
2. I prefer animals to humans.	☐	☐	☐	☐
3. I try to keep up with the current trends and fashions	☐	☐	☐	☐
4. I find it difficult to explain to others things that I understand easily, when they don't understand it the first time.	☐	☐	☐	☐
5. I dream most nights.	☐	☐	☐	☐
6. I really enjoy caring for other people.	☐	☐	☐	☐
7. I try to solve my own problems rather than discussing them with others.	☐	☐	☐	☐
8. I find it hard to know what to do in a social situation.	☐	☐	☐	☐

	strongly agree	slightly agree	slightly disagree	strongly disagree
9. I am at my best first thing in the morning.	☐	☐	☐	☐
10. People often tell me that I went too far in driving my point home in a discussion.	☐	☐	☐	☐
11. It doesn't bother me too much if I am late meeting a friend.	☐	☐	☐	☐
12. Friendships and relationships are just too difficult, so I tend not to bother with them.	☐	☐	☐	☐
13. I would never break a law, no matter how minor.	☐	☐	☐	☐
14. I often find it difficult to judge if something is rude or impolite.	☐	☐	☐	☐
15. In a conversation, I tend to focus on my own thoughts rather than on what my listener might be thinking.	☐	☐	☐	☐
16. I prefer practical jokes to verbal humor.	☐	☐	☐	☐
17. I live life for today rather than the future.	☐	☐	☐	☐
18. When I was a child, I enjoyed cutting up worms to see what would happen.	☐	☐	☐	☐
19. I can pick up quickly if someone says one thing but means another.	☐	☐	☐	☐
20. I tend to have very strong opinions about morality.	☐	☐	☐	☐
21. It is hard for me to see why some things upset people so much.	☐	☐	☐	☐

The Empathy Quotient (EQ)

	strongly agree	slightly agree	slightly disagree	strongly disagree
22. I find it easy to put myself in somebody else's shoes.	☐	☐	☐	☐
23. I think that good manners are the most important thing a parent can teach their child.	☐	☐	☐	☐
24. I like to do things on the spur of the moment.	☐	☐	☐	☐
25. I am good at predicting how someone will feel.	☐	☐	☐	☐
26. I am quick to spot when someone in a group is feeling awkward or uncomfortable.	☐	☐	☐	☐
27. If I say something that someone else is offended by, I think that that's their problem, not mine.	☐	☐	☐	☐
28. If anyone asked me if I liked their haircut, I would reply truthfully, even if I didn't like it.	☐	☐	☐	☐
29. I can't always see why someone should have felt offended by a remark.	☐	☐	☐	☐
30. People often tell me that I am very unpredictable.	☐	☐	☐	☐
31. I enjoy being the center of attention at any social gathering.	☐	☐	☐	☐
32. Seeing people cry doesn't really upset me.	☐	☐	☐	☐
33. I enjoy having discussions about politics.	☐	☐	☐	☐
34. I am very blunt, which some people take to be rudeness, even though this is unintentional.	☐	☐	☐	☐

The Empathy Quotient (EQ)

	strongly agree	slightly agree	slightly disagree	strongly disagree
35. I don't tend to find social situations confusing.	☐	☐	☐	☐
36. Other people tell me I am good at understanding how they are feeling and what they are thinking.	☐	☐	☐	☐
37. When I talk to people, I tend to talk about their experiences rather than my own.	☐	☐	☐	☐
38. It upsets me to see an animal in pain.	☐	☐	☐	☐
39. I am able to make decisions without being influenced by people's feelings.	☐	☐	☐	☐
40. I can't relax until I have done everything I had planned to do that day.	☐	☐	☐	☐
41. I can easily tell if someone else is interested or bored with what I am saying.	☐	☐	☐	☐
42. I get upset if I see people suffering on news programs.	☐	☐	☐	☐
43. Friends usually talk to me about their problems—they say that I am very understanding.	☐	☐	☐	☐
44. I can sense if I am intruding even if the other person doesn't tell me.	☐	☐	☐	☐
45. I often start new hobbies but quickly become bored with them and move on to something else.	☐	☐	☐	☐
46. People sometimes tell me that I have gone too far with teasing.	☐	☐	☐	☐
47. I would be too nervous to go on a big roller coaster.	☐	☐	☐	☐

	strongly agree	slightly agree	slightly disagree	strongly disagree
48. Other people often say that I am insensitive, though I don't always see why.	☐	☐	☐	☐
49. If I see a stranger in a group, I think that it is up to them to make an effort to join in.	☐	☐	☐	☐
50. I usually stay emotionally detached when watching a film.	☐	☐	☐	☐
51. I like to be very organized in day-to-day life and often make lists of the chores I have to do.	☐	☐	☐	☐
52. I can tune in to how someone else feels rapidly and intuitively.	☐	☐	☐	☐
53. I don't like to take risks.	☐	☐	☐	☐
54. I can easily work out what another person might want to talk about.	☐	☐	☐	☐
55. I can tell if someone is masking their true emotion.	☐	☐	☐	☐
56. Before making a decision I always weigh up the pros and cons.	☐	☐	☐	☐
57. I don't consciously work out the rules of social situations.	☐	☐	☐	☐
58. I am good at predicting what someone will do.	☐	☐	☐	☐
59. I tend to get emotionally involved with a friend's problems.	☐	☐	☐	☐
60. I can usually appreciate the other person's viewpoint, even if I don't agree with it.	☐	☐	☐	☐

The Empathy Quotient (EQ)

HOW TO SCORE YOUR EQ

❖ Score two points for each of the following items if you answered "strongly agree" or one point if you answered "slightly agree": 1, 6, 19, 22, 25, 26, 35, 36, 37, 38, 41, 42, 43, 44, 52, 54, 55, 57, 58, 59, 60.

❖ Score two points for each of the following items if you answered "strongly disagree" or one point if you answered "slightly disagree": 4, 8, 10, 11, 12, 14, 15, 18, 21, 27, 28, 29, 32, 34, 39, 46, 48, 49, 50.

❖ The following items are not scored: 2, 3, 5, 7, 9, 13, 16, 17, 20, 23, 24, 30, 31, 33, 40, 45, 47, 51, 53, 56.

Simply add up all the points you have scored and obtain your total EQ Score.

HOW TO INTERPRET YOUR EQ SCORE

❖ 0–32 = low (most people with Asperger Syndrome or high-functioning autism score about 20)

❖ 33–52 = average (most women score about 47, and most men score about 42)

❖ 53–63 = above average

❖ 64–80 = very high

❖ 80 = maximum

APPENDIX 3
the systemizing quotient (SQ)

Read each statement very carefully and rate how strongly you agree or disagree with it.

	strongly agree	slightly agree	slightly disagree	strongly disagree
1. When I listen to a piece of music, I always notice the way it's structured.	☐	☐	☐	☐
2. I adhere to common superstitions.	☐	☐	☐	☐
3. I often make resolutions, but find it hard to stick to them.	☐	☐	☐	☐
4. I prefer to read nonfiction over fiction.	☐	☐	☐	☐
5. If I were buying a car, I would want to obtain specific information about its engine capacity.	☐	☐	☐	☐
6. When I look at a painting, I do not usually think about the technique involved in making it.	☐	☐	☐	☐
7. If there was a problem with the electrical wiring in my home, I'd be able to fix it myself.	☐	☐	☐	☐
8. When I have a dream, I find it difficult to remember precise details about the dream the next day.	☐	☐	☐	☐

	strongly agree	slightly agree	slightly disagree	strongly disagree
9. When I watch a film, I prefer to be with a group of friends rather than alone.	☐	☐	☐	☐
10. I am interested in learning about different religions.	☐	☐	☐	☐
11. I rarely read articles or Web pages about new technology.	☐	☐	☐	☐
12. I do not enjoy games that involve a high degree of strategy.	☐	☐	☐	☐
13. I am fascinated by how machines work.	☐	☐	☐	☐
14. I make a point of listening to the news each morning.	☐	☐	☐	☐
15. In math, I am intrigued by the rules and patterns governing numbers.	☐	☐	☐	☐
16. I am bad about keeping in touch with old friends.	☐	☐	☐	☐
17. When I am relating a story, I often leave out details and just give the gist of what happened.	☐	☐	☐	☐
18. I find it difficult to understand instruction manuals for putting appliances together.	☐	☐	☐	☐
19. When I look at an animal, I like to know the precise species it belongs to.	☐	☐	☐	☐
20. If I were buying a computer, I would want to know exact details about its hard drive capacity and processor speed.	☐	☐	☐	☐
21. I enjoy participating in sports.	☐	☐	☐	☐
22. I try to avoid doing household chores if I can.	☐	☐	☐	☐

	strongly agree	slightly agree	slightly disagree	strongly disagree
23. When I cook, I do not think about exactly how different methods and ingredients contribute to the final product.	☐	☐	☐	☐
24. I find it difficult to read and understand maps.	☐	☐	☐	☐
25. If I had a collection (e.g., CDs, coins, stamps), it would be highly organized.	☐	☐	☐	☐
26. When I look at a piece of furniture, I do not notice the details of how was constructed.	☐	☐	☐	☐
27. The idea of engaging in "risk-taking" activities appeals to me.	☐	☐	☐	☐
28. When I learn about historical events, I do not focus on exact dates.	☐	☐	☐	☐
29. When I read the newspaper, I am drawn to tables of information, such as football scores or stock market indices.	☐	☐	☐	☐
30. When I learn a language, I become intrigued by its grammatical rules.	☐	☐	☐	☐
31. I find it difficult to learn my way around a new city.	☐	☐	☐	☐
32. I do not tend to watch science documentaries on television or read articles about science and nature.	☐	☐	☐	☐
33. If I were buying a stereo, I would want to know about its precise technical features.	☐	☐	☐	☐
34. I find it easy to grasp exactly how odds work in betting.	☐	☐	☐	☐
35. I am not very meticulous when I carry out do-it-yourself projects.	☐	☐	☐	☐

The Systemizing Quotient (SQ)

	strongly agree	slightly agree	slightly disagree	strongly disagree
36. I find it easy to carry on a conversation with someone I've just met.	☐	☐	☐	☐
37. When I look at a building, I am curious about the precise way it was constructed.	☐	☐	☐	☐
38. When an election is being held, I am not interested in the results for each constituency.	☐	☐	☐	☐
39. When I lend someone money, I expect them to pay me back exactly what they owe me.	☐	☐	☐	☐
40. I find it difficult to understand information the bank sends me on different investment and saving systems.	☐	☐	☐	☐
41. When traveling by train, I often wonder exactly how the rail networks are coordinated.	☐	☐	☐	☐
42. When I buy a new appliance, I do not read the instruction manual very thoroughly.	☐	☐	☐	☐
43. If I were buying a camera, I would not look carefully into the quality of the lens.	☐	☐	☐	☐
44. When I read something, I always notice whether it is grammatically correct.	☐	☐	☐	☐
45. When I hear the weather forecast, I am not very interested in the meteorological patterns.	☐	☐	☐	☐
46. I often wonder what it would be like to be someone else.	☐	☐	☐	☐
47. I find it difficult to do two things at once.	☐	☐	☐	☐

	strongly agree	slightly agree	slightly disagree	strongly disagree
48. When I look at a mountain, I think about how precisely it was formed.	☐	☐	☐	☐
49. I can easily visualize how the freeways in my region link up.	☐	☐	☐	☐
50. When I'm in a restaurant, I often have a hard time deciding what to order.	☐	☐	☐	☐
51. When I'm in a plane, I do not think about the aerodynamics.	☐	☐	☐	☐
52. I often forget the precise details of conversations I've had.	☐	☐	☐	☐
53. When I am walking in the country, I am curious about how the various kinds of trees differ.	☐	☐	☐	☐
54. After meeting someone just once or twice, I find it difficult to remember precisely what they look like.	☐	☐	☐	☐
55. I am interested in knowing the path a river takes from its source to the sea.	☐	☐	☐	☐
56. I do not read legal documents very carefully.	☐	☐	☐	☐
57. I am not interested in understanding how wireless communication works.	☐	☐	☐	☐
58. I am curious about life on other planets.	☐	☐	☐	☐
59. When I travel, I like to learn specific details about the culture of the place I am visiting.	☐	☐	☐	☐
60. I do not care to know the names of the plants I see.	☐	☐	☐	☐

The Systemizing Quotient (SQ)

HOW TO SCORE YOUR SQ

❖ Score two points for each of the following items if you answered "strongly agree" or one point if you answered "slightly agree":

1, 4, 5, 7, 13, 15, 19, 20, 25, 29, 30, 33, 34, 37, 41, 44, 48, 49, 53, 55.

❖ Score two points for each of the following items if you answered "strongly disagree" or one point if you answered "slightly disagree":

6, 11, 12, 18, 23, 24, 26, 28, 31, 32, 35, 38, 40, 42, 43, 45, 51, 56, 57, 60.

❖ The following items are not scored:

2, 3, 8, 9, 10, 14, 16, 17, 21, 22, 27, 36, 39, 46, 47, 50, 52, 54, 58, 59.

Simply add up all the points you have scored and obtain your total SQ score.

HOW TO INTERPRET YOUR SQ SCORE

❖ 0–19 = low

❖ 20–39 = average (most women score about 24, and most men score about 30)

❖ 40–50 = above average (most people with Asperger Syndrome or high functioning autism score in this range)

❖ 51–80 = very high (three times as many people with Asperger Syndrome score in this range, as compared to typical men, and almost no women score in this range)

❖ 80 = maximum

bibliography

Annis, Barbara. *Same Words Different Language: Why Men and Women Don't Understand Each Other and What to Do about It.* London: Judy Piatkus (Publishers) Limited, 2003.

Babcock, Linda, and Sara Laschever. *Women Don't Ask: Negotiation and the Gender Divide.* New Jersey: Princeton University Press, 2003.

Banerjee, Neela. "Toughness Has Risks for Women Executives," *New York Times.* Aug. 10, 2001 p. C1.

Baron-Cohen, Simon. *The Essential Difference: The Truth about the Male and Female Brain.* New York: Basic Books (Perseus Books Group), 2003.

"Barriers and Opportunities: Results and Strategic Recommendations from Dial Groups." Research: Barriers and Opportunities to Women's Executive Leadership. The White House Project.org. The White House Project. Online. Internet. Available: www.thewhitehouseproject.org

Barry, Ellen. "Mars and Venus Go to Work," *The Boston Phoenix.* (Jul. 27, 1998): Online. Internet. Mar. 2, 2004. Available: http://weeklywire.com

Bell, Ella L., J. Edmondson, and Stella M. Nkomo. *Our Separate Ways: Black and White Women and the Struggle for Professional Identity.* Boston: Harvard Business School Press, 2001.

Blum, Deborah. *Sex on the Brain: The Biological Differences Between Men and Women.* New York: Viking (Penguin Putnam), 1997.

"Bootcamp: Kicking Off Springboard's Coaching Program." *Boston Business Journal Advertising Supplement.* Oct. 25–31, 2002.

Boyles, Salynn. "Findings Could Explain Why Depression Is More Common in Women." *WebMD Medical News.* (December 3, 2003): Online. Internet. Feb. 11, 2004. Available: www.webmd.com

"The Brain Game: What's Sex Got to Do With It?" *ABC News* (Jul. 31, 2003): Online. Internet. Available: www.abcnews.com

Branswell, Helen. "Women's Brains More Densely Packed in 'Executive' Portion of Brain," *Canadian Press,* Nov. 16, 2001. www.canoe.ca

"Capturing the Impact: Women-Owned Businesses in the United States." Fact Sheet. *Center for Women's Business Research.* 2004.

Catalyst Fact Sheet. October 2003: www.catalystwomen.org/bookstore/files/fact/ snapshot%202003.pdf

Centofanti, Marjorie. "Study Shows Brain Switch in Men with Schizophrenia." *The Gazette Online*. The Newspaper of the Johns Hopkins University. (29), 28 (Mar. 20, 2000): Online. Internet. Available: www.hopkinsmedicine.org

Chambers, Veronica. *Having It All? Black Women and Success* New York: Doubleday, 2003.

Cialdini, Robert B. "Harnessing the Science of Persuasion." *Harvard Business Review*. Oct. 2001. pp 72–79.

Cleveland, Jeanette N. et al. *Women and Men in Organizations: Sex and Gender Issues at Work.* Mahwah, NJ: Lawrence Erlbaum Associates, 2000.

Cohen, Herb. *You Can Negotiate Anything*. New York: Bantam Books, 1989.

Damiani, Lisa. "Deciphering How the Sexes Think." *The Scientist*, 16, 2, Jan. 21 2002.

Davis, Jeanie. "Women, Men and Approaches to Stress." *WebMD Medical News*. T.L.C. Stress Management Services. (Sep. 8, 2000): Online. Internet. Available: www.stress-help.co.uk

DeAngelis, Tori. "Are Men Emotional Mummies?" *Monitor on Psychology*, Dec. 2001, Vol. 32. No. 11.

"Despite Women's Gains in Business, Their Representation on America's Corporate Boards Barely Improves." News Release. *Catalyst*. Dec. 4, 2003.

Dionis, Kim. "Women React Differently Than Men to Stress." *Penn State Intercom*. (Feb. 8, 2001): Online. Internet. Available: www.psu.edu

Eagly, Alice H., and Blair T. Johnson. "Gender and Leadership Style. A Meta-Analysis." *Psychological Bulletin*. 108.2 (Sept. 1990): pp 233–256.

Eagly, Alice H, Mona G. Makhijani, and Bruce G. Klonsky. "Gender and the Evaluation of Leaders, A Meta-Analysis." *Psychological Bulletin*. 111.1 (Jan. 1992): pp 3–22.

Ellin, Abby. "When It Comes to Salary, Many Women Don't Push," *New York Times*. (Feb. 29, 2004): Online. Internet. March 1, 2004. Available: www.nytimes.com

Ely, Robin et al. *Reader in Gender, Work, and Organization*. Malden, MA: Blackwell Publishing, 2003.

Epstein, Cynthia Fuchs. "Ways Men and Women Lead." *Harvard Business Review*, Jan./Feb. 1991, 69.1, p 150.

Evans, Gail. *Play Like a Man, Win Like a Woman: What Men Know about Success That Women Need to Learn*. New York: Broadway Books, 2001.

"Exploring Your Brain: Men, Women & the Brain." With: David Mahoney; Garrick Utley; Martha Denckla, M.D.; Paul Mulvey; Ruben Gur, Ph.D.; Sandra Witelson, Ph.D.; Stephen Suomi, Ph.D. WETA-TV, Washington, DC. (Feb. 1998): Transcript. Dana.Org. Books, Publications and Broadcasts: Radio and TV. Dana Foundation. Online. Internet. Feb. 2, 2004. Available: www.dana.org

Falbo, T., M. Hazen, and D. Linimon. "Costs of selecting power bases associated with the opposite sex." *Sex Roles*, 8: pp 147–57. 1982.

Farrel, Bill and Pam. *Why Men and Women Act the Way They Do*. Eugene, OR: Harvest House Publishers, 2003.

Fisher, Helen E. *The First Sex: The Natural Talents of Women and How They Are Changing the World*. New York: Random House, 1999.

Fletcher, Joyce K. *Disappearing Acts: Gender, Power, and Relational Practice at Work*. Cambridge, MA: MIT Press, 2001.

Frasca, Alex. "Where the boys aren't: the consequences." *The American Thinker*, April 29, 2004.

Gavin, Kara. "Pain and the Brain." *University of Michigan Health System Web site.* (Feb. 18, 2003): Online. Internet. Available: www.med.umich.edu

Gazzaniga, Michael S. *Nature's Mind: The Biological Roots of Thinking, Emotions, Sexuality, Language, and Intelligence.* New York: Basic Books, 1994.

Gewirtz, Paul. "On 'I know it when I see it'." *Yale Law Journal.* (Jan. 1, 1996): Online. Internet. The Yale Law Journal: Back Issues. Mar. 11, 2004. Available: www.yale.edu

Gilbert, Jennifer. "Lonely at the Top." *Sales & Marketing Management*, Jul. 2003, 155.7: p 46.

Gilbert, Susan. "New Clues to Women Veiled in Black," *New York Times.* (Mar. 16, 2004): Online. Internet. Mar. 16, 2004. Available: www.nytimes.com

Goleman, Daniel. *Emotional Intelligence.* New York: Bantam Books, 1995.

Goleman, Daniel. *Working with Emotional Intelligence.* New York: Bantam Books, 1998.

Gray, John. *Mars and Venus in the Workplace: A Practical Guide for Improving Communication and Getting Results at Work.* New York: HarperCollins, 2002.

"Gray Matters: Men Women and the Brain." With: Larry Massett, Phil Proctor, Melinda Peterson. *Public Radio International.* (Feb. 2001): Transcript. Dana.Org. Books, Publications and Broadcasts: Radio and TV. Dana Foundation. Online. Internet. Feb. 11, 2004. Available: www.dana.org

"The Growth of Women in 'Non-Traditional' Industries." Issue in Brief. National Women's Business Council. Mar. 2004.

Gurian, Michael, and Patricia Henley. *Boys and Girls Learn Differently!* San Francisco: Jossey-Bass, 2001.

Hardy, Rob. "The Sordid Story of the Empire State Building." Rev. of *Empire: A Tale of Obsession, Betrayal, and the Battle for an American Icon*, by Mitchell Pacelle. Non-Fiction Reviews.com. (Jul. 10, 2002): Online. Internet. Feb. 12, 2004. Available: www.nonfictionreviews.com

Harris, Gardiner. "Pfizer Gives Up Testing Viagra on Women," *New York Times.* (Feb. 28, 2004): Online. Internet. Mar. 2, 2004. Available: www.nytimes.com

Heatherington, Laurie, Laura S. Townsend, and David P. Burroughs. "'How'd you do on that test?': The effects of gender on self-presentation of achievement to vulnerable men." *Sex Roles: A Journal of Research.* (Aug. 2001): Online. Internet. Mar. 10, 2004. Available: www.findarticles.com

Heim, Pat, Susan Murphy, and Susan K. Golant. *In the Company of Women: Turning Workplace Conflict into Powerful Alliances*, New York: Jeremy P. Tarcher/Putnam (Penguin Putnam), 2001.

Heim, Pat, Susan K. Golant. *Hardball for Women: Winning at the Game of Business.* Los Angeles: Lowell House, 1992.

Helgesen, Sally. *The Female Advantage.* New York: Currency, 1995.

Henning, Margaret, and Anne Jardim. *The Managerial Woman.* New York: Simon & Schuster, 1977.

Hines, Melissa. *Brain Gender.* New York: Oxford University Press, 2003.

Hopkins, Jim. "More Daughters Get Keys to Family Firms," *USA Today.* Online. Internet. Dec. 9, 2003. Available: usatoday.com

"Hormone Levels Affect Structure of Adult Brain." *Proceedings of the National Academy of Sciences*, USA (1999;96): pp 7128–7130, 7538–7540. Online. Internet. Available: www.transgendercare.com

Hotz, Robert. "Women Use More of Brain When Listening," *Los Angeles Times*. Nov. 29, 2000. pp A1, A18, A19.

Hymowitz, Carol. "Women Put Noses to the Grindstone, and Miss Opportunities," *The Wall Street Journal*. (Feb. 3, 2004)

Jackson, Derrick. "Ladylike in a Man's World," *Boston Globe*. Aug. 22, 2001: p A.23.

Joyce, Amy. "Women need to stand tall: Nothing wrong with bragging a little. If a female works hard and achieves, but keeps her head down, she won't get credit, author says." *Washington Post*. 2003.

Kanter, Rosabeth Moss. *Men and Women of the Corporation*. New York: Basic Books, 1993.

Kaye, Ellen A. *Maximize Your Presentation Skills: How to Speak, Look, and Act on Your Way to the Top*. Roseville, CA: Prima Publishing, 2002.

"Key Facts about Women Business Owners and Their Enterprises." *National Women's Business Council*. Mar. 2004.

King James: The book of Judges 16 "Samson & Delilah." Online. Internet. Mar. 17, 2004. Available: www.godrules.net

Kolb, David A. *Experiential Learning*. Upper Saddle River, NJ: Prentice Hall PTR, 1984.

Kolb, David A., and D.M. Smith. *User's Guide for the Learning Style Inventory*. Boston: McBer and Company, 1985.

Kolb, Deborah M., and Judith Williams. *The Shadow Negotiation: How Women Can Master the Hidden Agendas That Determine Bargaining Success*. New York: Simon & Schuster, 2000.

Kraemer, Sebastian. (2000) "Lessons from Everywhere." *British Medical Journal*, 321: pp 1609–1612.

Kreeger, Karen. "Deciphering How the Sexes Think." *The Scientist*, Jan. 21, 2002.

Krueger, Alan B. "He Dickers, She Doesn't," *New York Times*. Aug. 21, 2003.

"The Leading Edge. Women-Owned Million-Dollar Firms." AT&T and KeyBank, underwriters. Jan. 2004.

Legato, Marianne J., M.D. *Eve's Rib: The New Science of Gender-Specific Medicine and How It Can Save Your Life*. New York: Harmony Books (Random House), 2002.

Lerner, Harriet. *The Dance of Anger*. New York: Quill, 1997.

Leung, Andrea. "Penn State Study Shows Men, Women React Differently Under Stress," *Daily Collegian*. Dec. 11, 2003.

LeVay, Simon. *The Sexual Brain*. Cambridge, MA: The MIT Press, 1993.

Ligos, Melinda. "For Her, U.S. Borders Are Profit Centers," *New York Times*. Jan. 29, 2004.

Lips, Hilary M. "Attraction and Ambivalence: Gendered Perceptions of Power." Public Lecture Presented at New Zealand Universities. (Feb.–Mar., 1999): Online. Internet. Mar. 9, 2004. Available: www.radford.edu

Llewellyn-Williams, Dr. Michael, ed. "The C200 Business Leaderships Index 2003: Annual Report on Women's Clout in Business." The Committee of 200. Northern Trust Corporation, 2001–2003.

Locke, Linda. "How Women Recruit Through Relationship Marketing." *MLM Know-How*. Online. Internet. Sep. 18, 2002. Available: www.mlmknowhow.com

Lublin, Joann S. "Women Managers Learn to Promote Themselves." *Career Journal. The Wall Street Journal Online*. Online. Internet. Sep. 26, 2002. Available: www.careerjournal.com

Manfer, Sam. "Go Straight to the Top." *Selling*, Jul. 2003.

McGinty, Sarah Myers. *Power Talk: Using Language to Build Authority and Influence*. New York: Warner Books, 2001.

McIntosh, Peggy. "Feeling Like a Fraud." *Work in Progress* series, Stone Center for Developmental Services and Studies, Wellesley Centers for Women, Wellesley College, Wellesley, MA, 1985.

Mestel, Rosie. "Brain Study Focuses on Gender Identity; Findings challenge the theory that hormones alone define male and female brain differences." *Los Angeles Times*. Oct. 20, 2003. pp A14.

Meyerson, Debra E., and Robin J. Ely. "Women Leaders and Organizational Change." *Working Knowledge*, Harvard Business School. (Dec. 15, 2003): Online. Internet. Dec. 17, 2003. Available: http://hbswk.hbs.edu

Miller, Jean Baker, M.D. "Women and Power," *Work in Progress* series, Stone Center for Developmental Services and Studies, Wellesley Centers for Women, Wellesley College, Wellesley, MA, 1982.

Mindell, Phyllis. *How to Say It for Women: Communicating with Confidence and Power Using the Language of Success*. Englewood Cliffs, NJ: Prentice Hall Press, 2001.

Moir, Anne, and David Jessel. *Brain Sex: The Real Difference Between Men and Women*. New York: Dell Publishing, 1991.

"Nearly Half of All Privately Held U.S. Businesses are Women-Owned." Fact Sheet. *Center for Women's Business Research*. Washington, DC (May 6, 2003): Online. Internet. Mar. 11, 2004. Available: www.womensbusinessresearch.org

"One in 18 U.S. Women is a Business Owner." Research. Center for Women's Business Research. Washington, DC (Jul. 16, 2002): Online. Internet. Mar. 11, 2004. Available: www.womensbusinessresearch.org

Otte, Jean. *Changing the Corporate Landscape: A woman's guide to cultivating leadership excellence*. Atlanta: Longstreet Press, 2004.

Peale, Cliff. "What Glass Ceiling? P&G Women on Rise," *The Cincinnati Enquirer*. (Jan. 26, 2003): Cincinnati.Com. Online. Internet. Mar. 10, 2004. Available: www.enquirer.com

Pease, Barbara and Allan. *Why Men Don't Listen and Women Can't Read Maps*. New York: Broadway Books, 2000.

"PET Brain Research Demonstrates Gender Differences in Pain Response." *SNM*. (Nov. 6, 2003): Online. Internet. Available: www.snm.org

Potier, Beth. Researcher: "Physics 'glass ceiling' intact," *Harvard University Gazette*. Jan. 8, 2004.

Price Waterhouse v. Hopkins. 490 U.S. 228 Certiorari to the United States Court of Appeals for the District of Columbia Circuit No. 87-1167. 1989. Online. Internet. Mar. 8, 2004. Available: http://caselaw.lp.findlaw.com

Raghunathan, Anuradha. "Women and Company in the News," *Dallas Morning News*. (Nov. 23, 2003): Women and Co. Online. Internet. Mar. 11, 2004. Available: www.womenandco.com

Raz, Tahl. "The 10 Secrets of a Master Networker." *Inc*. (Jan. 1, 2003): Inc. Online. Internet. Jun. 24, 2003. Available: www.inc.com

"Research probes sex-based brain differences." *CTVNews.com*. (Nov. 23, 2001): Online. Internet. Available: www.exn.ca/brain/stories/

Reskin, Barbara, and Irene Padavic. *Women and Men at Work*, second edition. Thousand Oaks, CA: Pine Forge Press (Sage Publications), 2002.

Rickert, Vaughn I., Rupal Sanghvi, and Constance M. Wiemann. "Is Lack of Sexual Assertiveness Among Adolescent and Young Adult Women a Cause for Concern?" *Perspectives on Sexual and Reproductive Health.* 34.4 (Jul./Aug. 2002): The Alan Guttmacher Institute. Online. Internet. Jan. 8, 2004. Available: www.guttmacher.org

Robinson, Ingrid. "Forming Strategic Alliances: Growing, Maintaining Market Share as a Women Business Owner." *Best Minds in the Business.* Women's Enterprise Texas. Diversity Publishing Group. Dallas, TX. (2003)

Rogers, Lesley J. *Sexing the Brain.* New York: Columbia University Press, 2002.

Rosener, Judy B. "Ways Women Lead." *Harvard Business Review,* Nov./Dec. 1990. 68.6: p 119.

Rosenthal, Patrice, David Guest, and Riccardo Peccei. "Gender differences in managers' causal explanations for their work performance: a study in two organizations." *Journal of Occupational and Organizational Psychology.* 69. 2: pp 145–7. Jun. 1996.

Rudman, L.A. "Self-promotion as a risk factor for women: The costs and benefits of counter-stereotypical impression management." *Journal of Personality and Social Psychology,* 74: pp 629–645. 1998.

Rudman, L.A., & Glick, P. "Prescriptive gender stereotypes and backlash toward agentic women." *Journal of Social Issues,* 57: pp 743–762. 2001.

Rudman, Laurie A., and Jessica B. Heppen. "Implicit Romantic Fantasies and Women's Interest in Personal Power: A Glass Slipper Effect?" *PSPB,* 29.10: pp 1–14. 2003.

Sabbatini, Renato. "Are There Differences between the Brains of Males and Females?" *Brain and Mind.* (1997)

"The Sales Process." SBA: *Online Women's Business Center.* (Aug. 10, 2001): Online. Internet. Sep. 18, 2002. Available: www.onlinewbc.gov

Sellers, Patricia. "Power: Do Women Really Want It?" *Fortune.* (Sep. 29, 2003): Online. Internet. Nov. 26, 2003. Available: www.fortune.com

Sellers, Patricia. "The Business of Being Oprah," *Fortune,* Apr. 1, 2002.

"Sexual differentiation of the brain, sex chromosomal influences on neural development." UCLA Department of Physiological Science. Faculty. Arnold, Arthur P. Online. Internet. Dec. 10, 2003. Available: www.physci.ucla.edu

Slater, L., J. Daniel, and A. Banks, eds. *The Complete Guide to Mental Health for Women.* Boston: Beacon Press, 2003.

SmartPros Editorial Staff. "AICPA Survey: 70% of Women Need Financial Help." SmartPros Ltd. Jan. 14, 2003.

Solomon, Muriel. *What Do I Say When . . . : A Guidebook for Getting Your Way With People on the Job.* Englewood Cliffs, NJ: Prentice Hall, 1988.

Steen, R. Grant. *DNA and Destiny: Nature and Nurture in Human Behavior.* Cambridge, MA: Perseus Publishing, 1996.

Strout, Erin. "Shrinking Violets?" *Sales & Marketing Management,* May 2003, 155. 5: p 46.

"Study: Wealthy women investors do not match stereotypes." *South Florida Business Journal.* American City Business Journals, Inc. Dec. 11, 2002.

"Style Matters: Why Women Executives Shouldn't Ignore Their 'Feminine Side'." *Research Brief.* HayGroup, Inc. Boston, 2003.

"Survey Says . . . " Results from the How Much is Enough? Survey. *Fast Company and Roper Starch Worldwide.* 26, (July 1999): p 110. Online. Internet. Available: www.fastcompany.com

Swiss, Deborah J. *The Male Mind at Work: A Woman's Guide to Working with Men.* Cambridge, MA: Perseus Publishing, 2001.

Tannen, Deborah. *Gender & Discourse.* New York: Oxford University Press, 1994.

Tannen, Deborah. *Talking From 9 to 5: How Women's and Men's Conversational Styles Affect Who Gets Heard, Who Gets Credit, and What Gets Done at Work.* New York: Morrow, 1994.

Tannen, Deborah. *That's Not What I Meant! How Conversational Style Makes or Breaks Your Relations with Others.* New York: Ballantine Books, 1991.

Thomas, David A., and John J. Gabarro. *Breaking Through: The Making of Minority Executives in Corporate America.* Boston: Harvard Business School Press, 1999.

Thurman, Judith. "The Handmaiden's Tale." Studies in Gender and Sexuality. 3.3: pp 309–320. The Analytic Press. 2002.

Tischler, Linda. "Where the Bucks Are." *Fast Company.* Mar. 2004.

Tremmel, Pat Vaughan. "Women Most Effective Leaders for Today's World." *EurekAlert!* (Aug. 4, 2003): Online. Internet. Mar. 9, 2004. Available: www.eurekalert.org

Tyson, Laura D'Andrea. "New Clues to the Pay and Leadership Gap." *Business Week.* Oct. 27, 2003 Issue 3855. p 36, 1p, 1c

Uhlenhuth, Karen. "Estrogen May Keep Women's Brains Going." *Seattle Times.* (Jun. 13, 2001): Global Action on Aging. Online. Internet. Feb. 11, 2004. Available: www.globalaging.org

Valentino, Todde. "Perception and Sensitivity to Horizontal Turbulent Air Flows at the Head Region." *Indoor Air.* 10. 4 (December 2000): p 297. Online. Internet. Available: www.blackwell-synergy.com

Wachs, Esther. *Why the Best Man for the Job Is a Woman: The Unique Female Qualities of Leadership.* New York: Harper Business, 2001.

Walker, Maureen. "Power and Effectiveness: Envisioning an Alternate Paradigm." *Work in Progress* series, Stone Center for Developmental Services and Studies, Wellesley Centers for Women, Wellesley College, Wellesley, MA, 2002.

Wellington, Sheila. *Be Your Own Mentor: Strategies from Top Women on the Secrets of Success.* New York: Random House, 2001.

Wellington, Sheila et al. "What's Holding Women Back?" *Harvard Business Review*, Jun. 1, 2003.

Weisinger, Hendrie. *Anger at Work: Learning the Art of Anger Management on the Job.* New York: William Morrow, 1996.

White, Kate. *Why Good Girls Don't Get Ahead but Gutsy Girls Do.* New York: Warner Books, 1996.

"Women Appointed to Presidential Cabinets." *Fact Sheet.* Center for American Women and Politics. Eagleton Institute of Politics. Rutgers, The State University of New Jersey. New Brunswick, NJ, Aug. 2003.

"Women-Owned Businesses in 2002: Trends in the U.S. and 50 States" Center for Women's Business Research. Online. Internet. April, 2003. Available: www.womensbusinessresearch.org

acknowledgments

It is a cliché to say that I couldn't have written this book without help, but the truth is that I couldn't, and wouldn't, have done it without the generosity and support of a lot of other people.

Brian DeFiore, my agent, hung in there with me, and believed in me when I didn't. Brian has the gift of giving really honest, tough feedback that inspires me to do my best.

The Rodale team is so terrific that I've had to pinch myself to believe they are for real. From the first day I met Stephanie Tade I felt nurtured and inspired by her. My dreams for what the book could be got bigger because of Stephanie, and she has been a true partner at every step along the way. Jennifer Kushnier, who had to edit under every possible constraint (including not enough time and an author who developed a sudden, dramatic allergy to lines being cut) managed to whip the manuscript into shape with grace and good humor intact.

Jessica Rossman, my assistant, has been involved in this book since even before I was willing to commit to writing it. Her incredible people and communication skills have been an enormous gift. Not only that, but she remained optimistic, cheerful, and enthusiastic throughout. Neil Cleary, my former assistant turned rock star, was also a big help when we were drowning in interview transcripts.

Edie Wiener suggested that I take a look at brain sex findings, and even gave me a couple of books to get started. Her instinct that this material would be key for me was unerring, as her instincts about the future usually are.

Dawn Raffel, my editor at *O* magazine, helped me find my writing "voice." Barbara Gottesman, of Woodmont Group, did most of the research for the book, and has a rare gift for being able to answer a broad research inquiry quickly, with exactly the right sparkling specifics. Thanks also to Karen Hansen for research and copyediting.

Diane Harris, editor, writer, and friend, was my guide and inspiration when the original structure I put together for the book just didn't work and I didn't know where to turn. She figured out a new structure, gave me confidence in all the workshop material I'd developed over the years, and helped me craft some of the how-to sections of the book. The joy of working with someone of Diane's caliber and character was one of the best parts of the project.

At HayGroup, Dr. Harvey Resnick and Annabelle Horowitz were also great supporters. My deepest thanks go to Dr. Steve Safier, my primary HayGroup business colleague, for being the "first reader" of this book. Steve really helped me clarify ideas, watch out for anything that seemed anti-male, and stay true to my voice. Because we pitch and work together so often, many of the ideas and concepts in this book first saw the light of day with him. He's a great coach as well, and really helped me through the tough spots.

Thanks also to my girlfriends, many of whom you met in the pages of this book, either as interviewees or as the inspiration behind the anecdotes. On my list of blessings, girlfriends rank near the top.

And finally, to my beloved husband Jimmy, who knew how demanding this project would be for me and, therefore, for him, and who nonetheless threw his support behind it, wholeheartedly.

Acknowledgments